THE SOUNDTRACK TO MY LIFE

DERMOT O'LEARY

HODDER &
STOUGHTON

First published in Great Britain in 2014 by
Hodder & Stoughton
An Hachette UK company

1

Copyright © Dermot O'Leary 2014

Catch Me If You Can, words and music by Bob McDill © 1980
Hall Clement Publications. Universal Music Publishing Limited.

A CIP catalogue record for this title is available from the British Library

Hardback ISBN 978 1 444 79018 4
Trade Paperback ISBN 978 1 444 79019 1
Ebook ISBN 978 1 444 79020 7

Typeset in Fairfield LH Light by Hewer Text UK Ltd, Edinburgh
Printed and bound by CPI Group (UK) Ltd, Croydon, CR0 4YY

Hodder & Stoughton policy is to use papers that are natural, renewable
and recyclable products and made from wood grown in sustainable
forests. The logging and manufacturing processes are expected to
conform to the environmental regulations of the country of origin.

Hodder & Stoughton Ltd
338 Euston Road
London NW1 3BH

www.hodder.co.uk

To Brendan, Terry, Bruce, Shane and the boys, Steven Patrick, and Johnny, to Guy and his brothers, Macca, and Joel and the good ship Athlete. May the wind always be at your back.
Go raibh maith agat.

CONTENTS

INTRODUCTION

•

SOUNDTRACK 1

'Catch Me If You Can' by Brendan Shine   9

•

SOUNDTRACK 2

'The Floral Dance' by Terry Wogan   23

•

SOUNDTRACK 3

'Ghost Town' by the Specials / 'Young Guns (Go For It)' by Wham!

/ 'I Can't Wait' by Nu Shooz   35

•

SOUNDTRACK 4

'Meeting Across The River' by Bruce Springsteen /

Sundry albums from the Britannia Music Club

(including a little bit of Phil Collins)   49

•

SOUNDTRACK 5

Queen at Live Aid (13 July 1985)   63

•

SOUNDTRACK 6

'Streams of Whiskey' by the Pogues   75

•

SOUNDTRACK 7

'November Rain' by Guns N' Roses (and a nod to Bob Marley)   85

•

SOUNDTRACK 8

'Gimme Shelter' by the Rolling Stones   99

SOUNDTRACK 9

'Protection' by Massive Attack (featuring Tracey Thorn)   111

SOUNDTRACK 10

'The Macarena' by Los Del Rio (I'm so very sorry)   123

SOUNDTRACK 11

'Frozen' by Madonna / 'It's Freezing' by Mel and Sue   141

SOUNDTRACK 12

'Stolen Car' by Beth Orton   157

SOUNDTRACK 13

(The middle eight): 'We Will Rock You' by 5ive (featuring . . . er, me)

/ 'Fear' by Ian Brown   171

SOUNDTRACK 14

'Newborn' by Elbow   183

SOUNDTRACK 15:

'Somewhere Only We Know' by Keane   197

SOUNDTRACK 16

'All These Things That I've Done' by the Killers   211

SOUNDTRACK 17

'Rehab' by Amy Winehouse   225

SOUNDTRACK 18

'Mysterious Girl' by Ant and Seb (Peter Andre) / 'Listen' by Beyoncé

/ 'Little Things' by One Direction   241

SOUNDTRACK 19

'You've Got The Style' by Athlete   267

•

SOUNDTRACK 20

Bonus Tracks   277

•

ACKNOWLEDGEMENTS   291

PICTURE ACKNOWLEDGEMENTS   294

INTRODUCTION

Well, hello. So, this is my book. Now, I didn't want to write an 'autobiography' in the classic sense (i.e. 'Read all about my struggle,' etc, etc) but, having worked on two of the biggest, weirdest but ultimately most rewarding TV shows of the last twenty years, and having had my own radio show but not having made a note in all that time, I thought I'd best put pen to paper . . . and with music-playing such an integral part in all that, and my actual life, I thought I'd link it to the songs that, intentionally or otherwise, have been the backdrop to my life. (Plus, I'm not so sure how much of this I'll remember in a couple of years' time. As it is, I'm pretty sure a lot of the early stuff is kind of sketchy, so you'll have to take my word for it, but rest assured I've always been very popular, and devilishly good-looking. At least, that's how I remember it.)

Here's the deal: we all have a soundtrack to our lives. Yours (which I hope for your sake is somewhat different to mine) is, well, *yours* – a unique series of musical markers that form a tuneful dot-to-dot pattern of your life. It's a bit like your DNA, only it can't be used to convict you for any crimes you might have committed years ago (musical or otherwise). So what do I think it actually is?

Well, it's easier to start by saying what it's not. The soundtrack to your life isn't your *Desert Island Discs* (now that radio show is an institution – it's been around since 1942! It's part of the fabric of our nation), and I harbour no desire to host a radio show for seventy years based on the STML. This, by the way, is what we're going to call the 'Soundtrack To My Life' from now on, largely because my typing is so bad it takes me at least thirty seconds to write 'Soundtrack To My Life'. Even more worrying is the fact that this page has so far taken me two hours so, right now, I can imagine you're reading this sometime in 2018. It's my bad and I'm working on it (that also just took twenty seconds). But, focus, O'Leary! Back to my STML (catchy, right?) and why it's not *Desert Island Discs*.

Your soundtrack doesn't require you to think in a sober and conscious way about the music you would want to listen to for the rest of your life, stranded on a paradise island with the complete works of Shakespeare, A.N. Other book (*South*, by Ernest Shackleton, since you're asking) and that one luxury item for company (which, while we're here, would be an endless supply of Cheval Blanc).

Also, this is no list of songs that you'd be happy and, be honest, sometimes smug about. A list to trot out when you're hosting a dinner party. You know the ones I'm talking about – something from the playlist of tunes you've been grafting on for over a week, so that when people come around to yours it will make you stand out from that friend who's playing that Kings of Leon album to deeeeath in his car, and thinks he can do a mean 'Sex On Fire' come karaoke time. We've all been there: you turn the volume up ever so subtly when what you consider to be a piece of bonafide gold comes on, you lean back with that post-dinner drink in your hand, smiling smugly like a Cheshire cat as you hear someone say, 'Oh, haven't heard this in ages' or the even better, 'This is great! Is it new?'

Furthermore, the soundtrack to your life is certainly not the list of songs you argue about in public when, God forbid, someone strikes up the 'greatest album/songs of all time' debate. Nor is it a list of your guilty pleasures. These are, after all, tunes you've still chosen to love and ones you know you'll sing when drunk or when prompted.

No, the soundtrack to your life is far deeper and in some cases darker than that, and the crucial difference between it and all of the above is . . . that *it* chooses you, not the other way round.

This is a fact. It's also, in many cases, nothing short of a disaster.

So, let's say that it's made up of between ten and twenty tracks that, for some reason, have a hold over us. (There are almost certainly more, but let's go with twenty musical signposts for our life.) And they have a hold on us because they have become inextricably linked to the most important moments and memories of our lives. So for example, they might remind you of your parents, your first day at school, the Blitz, dead people, the smell of cut grass, the beach, beer-soaked kisses, the smell of hot tarmac, being angry with the world, bad fashion choices, getting dumped, scoring a goal, etc, etc.

That's a pretty diverse list that a psychiatrist would probably have fun/a laugh analysing, but it's just what popped into my head in the thirty seconds (fifteen minutes) it took me to type it. And that's my point. Through your soundtrack, you can chart your own life and experiences, and thus the story of you unfolds.

All mass media has an emotional hold over us. We're bombarded with it, and we tend to hold on to the stuff we actually like. Films, books, television programmes can all take us back to a time and a place, but there's something about a three and a half minute song that can also elevate you and take you somewhere else, somewhere less specific. You can get lost in a song and somehow remember words, melodies, choruses you haven't heard or spoken or sung for twenty or thirty years. Sometimes they just inexplicably pop into your head, along with the warm, fuzzy feeling you got from that party, person or place they're associated with. There can also be – dear God – the excruciating embarrassment attached to an ill-advised dance move from a craze long since forgotten.

Last week, for example, I found myself on a car ferry and German band Opus's 'Live is Life' (circa 1985) came on the radio. Even though I hadn't heard it for almost thirty-odd years, I remembered the words – all of them. I also remember a kid at school called Chris Benge and he hated it, if you sung it anywhere near him he'd go nuts. It's no 'Space Oddity', but those words were still trapped up there in my head somewhere.

This incredible feature of the classic ear/brain/heart combo is sometimes great, à la Springsteen (a LOT more of whom we'll be talking about later); sometimes quite good, à la Jan Hammer's 'Crockett's Theme' from *Miami Vice*; and in some cases, brilliantly bad à la an advert for Coke you heard when you were eleven: 'First time, first love, Oh, what a feeling is this . . .' But whichever combination it is – and I sincerely hope there's more good than bad in your soundtrack – I repeat, it's yours.

You don't have to be proud of it – I'd argue that you shouldn't even *like* some of it, but it is unequivocally yours, and it's not going anywhere. In fact, it's only going to get added to. You're stuck with it, like your family, your football team or your criminal record (should you have one).

To prove my point, here are some common examples that I think work for most people of a certain generation (mine) from film soundtracks that I grew up listening to. The first is a song that almost made it onto my soundtrack: the stirring Peter Cetera's 'Glory Of Love'. If you're not that familiar with it/haven't slow danced to it, it's a classic eighties power ballad with overproduced synths and a heck of a chorus that kicks in at 1.06. What are you waiting for? Go and have a listen. Woo! Yeah! *The Karate Kid!* 'Get him a body bag!' etc!

Unless you're very young (in which case, you've probably bought this book under false pretences, thinking I am going to spill all about my relationship with Harry and the rest of the 1D guys and are now supremely miffed at me – though, by the way, if you're still here, and I haven't already been tossed in the fire as you 'Unfollow' me, *The X Factor* stuff comes a bit later), this track proves my point. Peter Cetera's 'Glory Of Love' might not appear on many 'greatest of all time' lists – maybe not even Peter Cetera's – and it might not be the best tune in the world (unless you're a tough young punk with a heart, and Elizabeth Shue for a girlfriend, about to open a can of whoop-ass on the unfortunate members of Cobra Kai), but you'd have to have a heart of stone for it not to take you back to playing on a green sometime in the eighties, pretending to be Daniel-*san*.

Karate Kid not your thing? (Loser.) OK, press play on the example/proving-my-point second track: Simple Minds' 'Don't You (Forget About Me).'

Now this is a cracker, appealing to both guys and gals out there. Once again, all you need to hear is Jim Kerr warbling: 'Hey, hey, hey, hey!' and you're there: *Breakfast Club*. You're Molly Ringwald placing a diamond earring into Judd Nelson's calloused hand; you're Ally Sheedy ripping a wrestling patch off Emilio Estevez's jacket; you're flipping the bird to Mr Vernon as you punch the air on the playing field of Shermer High. Or you're me, sitting in my parents' front room watching a third-generation copy on VHS, dreaming of Molly realising I was helplessly in love with a fictional character.

As I said, films are a terrific example as they are a common experience. But any song can have that effect on you. Four bars from a recognisable tune, and you'll be back to your first kiss, a family holiday, your first car, your grandparents . . . in short, your life.

So that's what this book is: a soundtrack to the milestones of my life; one half of which has been a lot of fun, and at times pretty surreal as I've been on the telly a fair bit, and the other half of which has been just as much fun, but with a lot less time on telly (apart from a cameo/pre-photo photobomb on *Newsround*, which came to my school when Live Aid was on – sorry John Craven).

Now, one disclaimer before we start: this is my first book, so my choices are all over the shop. There is often more than one musical choice per chapter, but that's the point; which, just in case you haven't been concentrating, I'll reiterate once more: you don't pick the soundtrack to your life; it picks you.

So, here's the story of me so far, with the music that's been my best friend, my confidante, my really annoying sibling and, at times, my tormentor. (Note to self, music isn't actually a person. Stop giving it a personality.)

SOUNDTRACK

1

'Catch Me If You Can'
by Brendan Shine

OK, to kick things off, I'm Irish. I know I don't sound it, but I am, and of all the rich and varied musical heritage the land of my parents and forefathers has given the world, of all the great folk that have sprung from the heartbreak of conflict, famine and emigration that mother Erin has had to endure, it's extraordinary that the track that is the first stop in my soundtrack is a song about a middle-aged farmer, effectively . . . pimping himself out.

Lisdoonvarna is a small town in the north-west of County Clare in Ireland. It holds no romantic attachment for me, and I have never even been there. My family's home is Wexford town and, like most second-generation Irish, if you ever go home and don't spend every waking moment drinking tea, being force-fed dairy in the kitchen while being interrogated as to why you STILL haven't brought a girlfriend home – 'Is there something wrong with you? Because . . . you know, it's fine if . . .' (i.e. 'Are you gay?') – and constantly being told, 'You're wasting away, you need to eat more butter,' if you turn your back on all that and instead decide to travel the country of your forefathers to better understand your heritage and tradition, then you are considered (quite rightly) to be a traitor to your kith and kin.

So, whilst I've never been there, Lisdoonvarna is legendary, and unwittingly played a huge part in my upbringing. Each September, it hosts a festival that is one of Europe's biggest matchmaking events: 40,000 farmers descend on a small town to try to find a wife, and from that has sprung one of the most important songs of my life . . . OK, if you're ready for this, it's time to press play on track one of my STML:

I'm a Páidín, from Tulla bhadín
I've got money and acres of land,
I'm looking for a honey, with a bit of money,
Catch me if you can, me name is Dan, sure I'm yer man.

I like the céilí, and the Stack of Barley,
I like the waltzes, the oul jigs and the reels
I like swinging, when Big Tom is singing
Catch me if you can, me name is Dan, sure I'm yer man.

And I'm off to Lisdoonvarna at the end of the year
I'm off for the bit of craic, the women and the beer!
I'm awful shifty for a man of fifty,
Catch me if you can, me name is Dan, sure I'm yer man.

I've got a brother, he's in the Gardaí
I've got an uncle, he's up there in the Dáil

He's quite a charmer, Geez a mighty farmer
Catch me if you can, me name is Dan, sure I'm yer man.

Now to conclude and finish my story
If there's a young one, looking for a man,
Take the bus from Bearna, down to Lisdoonvarna
Catch me if you can, me name is Dan, sure I'm yer man.

And I'm off to Lisdoonvarna at the end of the year
I'm off for the bit of craic, the women and the beer!
I'm awful shifty for a man of fifty,
Catch me if you can, me name is Dan, sure I'm yer man.

There it is. Two minutes and nineteen seconds of sheer heaven.*

Hmm, where to start . . . Well, if we just strip the song back, at face value it's simply a lot of fun. Here's a guy who is approaching fifty, he's obviously done well for himself and is big in farming circles, but as is often the case, has neglected his personal life. Who can blame him – he's a rural career guy! And by the sounds of it, he's well connected. He's got a brother in the police, and an uncle who's an MP. So the short story is, he's a good package who's just a bit lonely. The best thing about the tune is that he laughs his way through it – he sounds like he loves his life, he just needs a girl. So it's a song full of hope, and excitement and expectation that only the promise of potential new love can bring.

* . . . to me (aged eight)

OK, so I might be going into this a liiiiittle too deeply, but the real reason it eclipses so many other truly great Irish songs that could have found their way on to my early soundtrack is that it's pretty much the first Irish song I ever heard, alongside Terry Wogan's rendition of 'The Floral Dance' (which is not actually an Irish song – Cornish, I think, but we'll hear more from Terry shortly).

The singer of this two-minute nineteen-second gem is an Irish Folk/Country heavyweight called Brendan Shine. He's been going for donkeys' years and is, to the best of my knowledge, still rocking/big banding on. But three decades ago, I'm pretty sure he had no idea that he was playing an integral part in my formative years.

It's a strange enough experience to be brought up Irish in Britain, but when you're brought up away from an area that has a big Irish population, such as London or Liverpool, then it's even weirder: not unpleasant by any stretch, just different to the urban centres that had considerably large Irish populations.

I grew up in semi-rural Colchester, Essex, in a village called Marks Tey, to be precise. It's a small village nestled between two main roads from London to East Anglia and surrounded by fields. My parents spotted it totally by chance on a train journey, on their way to see my Uncle Bill, and Aunty Nelly (an old Irish matriarch aunty of my dad's who had retired to a well-kept rose-bedded bungalow in Brightlingsea). Having decided to leave Ireland, my parents couldn't afford to buy in London, and fancied some fresh air and green fields in which to bring up their kids, so Marks Tey became home. Pretty soon after that I was born, although I have it on good authority I was 'Made in Ireland'. Something I dread to even think about.

My mam (Irish spelling of 'mum') and dad (universal spelling of 'dad') were a pair of young Irish kids who had come over here to make a better life for themselves.

They love to move, love to dance – always have done. They met in Wexford when my mam was still in her teens and have been together ever since. They married in 1968 and my mam had my sister, Nicola, and I by the time she was in her mid-twenties. She was and still is a beauty, with beautiful black hair and olive skin (Lord alone knows where her ancestors were from).

My father was the oldest of five children, and is the hardest-working man I know. He was known in Wexford as 'Locksy' (everyone has a nickname), due to his curly hair, which might sound like a curse, but while his ginger afro period of the seventies was, I'm sure he'd admit, regrettable, he's still not grey now, so I'm also pretty sure he's not complaining. He was a star hurler – Ireland's national game – back in the sixties and had to give up playing at the highest level when he and my mam moved to England (missing out on playing in what was a championship-winning team the year after he moved). He night-schooled himself while we were growing up, getting a Masters in Business. He's never smoked or drunk – a combination of sporting prowess and taking 'the pledge' – but he has a love for life and fun of a man half his age.

You never give your parents enough credit, do you? For two kids like they were to up sticks, leave Ireland with not an awful lot and set up home in a country where they hardly knew a soul and raise a family is a big deal. Keeping in touch with home in whatever shape or form was important to them, and it rubbed off on us. While they were still active members of the local community (who can forget the street party when Charles and Diana got married, and the slightly less successful one when Andrew and Fergie got hitched), they, above all, loved and cherished the music of their homeland.

We lived on a purpose-built estate where everyone knew everyone. I know it's a cliché now to say that you used to be able to keep your doors unlocked, but it *was* pretty much that kind of thing back then. There was one school in the village, three pubs – the Spaniard, the Red Lion and the Prince of Wales – and a big primrose nursery that the mums went to work in when us kids were at school – which might explain why our house was always swimming in primroses of all shades and hues. What Marks Tey was most definitely NOT, though, was what you would call an Irish enclave.

There was, however, like most places in Britain, an Irish population that, how shall we say, punched above its weight. It was centred around the church – unsurprisingly – a hotel bar called the George – also unsurprisingly – and, for a short, ill-advised period, a stable yard where one of our friends had bought a horse, a nag called Firetrack – and, of course, our house, where an awful lot of what I suppose you'd call ad hoc céilís took place.

These involved all the Irish in town coming round (people who essentially had little in common other than actually being Irish) and drinking the old, canned, gassy Guinness – the one they had before they invented widgets – singing heartily themselves and listening to their/somebody else's kids sing pretty bad renditions of Irish standards – which was where I came in. The songs that were my (happily enforced) party pieces were staid old Irish standards, and generally they were pretty free of controversy/rebellion – the ones that were, were about the Wexford Rebellion of 1798, and therefore not current nor too threatening in 1970s Colchester.

And it was at these get-togethers where I first realised my weekends were panning out slightly differently to those of my friends.

To start with, growing up as a second-generation kid, you kind of live two lives. On the one hand, my real-world Colchester life was a pretty straightforward small-town upbringing in Britain in the seventies and eighties. We had all the usual stuff that go to make up your traditional nostalgia: endless summers, the smell of freshly cut grass, your dad owning British Leyland cars, the occasional dead animal found in a ditch and duly poked by every boy in the estate with a stick . . . all the classics. Whereas my home life included things like: the Pope, the Pope defeating communism, the Pope getting shot, the Pope forgiving the guy who shot him, First Communion, pouring Guinness for old men (who always looked older than they actually were), singing songs about places and people you didn't know, learning and reading – courtesy of my father – about a different history and literature than I was learning about at school (something for which I will always be eternally grateful, although he could have gone a little easier on the James Joyce), and twice-monthly trips to north-west London to see my dad play hurling and visit family, and the once-a-year endless summer trips back to see relatives in Ireland.

The brilliant contradiction in being a second-generation

Irishman (or, to that end, I'm guessing second-generation anything), was that, when you were back in Ireland, the Irish family always saw you as English, and you were treated as such, i.e. teased, and beaten (in a wholesome, cousin-like way, of course, until someone else, outside the family, called you English, at which point *they* became the subject of the family's abuse); whereas, back home in England, I was just a kid that had a slightly unusual name, and went to a different church, and who at times the teacher asked to explain who the Pope was, or what Holy Communion was. Heavy stuff for an eight-year-old.

Now, before the If-you-don't-like-it-over-here-why-don't-you-eff-off-back-to-your-own-country brigade starts (although I sincerely hope none of them are actually reading this book), our upbringing was a pragmatic affair. My parents LOVED it in England, and still do. My parents brought my older sister, Nicola, and I up to be proud of our heritage, whilst also embracing the culture we were living in, and they were treated with nothing but warmth and hospitality from the moment they got here (apart from the obligatory 'No Blacks, No Dogs, No Irish' door signs in London, and some ignoramus who rang my mother after an IRA bomb had gone off in London and said she was next, although I'm sure the idiot had got a bit confused and got it the wrong way round – what, my mam is next? For what? To get blown up by the IRA?). Anyway, the point is, for the most part, it was an overwhelmingly welcoming environment.

Reading back over what I've written so far, I feel I might have painted a bad picture here. Back in Ireland it wasn't all sitting around the peat fire, eating bacon and cabbage. (Well, some of it was, and it was great.) According to my parents, Ireland in the sixties was an exciting place to grow up. Just like Britain, kids were into the Beatles, and flocked to see the usual massive bands when they toured over there, which they did. My parents saw Gerry and the Pacemakers, the Searchers, Gene Pitney, and my mam still claims she did the twist with Chubby Checker, although my sister and I always suspect that was the Piesporter Michelsberg talking.

My dad also tells me that, exclusive to Ireland, they had the showband scene. These were big bands, such as Big Tom and the Mainliners (who are also still going – what do they make these guys *from*?) who played the most popular tunes of the day, and toured constantly. These bands and this music, exported to London, formed a big part of the music scene for the Irish diaspora in clubs like the Galtymore, and it's where, in the sixties, many a young Irish couple met, courted and cemented their relationships.

So although we listened to a lot of current music when I was growing up, my parents, and by extension my own music taste, was driven by nostalgia. Which is where my love of Brendan Shine comes in.

See, you don't pick it; it picks you.

In the midst of all these old rebel songs, which even at an early age I realised were beautiful – about struggles for freedom from unscrupulous landowner types, longing for home, missing families and loved ones, and such like – this song was pretty much the only happy one I can remember. I suppose it was my seventies version of the Tweenies. It was always on the record player on a Sunday night. My parents would play it to me, perhaps because they consciously (or subconsciously), after a typical weekend, didn't want their kid going to school on a Monday morning thinking about a rebellious priest who died in the Wexford uprising of 1798 (Father John Murphy, by the way, and I *did* go to school thinking about him ... thanks, Catholicism!) So, it's a Sunday afternoon/evening, we're having one of our many O'Leary family *céilís*, where post-dinner chairs are cleared back in our snug front room and the records come out. At a certain point, the 33RMP/LP of the Clancy Brothers and Tommy Makem singing 'The West's Awake' (yes, it's a rebel song) would be taken off the record player and replaced by Brendan's neo-classic. At which point the dancing would start.

For people who might not know, Irish dancing in a family context is a more anarchic version of Scottish dancing – everyone's up doing their own thing, which in my dad's case involved an awful lot of erratic leg kicks; normally, inches away from Aunty Nelly's face. (More about my dad's Dad-dancing antics later.)

The putting on of Brendan's song was a moment I always looked forward to. Getting up and throwing myself around in a room full of my relatives doing the same thing felt very warm and safe – things that are important to an eight-year-old (and a forty-year-old man).

We actually had two of Brendan's records – 'Catch Me If You Can' had him on the cover with a thousand-yard stare, smiling and wearing a cream turtleneck, whilst the other, 'Do You Want Your Old Lobby Washed Down, Con Shine' (it really is called that and, no, I have no idea what it means, either), featured him staring in exactly the same way, only this time wearing a blue turtleneck. (Even as a child, I thought someone should have had a word with Brendan's marketing people.)

This 'blue turtleneck' song is, as far as I can fathom, about a man who can't pay his rent and offers to clean a lobby by way of recompense. Sounds fair, but no matter – I thought he was singing 'lavvy', not 'lobby', which for an eight-year-old was *the* best form of toilet humour and therefore the second most brilliant thing I had ever heard, after 'Catch Me If You Can'. Obvs.

So, after a year or so of hearing Brendan's song practically every weekend, when we heard that the man himself was actually coming to town (well, Chelmsford), you can guess who was begging his parents to take him to the concert. And I must have been a pretty good beggar because Dad got tickets, even though I am pretty sure I was the main Brendan cheerleader in the house and my parents would have preferred something a bit more authentic and Dublinersy. Nonetheless, Daddo got the tickets and we were off to the ... hold on to your hats ... Chelmsford Civic Centre, and I was going to see Brendan! My first live concert (if church every Sunday doesn't count, which it probably doesn't)!

Now, being an Irish do, it was always due to be a late night, with a Rhianna-style stage time, but before we go any further about said concert, it's important to explain how the Irish are with their children and their attitude to sleep.

Whilst I stress that the Irish are great with kids – playful, warm, encouraging, great huggers – I have never seen children go to bed later in any other northern European country. It's like the Irish are permanently on holiday and have adopted a Spanish or Italian attitude to their kids' bedtime, only they're not in Spain or Italy, but cold, rainy Wexford town. To make matters worse, I'm from a family of nightbirds (nightbird squared). My wife, who is Norwegian, and therefore used to spending half the year in darkness, is bewildered by my family's socially acceptable insomnia, and will often raise the white flag and drift into the Land of Nod as they/we launch into another hearty debate (about ANYTHING) at two in the morning. To be fair, my mam was a pretty good sergeant major (he says, in fear of an imminent clip round the ear for this and the earlier Piesporter Michelsberg comment), but the point is, on the night of the Brendan Shine concert, even for an Irish kid I was allowed to stay up even later than usual.

Picture the scene then. After a long journey (for an eight-year-old), a support act and a truckload of crisps and Coke, an already late night is compounded by a late stage time. Inevitably, a crash was coming. So, what happened as my idol walked on stage; what happened when the moment I'd been dreaming of for months (well, days, but you know how much slower time passes when you're a kid) finally came to pass? I fell asleep! ASLEEP! In that classic kid/meerkat-at-nap-time, nodding-off-style way, between two really uncomfortable orange plastic chairs – chairs that no human being could possibly fall asleep on. I completely missed my idol performing. All I remember was waking up with a Coca-Cola/Tayto crisps-induced sugar/salt hangover and hearing, 'Goodnight Chelmsford.'

As you can imagine, I was in bits, devastated – it was the modern-day equivalent of taking one of your children to a Justin Bieber concert only for them to conk out at the start of 'Baby' (though in this day and age you'd be slightly more annoyed because the whole thing would have cost you the best part of 200 quid).

However, thankfully, there was to be a silver lining to this dark grey cloud. Somehow my dad was the most charming Irishman in a room full of charming Irishman – which takes some doing – and sweet-talked himself and his semi-comatose eight-year-old son past whatever security Brendan had – I imagine it was extensive – to the backstage area to meet the man himself. I woke up just long enough to get a pat on the head and an autograph from a jolly, white turtlenecked (yes, he was wearing one) troubadour before I passed out again, and woke up the next day with a big smile on my face and my dad's hero status securely cemented in my mind.

So there you have it. You know, there were so many Irish songs that I wanted to start with. Classic folk ballads that meant so much, and still do. I could have used my first choice to show you the breadth of brilliant Irish music that so many generations have been brought up listening to and singing along with. Songs that have had international recognition and are now regarded as timeless classics: 'The Green Fields Of France', 'The Auld Triangle', 'A Song For Ireland' . . . from voices that reshaped the way the Irish are seen over the world: the Dubliners, the Fureys and more.

But no. For reasons which I think are pretty clear now, I offer up to you the first track in the soundtrack of my life: 'Catch Me If You Can'.

SOUNDTRACK

2

'The Floral Dance'
by Terry Wogan

OK, I get it – I know it's only the second song, but you might already be getting a little worried about the choices of my soundtrack. Well, don't. This isn't going to be a collection of random, novelty Irish tracks. Well, OK, up to NOW it is, but things will pick up musically and become more eclectic, I promise. But if we're telling my story through random pieces of music – which we are – then we cannot discount this . . . classic.

I appreciate, however, that this might be one of my more questionable choices, being as it is, essentially, a novelty track. That said, it's a novelty track that was made (marginally) famous by the man you have to thank for giving me the inspiration to get into TV and radio in the first place. So if you're not keen on seeing me on the telly (and if you're not, that's cool, can't please all of the people all of the time, etc, etc. But then why are you reading this book?) then the man you have to blame is the Lord of Limerick – Sir Terry Wogan.

I can't tell my story without giving a fairly hefty nod to Terry, both as a kid and an adult; he is to me a hero . . . sort of like the legendary polar explorer Ernest Shackleton, but a lot less chilly.

This song, or least Terry's version of it, is God-awful. The original, slightly-less-God-awful version was written in 1911 by Kate Moss (probably not the model, but I'll check . . . it's not) to celebrate Cornwall's annual Fury Dance (sometimes known as the Flora, hence it's incorrect title, 'The Floral Dance'). It's been recorded a number of times by different folk, but most notably, as far as we're concerned, in 1977 by the Brighouse and Rastrick Brass Band, whose version got to number two at Christmas that year.

It was what it said on the tin (no Cornish tin-based pun intended) – a reworking of an old Cornish folk song. So far, so novelty Christmas single – think 'Mistletoe And Wine' for the seventies. Now, at the time, Wogan was hosting his breakfast show on Radio 2 and when he played this track he sang along to it. His accompaniment obviously set someone's synapses twitching because somehow, somewhen (actually in 1978), whoever this person was came up with the idea of Terry releasing his singalong version, which he did, even though the Brighouse and Rastrick version had only been released a couple of months before – so, you know, you'd think maybe people might not need another version of it? Well, they didn't, but they obviously did, because it got to number twenty-one, which in this day and age would have had you sharpening the guillotine, but in 1978 was no bad thing.

Now, if you ever want to see three minutes and one second of a man thinking, 'What have I done – this seemed quite a fun idea when we were in that meeting – but here I am like a berk – holding a bunch of flowers on *Top of the Pops* – without even Legs & Co for company – my ass is on the line here – and who's helping me? No one!' then check out Terry's performance online (or as my friend, Moonman's granny used to call it, 'The web web web'). It's here: http://www.youtube.com/watch?v=ElnCI1fkfFM

It's brilliant! So awkward! Terry is the antithesis of a pop star in his beige suit and perfectly side-parted hair. The only nod to any sense of glamour is his stencil-patterned white shirt, which he wears with no tie and open at the neck (steady, Terry), and the bunch of flowers he's holding, which appear to visibly wilt as the performance continues. In a magnificent study of restraint, I imagine Terry celebrated afterwards with an especially strong cup of tea.

I also like the fact that, back in the seventies, kids didn't care two hoots about what they were actually watching when they went to *TOTP*; all that mattered was that they were at *TOTP*, the coolest show in the universe at the time. You could have put a butchery course to music on there, and they'd still have been bopping away.

Anyway, I first heard Terry's version as a four-year-old, hiding in a cupboard from the bread man (yes, I do mean the man who delivered the bread . . . for some reason to me he was the most terrifying man in the world due to his friendly smile, white British Leyland van and sliced bloomer). In our house, 'The Floral Dance' was a permanent fixture, the radio was always on in the background, and this song was always on the radio. It had everything you could possibly want from a novelty hit: it was easy to sing along to, rhythmic enough for your dad to do a slightly embarrassing (OK, very embarrassing) dance to (and believe you me, my dad did – like the majority of his dances, it was a kind of amateur Irish jig with added Cornish gusto, like a deranged Morris dancer) and, like any great novelty hit, you could sort of make up all the words as long as you knew the actual words to the last line, which are of course: 'All together for "The Floral Dance"!'

But it's not really the song (thankfully) that defines my love for Wogan. As with all the songs in this tome, it's less about them and more about what they signify, the connections and meanings they have for me. Irrespective of the fact that I've come to know Terry through work, and could dare to call him a friend (OK, a friendly colleague), I can trace my admiration for him (not obsession, thank you) back to being that kid hiding from the bread man.

Without meaning to bang on about the whole Irish thing too much ('Here he goes again . . .!'), the UK broadcasting industry has always been home to Irish entertainers, and still is, from Eamonn Andrews through to Graham Norton.

In the seventies, if you were part of an Irish family living in England (which, in case it's escaped your attention, I was), Wogan was kind of like your connection to home. If my dad was lucky he'd call home to Ireland once a week, and write a weekly letter to my grandmother. There was obviously no email, no Skype; quite often when you left home, that was it, you never went back. So an Irish voice and face made people a little less homesick. Terry felt like part of the furniture over here, he was accepted; he was our boy . . . one of us who'd made good.

Actually, he'd made very good indeed. Terry was a big success. He was on the radio, he had his own talk show, he wasn't afraid to make himself look silly (see above), and perhaps most notably, he made the Eurovision Song Contest worth watching. There was always an underlying wit that let you know that whilst he wasn't taking *himself* too seriously, he was taking what he was doing seriously (apart from the Eurovision Song Contest, obviously, where all bets are off). There was an intelligence behind those steel-blue eyes. He might act the eejit, but he was no one's fool.

The hardest thing any broadcaster can do is make the job look easy. OK, it's not a hard job in the way that busting your chops on a building site or factory is, but to make TV and radio look and sound easy, when inside you're quite often thinking, 'SHIIITTTT, what am I doing?' is no mean feat. Terry is by far and away the most effortlessly gifted radio broadcaster I've ever seen work.

I'm often asked what I find more enjoyable: TV or radio, and my answer is always, 'Whatever is live.' Which I know is side-stepping the issue, but that's my answer. Nothing comes close to live broadcasting. At one and the same time it's the greatest buzz and most terrifyingly exciting sensation I've experienced, and I want to do it until I die, or retire (or, more likely, until it retires me).

OK, getting off the fence, TV is probably my first love, but nothing is more terrifying in broadcasting than being on your own, live on national radio, when it's just you, the mic, the listener, and, and, and . . . you can't think of anything to say! By comparison, the fact that TV is a visual medium and therefore physical, means you can pace it all out and enjoy a silence from time to time – and you can breathe, because, frankly, people can see you breathe!

Radio, live radio, is a whole different ball game. When I was first given my very own Radio 2 show, I had the amazing experience of finding myself sitting near to Wogan at the station's Christmas party at the Criterion. He probably won't remember, but that night he gave me the most simple and yet best piece of advice about radio that I've ever been given. It's also, instinctively, the hardest thing to do on radio . . . Ready for this? Good. Here goes: 'Never be afraid of the silence.' See, it sounds spectacularly simple, doesn't it? But it's so hard to put into practice.

Just for a minute, imagine you've got your own radio show (feels good/terrifying, doesn't it?). A song has just finished and you open the mic (that's a technical term which means 'start'). Now, count in your head for five seconds before saying anything . . . Bear in mind that, for someone like Wogan or the BBC Radio 2 breakfast show, there could be upwards of eight or nine million people listening . . . there's no music in the background . . . there's no posse to bounce off . . . ready . . . do it . . . 5, 4, 3, 2, 1.

There, five seconds. The fastest man in the world can run over fifty metres in that time, but in the middle of a radio show it can seem like an eternity. Of course I'm not actually suggesting that you should do that, and neither was Terry (unless I completely misunderstood what he meant). The essence of his advice is: take your time – the faster you talk, the faster you get. If you fill the airwaves with mindless nonsense, then the whole show will become nonsense, so better to pace yourself, relax and, as the great man said, embrace the silence.

Wogan didn't need to help a young broadcaster out. In this industry, it's pretty sink or swim (that said, all my brethren, and sistren, at Radio 2 have been like parents to me – almost literally, as when I started I was pretty much the youngest person there by about thirty-five years), so for someone to go out of their way to help me, to offer a couple of words of kindly advice, made a real difference.

There was also something I wanted to say to him that night at the Criterion, but I didn't say it to him that evening, or indeed any other evening because it just didn't feel right (and for that read, 'It felt wrong, in a kind of stalker-like way.') You see, having fallen for Terry's soft, lilting tones as he sang along to 'The Floral Dance' and quashed my four-year-old-boy's fear of that bread man, one night at the BBC Television theatre in Shepherd's Bush a few years later, circa 1980, he changed my life *again*. (Now you can see why I didn't mention that to him . . . bit weird.)

To explain, my Uncle Frank, and Aunty Angela (my mam's older sister) came over from Ireland in the late sixties. They've always been very close, and they were already in England by the time my parents arrived, and were very supportive of them, in all the ways families are. Especially when my parents were starting out over here and my dad was working on the building sites. Frankie sadly passed a while ago, but he was in many ways both the antithesis and archetype of an Irishman: he had the heart of a lion; razor-like wit – dry as a bone; and he smoked sixty a day – proper fags as well, Superkings, or Raffles when they weren't available – none of your menthol rubbish. I know because he would send me round to the corner shop to buy a packet when I was eight (it was a different time) and in a masterstroke, he once gave me a sly puff on a cigarette at that age, knowing full well it would put me off for life. Which it did. The other side of the Frankie coin was that he never touched a drop of alcohol and, if you put him in a party situation, he was as shy as a dormouse. He was just a really lovely, warm and intelligent man. He was of that breed of dads/uncles that never seems to age, always permanently about fifty-five to sixty, with thinning hair, smart trousers, vest underneath a white shirt (classic), but never unkempt, always smart. He was a legend.

Frankie was an electrician and did very well over in England. He always drove Fords (love the brand loyalty). He had a Ford Capri – the Professionals drove a Capri, so for an eight-year-old child (and, come to think of it, a grown man in his forties), that was very cool. He also drove, for work, a British Leyland Sherpa van with a slide door which he kept open when he drove, à la *The Spy Who Loved Me* – he couldn't have been cooler. His partner in crime was my Aunty Angela.

She was everything to us: big sister, aunty, grandmother, bacon/dairy pusher . . . I knew that as soon as I walked through the door there'd be at least four rashers of Irish smoked bacon waiting for me (I'd always eat them straight, no ketchup or brown sauce chaser) and, get this, *she cooked it in a microwave*. Because she could, and because it was the eighties. Plus, she did a hell of a roast, which was our reward on a Sunday having driven up to their place in Queen's Park in London (at the time a big Irish enclave – that's gentrification for you!) from

Colchester, post-Mass. She was a gravy alchemist, and like any self-respecting Irish cook, made sure that no roast was complete without two different types of potato.

I swear, the whole Irish thing about being obsessed with potatoes is God's honest truth. On one of my wife's first trips to Ireland, she pointed out to five members of my family (including Aunty Angela) that we'd been debating the relative strengths and weaknesses of varieties of potatoes for half an hour. Not, you understand, how you like them served: boiled, mashed, etc. No. *Types* of potato – surely the kind of conversation you can only be born into. Worse still, I was part of that debate. I guess you're either part of the problem or part of the solution, man. (For the record, I'm a Kerrs Pink man.)

Angela was glamorous, in an aunty sort of a way. She was obsessed with Marks and Spencers – still is. Quite rightly. She thought it was the height of everything. If you were doing well, you shopped at M&S . . . it was their one indulgence. Like most immigrant families, they worked hard, saved hard and sent money home. She was a manageress at the LEB (London Electricity Board) showroom in Kilburn High Road and the thing I remember about her most was the lipstick and perfume she wore – when you're a kid, it's the little things you remember about people. It was different to my mam's (which was Opium – still is) and I can smell it now . . . It just made you feel *warm*.

The reason why Aunty Angela and Uncle Frank appear in chapter two isn't just because I love them, but because after Frank retired, sometime in the eighties, he got a job as a security guard. (Hang in there, it'll all become clear.) Like most people, when Uncle Frank retired he realised that smoking sixty a day, growing some pretty kick-ass geraniums and the occasional fishing trip wasn't going to cut it, so he got what I considered to be the most glamorous job in the world – being a security guard at the BBC Television Theatre, and that meant an intro into Woganville . . . (No, not the theme park, the man himself.)

As with any TV studio/show, people who work on it get comp'd a couple of tickets from time to time – the yearly rush for *The X Factor* tickets in my family is reminiscent of wildebeest stampeding in the Serengeti – and when Frankie got us a couple of family tickets to Terry Wogan's chat show, *Wogan*, it was a big deal.

I was about ten at the time and, if I'm honest, I can't remember all that much about the night (I can't even recall the guests), but it didn't matter because what I can remember is that it was the first moment I ever thought, 'I want to do this for a living.' I had no idea what 'this' was, but I just knew I wanted to be part of it. Whether it was the smell of the theatre, the lights, the cameras, the Maltesers . . . Most likely, in fact, 'this' was the moment when I actually met Terry himself (and the Maltesers). So, not meaning to gossip, but picture the scene, reminiscing fans . . .

We were sitting in our seats at the back of the BBC theatre (Frank could get us in, but the choice of seats was out of his hands). I don't quite know how this happened, but there was some sort of murmur in the audience and suddenly Terry Wogan walked around the back of the stalls, right past us, a glass of fine red in hand, nonchalant and confident as you like. Now, I can't quite remember if this was my mam or my aunty – though knowing them both as I do, it was almost certainly my mam, being the slightly more outgoing of the two – but once we'd regained a modicum of composure . . . she asked Terry for his autograph.

Obviously Terry obliged: he handed said glass of fine red to either my mam, my aunty or our next-door-neighbour who was also with us, Daphne Dufton (also Irish, from Gorey, north of Wexford town and a Protestant, if you don't mind). Anyway, the upshot was that the ten-year-old me got a smile and a pat on the head.

It was incredible – it felt as if I was being knighted. I'd like to say that after that I didn't wash my hair for months, but sadly, after the Colchester nit epidemic of the late seventies, that wasn't possible. It was a memorable day, though (the bits I can remember) – the day that I was introduced to three of the great loves of my life: Wogan, red wine and television, in that order.

After that night at the Criterion, when Terry was still working regularly at Radio 2, I used to see him a lot and even though they say you should never meet your heroes, in this case I'm very pleased I did. When I meet him now we talk about the Irish rugby team and make general chit-chat, but to this day I'm still in awe of the great man, and secretly wish he'd pat me on the head again. (Note to Terry: I'd settle for a glass of red.)

So when I hear 'The Floral Dance' today – and, yes, I do from time to time – I don't think of that eggy *Top of the Pops* performance or a Radio 2 DJ enjoying a novelty blip. I think of that moment in Shepherd's Bush theatre and how it set me on the path to where I am today.

SOUNDTRACK

3

'Ghost Town'

by the Specials

'Young Guns (Go For It)'

by Wham!

'I Can't Wait'

by Nu Shooz

On paper I shouldn't really relate to 'Ghost Town'. It came out in 1981, so I was nine which is hardly the age for fervent political activism (certainly not in Colchester, which wasn't exactly what you'd call a hotbed of extremism). Like many of my friends, I had a lower-middle-class upbringing with working-class values. My parents came from solid, hand-to-mouth working-class families but I didn't live in inner-city Coventry or London, so the full impact of Margaret Thatcher, her government and all that free market jazz seemed less apparent (although I'd be lying if I said the 'Margaret Thatcher Milk Snatcher' scandal didn't send St Andrew's Primary school into pre-pubescent anarchy).

My dad was, if not motivated, then politically engaged. He was always, and is still to this day, engrossed in the daily paper, although oddly always last thing at night (when it's not really news any more), and always, always, over a bowl or two of cereal. He has a thirst for news, history and politics that I inherited; but, back on the mean streets of Colchester in the early eighties, that hadn't quite filtered down to me and my friends, and we were still very much playing cops and robbers, not unions versus Tories.

So, rather than opening my eyes to the great inequalities of Thatcher's Britain, this song was for me the gateway into the great communal joy that was music on TV, and more specifically *Top of the Pops*, the show that determined how my generation saw, consumed and became obsessed with music.

In fact, such was the influence *TOTP* had on me and many, if not most, of my age, it is the source of many other tracks I could have picked to be on my soundtrack. Here are just a couple:

A-ha's 'Take On Me'. This deserves a nod just for the incredible video, and for the quite incredible effect lead-singer Morten Harket had on the girls at secondary school. Such was their adoration of this Norwegian Adonis that every boy in my year/ youth club tried to dress like him (pinched leather – or, more affordable and therefore likely – ski jacket) in an attempt to look like they were in a black and white animated video. I actually remember a girl called Claire Keeble – who left school to move to Hong Kong, which immediately made her more mysterious and therefore attractive – literally running around in circles, doing a half-decent impression of the impressively named Bunty

Bailey, Morten's girlfriend at the time who featured in the video, because A-ha were in the charts at number two.

Michael Jackson's 'Thriller'. While admittedly it might not need the plaudit, truly there was never a more exciting night than sitting in the front room, waiting for the countdown on telly and being scared shitless by the fourteen-minute epic premiere of 'Thriller', which was shown on Channel 4 at some ungodly hour.

But no, I've settled on 'Ghost Town'. The scene couldn't be any less urban decay if it tried. More often than not my sister, Nicola, and I would watch *Top of the Pops* round at our neighbour, Sylvie Webb's house. Sylvie and her husband, Clarence, lived across the road and immediately became my mam and dad's surrogate family when they first arrived from Ireland. Clarence even drove my mam to the hospital when I was born – ironically (for my love of military history) in a military hospital, as Colchester Maternity was full.

It's impossible to overstate how instrumental Sylvie and Clarence were in my upbringing. They were your neighbours from heaven, always babysitting and playing host to my sister and me, to the point where eventually you didn't really ask, you just went round after school. Sylvie was the friendly matriarch of the street, always travelling round on a pushbike with a scarf wrapped around her head, like she'd survived and thrived in the Urals under Stalin.

Pretty much everyone in the village had moved there as soon as the estate was built. Some had moved from the East End of London, some retirees, but mostly it was young families whose kids could go to the local school and whose dads could commute to London, if they didn't have local jobs in Colchester. With us being pretty much the only Irish family in the village, it wasn't exactly a meeting of bedfellows, but somehow it worked. Sylvie's family, however, were more old-school Essex/Suffolk land folk farm types (which kind of made them local royalty).

So, growing up, me and my sister quickly became a fixture around Sylvie's house, post-school, if my mam was at work. Sylvie was a silver-haired, hard-working, sleeves-rolled-up type of mother, who would go out to work at the local flower nursery every day, but would always make sure Clarence had chops and veg on the plate by five o'clock (country folk ate so early) when he came home from his job as an electrician.

Clarence was an extraordinary man. He never complained (he'd never dare – Sylvie was the boss) about the number of local children climbing all over his kitchen, alongside his own two kids. He was also extraordinary-looking. Anyone from the country will know what I mean when I say he had country skin – a beautiful olive-brown from a life of being outside. He looked like he should have been tending a flock of sheep in Tuscany, not rewiring a house in Great Tey (the village up the road, that us Marks Tey-ers had a Sharks and Jets relationship with).

There were many things I loved about going to Sylvie's, though possibly the thing I loved the most was that she used to ply us with sweetened coffee at an impossibly early age . . . which maybe explains why I was such an active child. But, trust me, with a runny nose and biting wind around your legs, a sweetened Nescafé or Mellow Birds after school was just the ticket.

It might sound odd, but writing this book (obviously, for me) conjures up a lot of nostalgia, and as much as the sound of a song can take you to someplace else, so too can a smell (though I'm not sure a 'smelltrack' to your life would work). The smell of a sweetened instant cup of Nescafé, and the aroma of Clarence's post-dinner cigarette, always made me feel cosy; it made me feel safe (though, obviously, I wasn't at all! I was actually in danger of contracting cancer from passive smoking, and possibly some caffeine-related illness, but hey, different times and all that).

Of course I also loved the communal experience of watching *TOTP* round at Sylvie's. There was always something a bit naughty and exciting about watching TV around someone else's house when you were a kid. For those of you under thirty-five, it's impossible to stress what an important part of the TV-watching and listening week *TOTP* was. Musically, it was the only vessel that allowed you to see the faces behind the songs. When you were into music as a kid, *TOTP* was both the appetiser to the forthcoming charts and the coronation of the previous week's charts. Also, before the days when you could illegally download everything under the sun, it also crucially determined how you spent your pocket money.

There seemed to be so much glamour to it. There were the bands, the – at the time – very cool DJs presenting it; some of whom we can't mention, but others we can, like Mike Reid, Simon Bates, Steve Wright, David 'Kid' Jensen and, of course, the dancing girls – Pan's People or Legs & Co. The idea of Legs & Co now seems utterly ridiculous. If the bands didn't turn up or an American artist wasn't in town, they just put on a group of scantily clad girls dancing to their song . . . Try and picture that now: 'Sorry, the Arctic Monkeys couldn't make it, but here are some dancing girls with their legs out, marching up and down to "Do I Wanna Know?" . . .' (OK, it's not without its virtues, and we pretty much do that every week on *The X Factor*, but you get my drift.)

TOTP also pulled off the incredible feat of going from ridiculous to credible in no time at all. You never knew what to expect on the show: as we huddled around the telly over at Sylvie's, hot sweet coffee in hand, watching a non-Operation-Yewtree-implicated presenter – Kid Jensen, one of the cuddly ones – suddenly, out of nowhere, you would hear a siren, and that was the start of the Specials' 'Ghost Town' . . . (https://www.youtube.com/watch?v=1WhhSBgd3KI&feature=kp)

I had never heard anything like it before. Up to then it had always been Irish music or American music that my mam played at home – Nat King Cole, Elvis, a cheeky Barbra Streisand album here and there (which, let me tell you, had a worrying impact on me, come talent-show time at school. You try telling a group of fifth years after performing the greatest hits from *Funny Girl* that you do really prefer girls.)

I was too young for punk or glam rock, so when 'Ghost Town' hit my nine-year-old senses, I was all, 'Cor blimey, that Thatcher woman seems a bit tough . . .' OK, maybe not that, but I was suddenly aware of *difference*. People weren't all happy: the song's video about urban decay and disenfranchised youth which was shown on *TOTP* didn't instantly politicise, but it did confuse me, opening my highly caffeinated eyes to a different, harsher world through music. These weren't smiling faces, or balladeers telling girls they loved them till the end of time. And they weren't throwaway, hedonistic, let's-dance-on-a-Friday-night sort of pop . . . this was real, and quite gritty and I loved it . . . I wasn't quite sure why I loved it . . . but I did. It was the first song of that kind that stuck in my memory: six blokes in a car driving around a desolate urban landscape saying, 'You know what? Life's pretty rubbish at the moment.' Ah, great stuff, happy memories.

The video also featured the first non-white faces I saw on TV other than comedian Kenny Lynch, and boxer John Conteh, both of whom I regularly saw on that classic of daytime telly, *Pebble Mill* (or, to give it its full title, *Pebble Mill at One*, a brilliant device which meant that no one ever forgot when it was on). Now, don't get me wrong: a Catholic school is always going to be a melting pot, and along with regular trips to London I had plenty of non-white friends growing up. It's just these guys were young adults talking about a place without hope and looking pretty unhappy about it, which was not what I had been used to seeing on TV until then. It just made me think, 'Blimey, this life thing obviously isn't as easy at it looks.'

The only reason I didn't buy 'Ghost Town' was because I didn't buy very much at that age as I was only nine, and my pocket money only extended as far as a quarter pound of wine gums after Mass on Sunday – as far as I was concerned, they were the body and blood of Christ's gums (very poor, sorry). But my years of playing fast and loose with the 7" single market were just around the corner . . . with tragic consequences. (Well, tragic for an eleven-year-old, so not really that tragic at all.)

It can only be described in my head as the Great Single

Swindle of '84 (or maybe the single greatest single swindle of '84). It ranks only alongside the great Canine Swindle of '87, when we moved house and my mother and father promised a dog and then reneged on it in such a way that I thought they had amnesia – the two greatest family-based injustices in my life (yes, I had a happy upbringing). But back to the single swindle. Nicola, my sister, is three years older than me, and as such we shared many things: pop-culture experiences, clothes (the borderline, androgynous stuff ie. Kids from Fame sweatshirt), parents, rabbits and – like most two kids not too far apart in age – some possessions, which were very much described erroneously as 'ours'. So when Nicky suggested we pool our pocket money to buy one of the standout hits of 1984, Wham!'s 'Young Guns (Go For It)', I was all ears.

This was, after all, my sister talking, my older sister – I could trust her, surely.

Of course I could: on my first day at secondary school, I felt like a made guy because of her, my Liotta to her Pesci in *Goodfellas*. Even though I'd gone to a local primary school, my parents had decided, in lieu of the possibility of my not passing the 11-plus (of which I could have told them there was a 100 per cent possibility), I should go to a local Catholic comprehensive. Now, any young kid's – but boy's in particular – first day at school is as terrifying as it is exciting. You're thrown into a bear pit where the rules of the playground need to be learnt quickly in order to survive (e.g. if a sixteen-year-old boy on the cusp of manhood gives you a clip around the ear, you don't grass on them). Added to that, I was starting in a school where I knew not one person apart from my sister. But as my mam dropped me off on that first day – me walking through the gates feeling like an extra in *The Green Mile* – it was soon made aware to me that my sister was looking out for me – i.e. I didn't get beaten up by anyone in her year (and she was in the fourth year). I was the school equivalent of a small-time Mafia hood, not untouchable, but protected. At least, until she left – then I was fair game. Which was obviously brutal.

Don't get me wrong: no fourteen-year-old girl should be nice to their younger brother, so I'm not saying she was especially nice to me at school; she just ensured I was safe, and that people with names like Wormy and Lugsy and Carlos didn't beat me up. To be honest, though, my sister and I have been really close all our lives, apart from an eighteen-month period where she was a truculent teenager (boys, vegetarianism, smoking) and in turn I played my part as an annoying little brother. (She at least grew out of her phase.) Even now, I defer to her better judgement and am incredibly proud of her achievements in becoming a doctor of criminology (she's a doctor, for God's sake, and I talk out loud for a living, so it's not too difficult to see who got the brains and, come to think of it, the looks).

So, when my sister, my trusted older sister, hit me with this Wham!-based pocket-money idea, who was I to refuse my protector? (A word from her, and old Luggy would be paying me a visit come break time.) Back then, my pocket money was something that most children these days would argue constitutes slave labour, but I duly handed over my meagre contribution to my sister, and she went to Andy's Records in Colchester to buy the Wham! classic.

Now, together with A-ha, Wham! was a massive deal at the

time, even though pretty early on you could tell that girls weren't really George's thing (I mean Pepsi and Shirlie? Who are these guys kidding?) Every girl at youth club was obsessed, and that meant, despite the fact that 'Young Guns' wouldn't necessarily have been *my* first choice of single to buy, I had to get in on the game.

And, thanks to my sister, as far as I was concerned, I was indeed now in on the game. I was very excited at the prospect of actually part-owning my first ever single and was looking forward to getting it on the turntable and hearing it. However, even though my sister bought it, and I did part-own it, I never got to hear it. Well, I did through walls, specifically my sister's bedroom wall (I could hear the muffled chants of 'Wise guys realise there's danger in emotional ties'), but it never made it in to my hands . . . She'd only gone and done the old 'older sibling possession is nine-tenths of the law' thing, and seeing as though she could still theoretically beat me up – and I had no idea what 'possession' or, indeed, 'law', were – it remained hers.

I was burnt by this, badly burnt, so when I was old enough to get the number 70 bus or, less conveniently and more round the houses, the number 53 bus, into town, I didn't pool my money with anyone. If I was going to buy my first outrightly owned single, it was going to be mine and mine alone and, furthermore, it was going to be one that would endure the test of time . . . and that single was 'I Can't Wait' by Nu Shooz.

Now the song itself is a piece of classic eighties pop and, as far as I'm concerned, it's clearly stood the test of time (surely I'm not alone in that?) but, as we've agreed by now, this isn't really about the song itself – it's about the time, the clothes and, in particular, the roller skates.

As a kid in Colchester – in fact, for any kid growing up – Saturdays are your Mecca. It's the free pass day, it's a bus into town, it's the wandering round the shopping centre, it's pretending you're fifteen to get in to see *Poltergeist 3*, it's buying your own clothes (mainly, as mentioned earlier, ski jackets) for the first time . . . and, as I'm sure was the case in so many other towns, it was about the roller rink, which in Colchester meant . . . hold on to your hats . . . the Triangle Roller Rink.

The Triangle Roller Rink was near an area called the Hythe (which I know lends itself to a wharfy image of dockers in gin houses). It was situated on the edge of an industrial estate, near a railway track and, frankly, you couldn't think of a more terrifying place for a suburban father to drop off their teenage daughter. So far, so 'over my dead body', but in mid-eighties Colchester, on a Saturday afternoon (evening if you were over eighteen), this was the only place to be. It was kind of our Hacienda, if you substitute cream soda for class-A drugs.

The Triangle was glamorous in that mid-eighties, edge-of-an-industrial-estate kind of way (if such a thing exists). It had bouncers, though for the life of me I was never sure why ('Kids Going Nuts On Cherry Cola' read the headline . . .). It was pitch-black inside, save for the classic neon, mind-throbbing disco lights, which the resident DJ held power over. There was a strict anti-clockwise directional flow to curb any anarchic clockwise skaters – oh, there were rules! But what it really had were *girls*. And not just the girls you knew from school, not the ones that had got to know you, sat in lessons with, been out

45

with your friends, and when you slow danced with them, told you how they saw you as a 'brother' (arrgghh, why was that always me?!); no, there were other girls, from other schools with strange names like Phillip Morant, and Sir Charles Lucas (that's the schools, not the girls). Girls who were new, who you hadn't made an idiot out of yourself in front of (yet), and who were therefore the MOST EXCITING HUMAN BEINGS OF ALL TIME.

There was, however, a problem. To impress said ladies, you had to be able to skate – or have your own motorbike (which was never going to happen, not least because I was about fourteen at the time), so skate it was. Preferably backwards.

Now I can't stress how important this was in 1980s Colchester. It elevated a 'Wouldn't look twice at him' kind of a guy to the status of, well, a backward-skating god and, let me tell you, that was about the highest status there was. This was a big problem for me, as I could barely roller skate in a forward direction (that's 'skate', not 'blade' by the way). So, each week, as I slipped the (slightly warm and damp, never a good combo) roller skates on, I had a sense of dread that I was going to spend the next hour of my life on my arse as boys skated around me, whisking the likes of Linzi Turner and the lovely Andrea (can't remember her second name, but I'm sure it was goddess-like) off their feet.

Irrespective of how bad I, or anyone else, was at skating, though, when Nu Shooz's timeless classic 'I Can't Wait' (I repeat the title here in case you've forgotten and it therefore hasn't stood the relatively short test of time since I first mentioned it) came on, it became like dance rush-hour on the roller rink. Which did always slightly confuse me, as unless you were part of the chorus line in *Starlight Express*, you didn't really dance to the music, you skated . . . the same way you skated to any other song. But when Nu Shooz was playing, you got your ass (literally, in my case), onto that plastic-covered concrete and went for it.

The rink would invariably smell of the detritus of a pubescent Saturday afternoon: sweat, cheap teenage aftershave (Insignia) and, for some reason, spilt, slightly off milk. It's an odd combination of odours, but to this day, whenever I hear 'I Can't Wait' – which to be honest, isn't all that often – I still get a faint whiff of it. And no, my skating never got any better; nor did my luck at the rink.

But it didn't matter: I had my first single, which my sister couldn't touch (although she did, often), and I was on my way. Only another twenty or so, and we've got ourselves a collection! Then . . . well, my friends, then there's a new player in town . . . (Most of that was internal dialogue at the time – I never actually said those words out loud.)

SOUNDTRACK

4

'Meeting Across The River'
by Bruce Springsteen
Sundry albums from the Britannia Music Club
(including a little bit of Phil Collins)

The Boss. Fortunately, a nickname given to him. (Could you imagine someone actually calling themselves that? Unless they were in fact some kind of boss, then I guess it would be OK.)

Bruce Springsteen has been the most important musical influence in my teenage life; and, twenty-five years later, probably still is. Now, before you start thinking, 'Oh, here we go, Springsteen, chest-thumping Reagan-era stadium rock, *Born In The USA*, down with the commies,' etc, let me stop you, and by stop you, I mean open a can of whoop-ass on you if you trash-talk the Boss.

Seriously.

Springsteen is *so* much more than just that album (and even if he wasn't, it wouldn't matter). Take the actual title track,

'Born In The USA' – it can be summed up as: a guy's born into a hard life, goes to Vietnam, loses his brother out there, comes home, can't get a job, ends up in jail . . . Not exactly the anthem of the American dream. More proof needed? *Nebraska*, the album he made before *Born In The USA*, was made in his bedroom on a four-track recorder, and featured songs about loners, small-time criminals and serial killers (a sure-fire hit with the American Right if ever there was one), while the title track of the album ends up with the main character being sentenced to death by electric chair. It's pure commercial gold!

Springers (my pet name for him – it never took off) has always been the hero of the underdog, the loser, the guy that can't get the girl; in short, most of us, and in even shorter, teenage me.

But, how did a kid growing up in a village in Essex become (mildly) obsessed with a blue-collar rock star from New Jersey? I'll tell you how: the Britannia Music Club.

Now, the first thing to make clear, to those not in the know, is that the Britannia Music Club was not a physical entity. It was not an actual building where bands played and the floor became sticky because so much beer had been spilt on it (or, like one of my favourite venues in London, the Garage, which gets so cramped that the sweat actually collects as condensation on the ceiling, and then drips into your beer . . . salty!) – alas, no. It was a mail-order music company that you joined, and when I say joined I actually mean you were press-ganged into joining by your friends (in some 18th century type way), because said friends were on a promise of an extra album or two for any new members they got on board.

It was simple and genius, like a teenage Ponzi scheme – you

heard about it from your friend, who heard about it from their friend, etc, etc . . . it was a suburban adolescent gold rush – people were plucking albums out of the ground (or rather, letter boxes). But, similar to California in the 1840s, it turned out to be too good to be true . . . why do we never learn from history?

I have no idea if the Britannia Music Club still exists (in fact, I do, as I've just looked it up, and it ran from 1969 to 2007 – R.I.P) or if anyone outside my group of friends were members, but unintentionally it is responsible for my musical tastes, and that of a lot of my peers. (It's got a lot to answer for.) So, in my case, Neil Butler got me involved. He's my oldest friend – I've known him since we met in an alleyway by his house aged five, when he attempted to bully me out of some bacon crisps, whereupon a strange five-year-old version of a Mexican stand-off ensued that went something along the lines of:

'I want your crisps.'

'They're mine, you can't have them.'

'But I want them,' etc, etc, and we were friends from that day forth. (Boys . . . very simple.) He was classic five: really blond hair, mothers loved him, and we've bonded ever since, on everything from pubescent rock, actual pubescence, *Vic Reeves Big Night Out*, and movies – in particular, the *Nightmare on Elm Street* films – and early John Carpenter. Neil had film parties around his place, about half a mile from mine, which, let me tell you, after you've watched *Nightmare on Elm Street 2* and have to walk (run) home on your own in the foggy dark, is a long half-mile.

Anyway, for his trouble, Neil received a Madonna album (*True Blue*, obvs); I, in turn, got Simon Johnson or Mark Ainsworth (can't quite remember which one) involved, and for my recruitment efforts, got Go West's *Go West*. Result! And so it went on, and on and on (I guess until 2007, when Britannia sent out it's last LP or CD, as it probably was by then, and went to that big HMV in the sky).

So, here's how it worked. It was a simple process. For about £5 (in today's money, a couple of hundred quid or thereabouts), you got three albums. That was the sweetener, and what's not to like? Well, I'll tell you: when you looked down the list of records that were on offer, it soon became clear that the three albums coming your way weren't current, out-at-the-moment, top-of-the-hit-parade type albums. No. They *were* albums by the really big stars of the time, but they were more your back-cataloguey than your latest-releasey, so, if you wanted the hot-off-the-press *No Jacket Required* by Phil Collins, tough luck . . . but if you wanted Phil Collins, *Hello, I Must Be Going!* (much maligned, but pretty dark – let's just say it's one of his 'divorce' albums, so, you know, not too light for a thirteen-year-old kid), then quids in.

Alternatively, you could also invest in some of their classical albums such as some obscure orchestra's version of Holst's *The Planets*, which in many cases, strangely, made the parents in our village more worried than they would have been if their sons had become goths (which as any self-respecting music lover knows involves the prerequisites of hanging around graveyards and drinking premium-strength cider whilst listening to the Sisters of Mercy, and latterly, the Mission). It was as though by listening to classical, parents were worried their children would become socially ostracised versions of Patrick Moore, hopefully without the questionable politics.

Now for someone who at the time only owned one album, the thought of quadrupling my collection, albeit with three not-so-current albums, was quite appealing. The one album I owned by then, by the way, was a compilation album, and only the finest compilation album of all time, called *The Heat Is On*. I bought it from the local Shell garage, entirely paid for in coppers (much to the bored cashier's chagrin), and it featured legendary power ballads like John Farnham's 'You're The Voice', Kenny Loggins' 'Footloose' and a bit of classic REO Speedwagon in the timeless shape of 'Keep On Loving You'. In fact, this was *such* a great album, let's get sidetracked for one minute to talk about it.

Now, vis-à-vis 'soundtrack' (i.e. this book) it's a toughie as, strictly speaking, I'm meant to be writing about *songs* that shape your life rather than albums, but it's a compilation album, so different rules apply (and, anyway, it's my book). So, think of this as a welcome diversion, like taking a drive to the coast and getting a portion of chips on the way, especially if you're not keen on blue-collar American rock/folk music.

My first ever job was a paper round – so far, so kid growing up. However, I had *the* paper round of all paper rounds. I'm talking the plum gig. There was no nepotism going on here, it was just plain luck. Rather than give me a regular paper round, on a Sunday, Wilby's the newsagents had me *drive* around in a tiny Honda van, so that I could deliver the other paperboys' papers . . . Thought you'd be impressed. This can only be described as a sweet deal. The guy driving the van was (I think) called Ian, with a perm that suggested Def Leppard roadie (that, I definitely remember). He was quite wide, in a small-town 'got to see a man about a dog' kind of way, but he liked me, largely because in a nerd-like way, I could remember exactly what paperboy did what route, which meant he didn't have to and could just drive the van, largely hung-over.

After we finished this route I then had my own paper round, which similarly involved a minimum of wear and tear on my shoes, as I also did this in the van (like I said – sweet gig). It was a rural route, so the papers I delivered were to a few farmers and country folk who would always pay in change and say, 'Thanking you,' in the broadest Suffolk accent, after which Ian dropped me home in time for a quick change before Mass and my altar boy duties (which is ANOTHER chapter, but we can't go off on another tangent, what with this already being a tangent and all).

So, before Ian (I think) would drop me home, he would take me to Marks Tey's only garage, where his girlfriend worked, doing the glamorous Sunday morning shift. He would then buy me sugary instant coffee (I was wired on caffeine for the best part of my childhood) and chocolate shortbread whilst he went and whispered sweet nothings to his gal.

Now, those of you who have spent hard time in petrol stations (you know who you are) will know that after filling up with petrol, and using the conveniences, there's not *that* much else to do. My attention shifted pretty rapidly from the rural *Essex A–Z* (a pretty thin read, to be fair) to car stereos, of which I happily knew/still know nothing, to finally, and most pleasingly, cassette albums, and there I saw it . . . *The Heat Is On*: sixteen tracks from Glenn Frey's title track to Loggins, interspersed with titans such as Survivor, the Cars, Mr Mister and Marillion thrown in.

One glance and I knew I had to have it, immediately. The only problem was a funding issue: I didn't have the cash, which I know was weird, seeing as how I'd just finished my paper round, but it was 1986, so cut me a little slack. Also, there was no way I was going to get burnt again after Wham!-gate (we didn't actually call it that), so asking my sister to come in with me was out of the question.

Rather than going to the local bank (my dad) for credit, however, I decided that the best plan of action was to empty the penny jar that had been collecting dust for some time in my bedroom at home (the contents of which I think were supposed to be destined for charity, but let's gloss over that for now). So, the very next day, I walked into that garage, straight up to Ian's (think that was his name) girl and splashed the cash. There was a new high-roller in town as £6.29 cascaded over the till area (all in coppers). I had arrived on the Marks Tey (if not Colchester) music scene. I had bought my first album.

And not just any album, mind – a compilation album, and one that was all killer, no filler. This meant popularity in the form of loads of friends making copies of said album on that weird cassette-to-cassette, high-speed setting that made the artists sound like they recorded the albums on helium (when in fact, what with it being the eighties and all, they most likely recorded on something else).

This was done in each other's bedrooms and usually took quite some time, so as we waited we indulged in the only other thing as important as music: playing computer games on our ZX Spectrums (for all you Generation One Directioners, that's the eighties version of PlayStation) which was a labour of love, taking so long to load it was the teenage equivalent of embarking on the Santiago de Compostela pilgrimage.

If you grew up in the eighties, the ZX Spectrum was the greatest invention of all time – I'll allow a Commodore 64 into the mix, but anyone whose parents bought them an Acorn or, worse, a BBC computer (a computer! What was the BBC thinking?) was rightly considered a social pariah with their limited games and even worse their educational ethos. There was one problem: to load a game was a simple but delicate affair as, after the game was set to load (on a cassette player!), the slightest movement would cause the computer to crash. It was essentially teenage bomb disposal – and not the thing to be doing when classic power rock anthems are playing in the background.

Anyhoo, first album secured, we rejoin our hero back at Britannia . . .

In the minds of us thirteen-year-old adolescents, joining the Britannia Music Club and getting those three albums was a win-win . . . win deal. In short, I couldn't lose. However, there was a catch. You see, the great three-album deal was, in fact, a joining sweetener (I know, who'd have thought?) and so, if you didn't tick the tiniest box at the very bottom of the joining form, you ended up being committed to having to buy at least one and possibly three albums a month. And, would you believe it, I and most of my friends didn't tick that box. So, as vinyl or cassettes from the likes of Prefab Sprout, Tears for Fears and Johnny Hates Jazz started dropping through our letter boxes on a regular basis for a tenner a pop (at the time, the equivalent sum of paying off a dodgy loan shark after a £2 investment), our parents quickly realised that we had made something of a schoolboy error (which, to be fair, was exactly what it was).

So, even though I loved the Boss and knew I wanted *Born In The USA* as the first non-compilation album to have in my collection (who wouldn't? It was cool, he was wearing jeans and a white T-shirt, he was kind of strutting, in a standing-like way, he had a red cap casually in his back pocket – what if he had sat down?! – but he didn't care, he was the Boss – and 'Dancing In The Dark', one of the main tracks on the album, was on TV all the time with that awesome Courtney Cox cameo . . .) I knew that, due to the offer, I had to get through *The Wild, The Innocent & The E Street Shuffle* first. Who? What?

Quite.

It was Bruce's second album, one from his back catalogue – that's how it worked, remember? I'm not sure how many copies it sold, but I think my purchase definitely helped get the sales up. In truth, I wasn't holding out much hope as I put the cassette on. I was fickle, I was a teenager, I wanted mid-eighties-stadium-rock Springsteen, not late-seventies-life-is-actually-pretty-hard-growing-up-in-New-Jersey Springsteen.

Was I ever wrong . . . It's still to this day one of my favourite albums, and it spurred me on to really get into Springsteen. (My other two sweetener albums, incidentally, were a Simply Red album classic, and the aforementioned *Hello, I Must Be Going!* by Phil Collins, which, being about middle-aged divorce, helped me, fairly inappropriately, through a fair bit of teenage heartache.)

So, I became obsessed with Springsteen, and when I say obsessed, I mean that, simply put, I just really liked him. I know that's hardly fanaticism, but I've never been the sort that needs one sole tribe to identify with, so I didn't hang with the other

'Springsteen kids', although to be fair I'm not sure there were any. Maybe a couple of dads.

My love also didn't extend to dressing like him (far too many ski jackets for that). I did, however, save up and buy the whole of the rest of his back catalogue, about six or seven albums. Now I have to be honest: it was for the most part pretty dark stuff, and having been raised on pretty happy or, if not happy, drunk Irish music up to then, it must have been disconcerting for my poor parents to hear stories of Vietnam, serial killers, and ghetto-doomed love stories coming from the stereo in my room. Still, as long as I wasn't into drugs!

From the first album *Greetings From Asbury Park, N.J.*, it gets steadily more brooding. From the heartbreaking 'Darkness On The Edge Of Town' through to the despair of 'The River', it was exactly the kind of thing that, as a music-loving parent, you'd be quite proud of your kid for listening to it, whilst simultaneously ever so slightly worrying about their mental welfare. Yes, Springsteen became my pre-Housemartins/Smiths go-to music for self-pity . . . and it was one song from *Born To Run*, probably my favourite album of all time, that got me right *there*, as they say.

'Meeting Across The River', like so many of Springsteen's songs, is a beautifully told story that is like a dagger through your heart, only one that you're grateful for. It's a song about two small-time hoods going from New Jersey to Manhattan to finalise a deal that they might or might not come back from (all pretty relevant stuff in Colchester when you're fifteen). With Springsteen, it's all about the detail, the minutiae: he's the Miss Marple of the American folk/rock scene. The little things the characters say are the things that stick in my mind, little throw-away lines like:

> 'And remember, just don't smile.
> Change your shirt, 'cause tonight we got style.'

While the song finishes with a kind of proclamation . . .

> 'And tonight's gonna be everything that I said,
> And when I walk through that door,
> I'm just gonna throw that money on the bed,
> She'll see this time I wasn't just talking,
> Then I'm gonna go out walking.

> Hey Eddie, can you catch us a ride?'

You see? YOU SEE?! There's no glamour in all of this: he wasn't Simon Le Bon in a beautiful suit prancing around on a yacht (which, incidentally, I did also love). He has to ask his mate for a lift – his song was real, I could relate to it . . . I had to ask *my* dad for a lift! Which made us practically *brothers*! (And admittedly, mine was only to the Odeon, not a contraband deal which I wasn't sure if I'd come back from.) But it was the sound of a broken heart, and if you can't relate to that as a teenager, you'll never relate to it.

I've long since come to the conclusion that happy, positive people like sad music, which admittedly is a handy piece of self-diagnosis, but it's one, out of self-interest, that I'm sticking to. There's something about a sad song that just hits me for six, well, for four minutes and thirty seconds at least, but after a little tear, and a touch of 'Woe is me', I'm back on my merry way. (And yes, I *am* aware this makes me sound like a simpleton.)

So, prior to Springsteen, all my reference points had been from my sister's record collection – and *Smash Hits* magazine. Don't get me wrong, I still loved all that stuff – your Curiosity Killed the Cat, your Kajagoogoo – but this was serious music I wasn't afraid to be into, the first music I'd listened to that gave me an identity, albeit a weird identity that I had nothing in common with.

To put this song into some kind of 'Why am I singing it outside my house in a cul-de-sac at 11 p.m. on a Friday night?' context, this was probably the first track to ease my broken (or what passes for broken) heart.

The village next to ours was Great Tey and, as I say, by virtue of that very fact – i.e. it being the next village along – we were naturally suspicious of each other. They were country folk, whereas we, with our two main roads and more than one shop, were veritable city slickers. They did, however, have one thing we couldn't match: a youth club. Every Friday night the place was rammed with coming-of-age guys and – more importantly for us – gals; all getting together, breaking up, making up, then breaking up . . . and so on. For my bunch of ZX Spectrum-playing pals it was heaven: more new girls who didn't know we weren't that cool (yet). It was the roller rink without roller skates – or a rink. In our eyes, they were country girls who were kind of glad you were there, and impressed that you went into town, by bus no less, on a Saturday. The first few times we went there, we thought we'd struck gold. A typical night would include a mixture of pool competitions, slow dances, a walk around the estate to the chip van, hanging out in the park, watching then breaking up a fight or two ('Leave it, he's not worth it,' etc, etc), all before a dad would come and pick us up (but waiting for us the obligatory two streets away).

Somehow, almost like feudal England, the choice of girl you were to go out with seemed to be pre-ordained – it had to be a certain girl from a certain clan. So, as all my friends found love (not in a hopeless place – well, in Great Tey) amongst a certain group of girls (the quite cool, but not Alpha set), so it was that Fate decided I was also to go out with a girl from that group. She was called Shaleen Aves (I know, what a name – I mean, honestly, how many Shaleens have you ever met?). This was fine by me, although if memory serves me correctly, Shaleen's dad did have a Status Quo poster above the mantelpiece, which even at fourteen was pretty disconcerting and didn't really bode too well for the future. (And, whilst we're on my memory, I'm now virtually certain that paper-round van driver's name *was* Ian.) Shaleen was a beauty: elven – the best way to describe her – and a really nice girl. The problem was . . . well, in a nutshell, she didn't really like me like that. Just more as a . . . wait for it . . . *friend.*

This was no big deal (obviously it *was* a big deal, but I was able to laugh that off, through my tears and Bruce Springsteen), except that this was what we did – go to the youth club – every week, for at least three years, and my crush lasted a while. So, instead of moving on and, like most sensible, well-adjusted young men, asking someone else out, I asked her out again, and again, and again . . . for about a year (yes, I can hear the cries of

'Loser!' and yes, I agree with you). My friends have subsequently worked out that I asked her out 156 times, and whilst I think there's an element of the Shroud of Turin about their estimations, it is true to say that I asked the poor girl out a lot, and she said no – a lot. Cue the *Groundhog Day*-like succession of rejection: 'No', 'No, thank you', 'I'll think about it' and 'Get away from me, I've said no over a hundred times now.' There might've even been a slap or two (but alas, never any tickle).

What there was, however, was my good self, running home, or more accurately, getting a lift from my dad, bless him, and as he put the car in the garage, me walking around the cul-de-sac singing this Springsteen song in my head about two gangsters from New Jersey about to get whacked. (Or at times *Crockett's Theme* but it didn't have any words, so that would've made me a kid just humming a song around a cul-de-sac at 11 p.m. at night . . . which would've been weird.) It definitely made me feel better and helped me get through the heartache . . . so I could recover enough to ask Shaleen out again the following week.

So, thank you, Boss (that's 'Bruce' to all you non-Bruce fans). You were there for me when it mattered. Which by the way, is still now.

SOUNDTRACK

5

Queen

at Live Aid (13 July 1985)

From musicians I have interviewed who were there in 1985, it's clear that Live Aid was one of those generation-, and in some cases, career-defining moments. For a twelve-year-old me, it wasn't the enormity of the day and the cause behind it that gets it onto my soundtrack; nor was it the fact that pretty much for the first time ever these names had been put together on one stage. It wasn't even the sheer effort that Bob Geldof, Midge Ure and Harvey Goldsmith went to, doggedly hunting down, educating and press-ganging pampered eighties musicians into performing. No, this is on my soundtrack for the simple reason that it's indirectly responsible for my becoming a TV host. So if you're looking for someone to blame for me being on the box (quite understandable), blame Freddie Mercury.

Now, obviously I wasn't there (I'm not certain, but I don't remember seeing many twelve-year-olds in the crowd); I was, however, transfixed, watching at home. As I recall the weather was beautiful for the concert, though I guess this is hardly a revelation as it took place in July, and, being young, every summer based memory from childhood involves a baking hot day . . . your memories can be blurred, and the images snatched here or there, but the sun is always shining: McEnroe crying at Wimbledon, Arsenal losing the FA Cup in '78 (boo), winning it in '79 (hurray), being allowed to watch *Tales of the Golden Monkey* whilst eating my dinner on my lap, my mam wearing a bikini doing the ironing in the garden (very seventies/eighties), all (especially the last one, thankfully) taking place on baking hot days.

However, if it was glorious sunshine outside, it meant that getting the TV turned on in our house was the equivalent of crossing from East to West Berlin in the late sixties – it simply wasn't on – with my mam playing the part of chief border guard (the Stasi would have snapped her up if she'd been born in East Berlin). It was always the way with my parents – well, my mam: you asked a simple question, e.g. 'Can I watch some TV?' and the answer would have made the inventors of the Enigma machine proud. It was always, 'We'll see' (We'll see what?) or the equally cryptic, 'Maybe/perhaps', just leaving the possibility hanging in the air, but still letting you know that there was pretty much no chance this TV-watching plan of yours was going to play out how you wanted it to.

So the fact I was able to even see Mercury and Co strutting their stuff rather than having to 'play outside' is a miracle. Or it could have been to do with the fact that Mam worked on Saturdays (one or the other). Saturdays followed a very similar pattern – Mam would go to work (BHS in Colchester) and my dad, my sister and I would go into town at the ungodly hour of seven in the morning, before we'd even had breakfast. The reason for this was that as I went to a C of E primary school, on Saturday mornings I had to go to Catechism classes at the local convent with the nuns in town to prepare for my First Communion. (Would it have been so bad if the sisters had allowed themselves a weekend lie-in and let us start at eleven?) As weird/bad as this sounds, I kind of liked it. My experience of nuns was always of the cuddly Irish ones, who were happy to give you a Murray Mint (from Jesus, obvs) rather than the *Philomena*-like ones. Despite this Holy minty enticement though, after a week at school, spending my Saturday mornings learning about the Gospels when knowing that most of my other friends from the village (with their C of E God – tsk!) were learning how to do wheelies on their bikes, was a bit of a slog.

So my parents, cannily, and rightly, thought they'd bribe me with an after-Catechism-class, slap-up breakfast. Post-nuns and mints, my dad would take me to BHS to say hi to my mam (this started at pre-Communion age, about six or seven, because at that age if you don't see your mam every couple of hours it feels as if they've been away for a few months/might have deserted you) and visit the canteen there, where I was allowed to eat ridiculous food that they'd lock parents up for feeding to their kids in public nowadays: strawberry flan – not cake, flan – for breakfast was a particular favourite. Not one of your five a day, and Jamie Oliver would have gone mental and rightly locked my parents up (if Jamie enjoyed custodial powers).

Saturday mornings then, like now, pretty much revolved around food, which continued on to lunch, when Dad would attempt the culinary version of the perfect crime. This involved us going to a fishmongers, picking up some cod roe (I know, were actual fish being rationed? What was he thinking?), frying it for lunch with chips (Dad chips were always a winner – universal truth), and then trying to clear up the kitchen (maybe), and get rid of the smell (never), before Mam got home. I mean, have you ever smelt cod roe? Do you even know what it is? Well, the unappetising definition would be fish eggs, but it's so much more than that. It's a beautiful, melt-in-the-mouth dish that I still love today, but it's one of those 'air the house' dishes, one where the smell doesn't really shift until twenty-four/forty-eight hours have passed post-fishy/eggy crime.

It played out the same each week. Every Saturday evening after work, my mam would smell the fried fish from the top of our street and, before she'd kiss any of us hello, she'd ask/state, 'Have you had cod roe for lunch again?' and bust my dad and his balls for stinking her house out. Eventually she won the battle, Smell-gate was no more, and cod roe was replaced by Findus Crispy Pancakes – odourless, but no less delicious – something that coincided with our house becoming a 'go-to' place for my friends (if a go-to place existed in Marks Tey).

By now my dad worked for British Telecom and commuted to London every day during the week, so even though I got to see him every night – cycling to the train station to meet him – those Saturdays became extra special. Post-Crispy Pancakes, a group of us: Neil Butler, Mark Ainsworth – the usual suspects – would settle down to watch the wrestling on telly, after which Dad would admirably take on the role of Giant Haystacks as a group of kids high on whatever was in a Findus Crispy Pancake would essentially assault him for hours in the thinly veiled guise of wrestling.

So although my dad wasn't necessarily a soft touch (far from it, when the occasion demanded, i.e. homework, bunking and the less serious, cautionable offence of scrumping), he was a bit more lax on the watching TV rule, and therefore on his shift (Saturday) I got to see a lot of *Grandstand* (I knew an unhealthy amount about the form of the runners and riders in the 3.15 at Haydock Park) and, more relevant for this chapter, Live Aid.

It's not that you remember the day itself. We didn't sit around the TV and say, 'Here we go, we're going to watch Live Aid together . . .' – it just sort of happened. We were aware at school about the famine in Ethiopia, and that the concert – in my twelve-year-old brain, at least – was the thing that was kind of going to sort it out once and for all, but I don't remember the Friday before, everyone being really excited about spending the next day watching this momentous event. So for me, it's not necessarily about vividly remembering that opening performance by Status Quo, and the sixteen – sixteen! – hours that followed. It's more about the feeling that came off the back of it, specifically, 'Blimey, that Freddie Mercury's good, isn't he?'

If you have the opportunity, or if you can't remember what a shift Queen put in and how Freddie stole the show, watch it now! http://www.youtube.com/watch?v=eQsM6u0a038

Have you done it? Excellent.

A bit like a young kid nowadays who's not entirely sure they have the actual memory of something, or if their memory comes from what's recorded on their parent's iPhone, similarly I don't know if I remember the performance vividly or whether I'm looking at it through rose-tinted spectacles because I've watched it on YouTube so many times . . . but, from the moment he comes on, with a ridiculous hand gesture where it looks as if he saying 'Up yours' to half the crowd, and machine-gunning the rest of them, Mercury was the master showman, owning Wembley and the watching world that day.

Since I've started in this business (of show), I've interviewed many people who knew Freddie Mercury and were there (or who were in Philadelphia, at the sister concert) – Elton John and Bob Geldof, to name but two. They all say the same thing: Mercury blew everyone away that day . . . people were scared to go on after him. Anecdotally, you hear that it turned Queen's career around, but for me, aged twelve, the fortunes of the band weren't foremost in my mind then.

Freddie's performance didn't make me want to be a rock star (well, OK, it did a bit, but even pre-voice breaking, my singing wasn't the best, only wheeled out for visiting Irish aunties with questionable taste and family sacraments); rather, it made me want to be an amalgam of Bob Geldof, Midge Ure and Harvey Goldsmith rolled into one, with a bit of Freddie thrown in as well.

I left school with two GCSEs. I'll understand if you think that makes me an idiot, but I prefer the term 'easily distracted' – five years at school and from the first to the last day, if there was more than one person in a corner talking, regardless of what I was meant to be doing (working), I'd find an excuse to go and see what they were up to. Generally though, my wanderings went unnoticed because St Benedict's R.C. Colchester didn't have the greatest academic reputation at the time. It was a bit of a waif-and-strays school – it was the only Catholic school in town, so any local left-footer could send their kids there, and what with Catholics being quite a diverse bunch, that meant it was something of a multicultural school and, aside from academia not being their – or my – strongest suit, in that very Catholic way it almost cared more about churning out pupils with a social conscience . . .

Student/me: 'Look, I'm not entirely blameless here, but I've only got two GCSEs.'

Careers advisor: 'Yes, but you understand the societal impact of the floods in Bangladesh and the complexities of a two-state solution. Off you go then, enjoy your adult life.'

Student/me: 'Oh, OK, thanks. Bye.'

Yes, we might not have been able to do algebra (and when I say we, I mean me) but we sure as hell knew who Lech Wałęsa was (and when I say we, in this case I do mean we). If that didn't stand you in good stead to get a job, then something was seriously wrong with the system.

And so, after watching Mercury et al at Live Aid, me and my best friend, Joseph Griffin, decided to do something about it. 'It' being famine.

I met Joseph in a classic secondary school case of mistaken identity: on the second day, I found myself standing next to him in the dinner queue and incorrectly took him for Michael 'Sharky' Larkin from my form. Joe couldn't be bothered to correct me, and we've been best friends ever since – boys, as I've said before, really are that simple/stupid.

I've got Joe to thank for a lot of my musical taste – he got me into the Smiths, the Housemartins, and even a bit of PWEI

(Pop Will Eat Itself for the uninitiated, or the 'I hadn't even been born in the eighties.') He had jet-black hair, was skinny as a beanpole, had the lungs of a thoroughbred and, for all you eye fans out there, possessed of a pair of steely-blue Paul Newman-like peepers. He also, like many kids at school, had somehow developed a kind of imaginary beef with another kid, a feud with no reason that lasted years. In Joe's case, he had an ongoing battle with Adam Butlin, which was unwise because Adam was what you'd call somewhat of a loose cannon in our year (no idea how it started, or if it ever ended. So Adam, if you're reading this, Joe will meet you on the playing field at 3.30 tomorrow, come tooled up.)

So, Joseph and I endeavoured, influenced by Freddie, Michael Burke and a junior membership of Amnesty International – like I said, why let a good academic education get in the way of social action? – to put on the finest fundraising concert that a Roman Catholic school in Colchester had ever seen . . . in the late eighties.

This was done with the help of the greatest teacher I ever had, Bob Hastie. Bob was head of RE and was a firebrand. He's one of the reasons I'm still a Catholic. For him religion, and religious studies, were all about social justice. It was about fairness, evolution (in all senses of the word) and society. In short, Bob was actually teaching politics. He had a shock of white hair, real firebrand stuff – which added to the message – and spoke with the conviction and passion of a politician: a Benn, or a Bevan. He encouraged students to think for themselves – not to judge but to question (almost unheard of in RE), and to come to their own conclusions, with their faith being a backdrop to this. Not a path to easy certainty. And we loved him for it. When he died (tragically young, from cancer) I'd left school, but hundreds of ex-pupils came back for his funeral, and the town stood still.

He was, however, a teacher – he helped get the hall, print the leaflets, etc – but he wasn't a theatre producer. And we had a problem. Talent.

We weren't exactly heaving with it at the school but, undeterred, and with that magnificent and deeply misguided self-belief that comes with youth, we decided to carry out an extensive search (which, to be fair, given that it was a school of 800, wasn't exactly that extensive), coming up with the brilliant idea of holding auditions . . . (I know, revelatory).

Think the Kids from 'Fame' crossed with *The X Factor*, crossed with dusty-village-hall am-dram, and you'd be right. Literally tens of people turned up to perform in front of Mr Hastie, Joe and myself and, as far as the final line-up went, we ended up with a veritable Vaudevillian cast of characters. I give you . . .

1) Alex Coster, the quietest bloke at school.

Alex was a sort of never-take-your-bag-or-duffel-coat-off type, and always stood outside the gym at break time. Whatever the weather. He was one of those *Fantasy Fighting* book types (but then, who were we to judge? Who didn't indulge in a little 'Fighting Fantasy' swordplay from time to time, and occasionally still do?). So, Alex was dead shy, but could play a passable synthesiser, which practically made him a member of Mensa at our school. He also, weirdly, would only play 'Love Me Tender' by Elvis, and, inexplicably for a kid who you couldn't get two words out of, was willing to do this in front of the whole school. Tick, he was in.

2) Orlando Reid, one of the most left-field characters in my form/school/life.

Always a little on the edge, he would veer between placid student and a wild, unpredictable Jack Nicholson-type from *One Flew Over The Cuckoo's Nest*. He'll always be remembered as a cult hero because when we had to dissect a bull's eye in Biology, Orlando decided to bring in a two-week-old shark's eye that he'd got from the fishmonger. It stank the place out something rotten (my dad would have been proud; my mam would have been livid). He could also move a bit, so for his audition he did a dance to Prince's 'Kiss'. Tick, he was also in.

3) Eugene Renford, the hardest guy in school, but also, and somewhat atypically, one of the nicest.

Eug was a legend – he could've ruled the school with fear, but instead he did so by being an incredible drummer. We would often while away a break time watching him drum to U2's 'Sunday Bloody Sunday' (like I said, Catholic school). So, for the concert, Eugene was a shoo-in. There was no band to play around him, but it didn't matter . . . he was Eugene Renford, and that snare drum sounded sweet! Tick, we had three acts.

4) Lastly, there was a young girl from the second year, who could play the flute, or clarinet (can't quite remember, but definitely

an orchestral instrument of some description), which in our school made her our Yehudi Menuhin (or Acker Bilk). Double tick, we had our line-up.

And so, with that veritable array of talent, the stage was set. But who could host . . . Who? we wondered . . . such an esteemed evening?

No, we couldn't think of anyone, so I ended up doing it.

I'd had some experience of being onstage before as part of a local am-dram group I was involved with called the Stane Street Players, but this was the real deal. You know what schools are like – get something wrong, or show some weakness, or one mistake, and you can be tarred with it for the rest of your school life. For example, on the second day of school, Gregory Rudd had a Cadbury's Caramel for his lunch which earned him the moniker 'Beaver' for the next five years (a beaver was in the advert for the chocolate bar at the time). And Gregory hadn't shown any weakness, he had just had a chocolate bar for his lunch, yet it had defined his whole school life. So, for me, hosting our version of Live Aid had to work.

And boy, did it (well, it kind of did).

For the teachers and any adults watching, I'm sure the night itself was awful, but for us – we felt like we were famine-busting impresarios.

It kicked off impressively with some sixth-form rock band we'd roped in at the last minute doing a more than passable version of 'Rockin' All Over The World'.

That set the stage for Alex Coster, who was on cracking form and did a Kraftwerk-inspired version of 'Love Me Tender' from behind his synthesiser.

Orlando, true to his mercurial left-field self, was given a red card by Bob halfway through his dance performance for turning it into a striptease, although luckily it was stopped before he got south of the equator.

And Eugene . . . well, he was just brilliant. And if he wasn't, he was the hardest kid in school, so no one was going to tell him otherwise.

That left the poor second year to close the show with a downbeat flute/clarinet-based number: something by the Chieftains, if memory serves me correctly.

There wasn't exactly a Queen moment, but we made a couple of hundred quid, which we were convinced would pretty much sort out Ethiopia, or at least Eritrea.

As for me, I suppose you could safely say I caught the hosting bug that day. I guess it was being on stage, talking to an audience, not getting booed by said audience, and putting the whole show together. It's all very well having lofty ideals when you're eight years old and watching Terry Wogan in Shepherd's Bush but, let me tell you, when you're at the coal face, staring into the whites of Orlando Reed's eyes as he's being hauled half-naked from the stage, it's a sink or swim moment. In truth, I trod water, but that was good enough for me.

So thanks, Freddie, for that baking-hot July afternoon when you ruled Live Aid and, for one afternoon, a little corner of Essex.

6

'Streams of Whiskey'

by the Pogues

It was the aforementioned, cherub-like, butter-wouldn't-melt-in-his-mouth, with head-boy good looks, Joe Griffin, of all people, who first got me into a life of crime. I sat next to Joe in English, always the best subject if you wanted to get away with some non-curricular chat as it was masked by the curricular chat, a prime example being when we did a class read-through of *Romeo and Juliet*. I played Mercutio, an easily distracted romantic (typecast) who's killed off early on, whilst Joe played Benvolio, Romeo's long-suffering best mate, which he did with his eyes shut, and therefore we had the opportunity to talk about whatever we wanted . . . including, sometimes, English.

It was through these non-timetabled chats that we discovered our friendship had more in common than the aforementioned mistaken identity in a dinner queue. Secondary school friendships really are the ones that burn the brightest – you haven't reached that compromise, live-and-let-live, flirt-with-Buddhism stage of your life yet (I believe they might call it middle age, but let's settle for adulthood), so your secondary school friendships are based on the honest parameters of things you like and dislike.

I was never part of any cool set at school; oddly, in my experience, no one who has ended up performing/showing off for a living was. The cool kids didn't need to be into anything other than themselves; they were attractive, they had each other and their good looks to . . . look at. They had the best spot in the common room; they had friends that picked them up on motorbikes – not Raleigh racers (Pursuits or Winners naturally), but motor-bloody-bikes! School was a mixture of the haves and have-nots. It was like the Edwardian class system that existed in, well, Edwardian times, only condensed down to secondary schools in the 1980s and 1990s. How could us lot 'downstairs' possibly compete with schools' versions of the landed gentry? As it turns out we couldn't, and it really didn't matter, because we were into . . . wait for it . . . *stuff*.

Yeah, that's right, cool kids! The rest of us actually *like* things – not so cool now, are you? Well, maybe you are, but we had things, and by things I mean pastimes: sports, books and, of course, music.

It's not that the insanely good-looking and overachieving set at school weren't into those things; it's that they didn't need them as much as anyone else (i.e. me). Looks and cool at school are like having a reserve of gold bullion in a safety deposit box in Zurich – if all else fails, you've always got something in reserve to fall back on. For me, not being one of the cool kids (as I think I've made clear), my 'thing' was music, with sports a close second, and books lagging a fair way behind in third.

The music that you get into, and the taste you develop in school during your teenage years through to your late teens, is probably the tone, taste-wise, that defines you for the rest of your life. These are the songs and bands that you still now jealously guard and are happy to go to the wall and take a bullet for in any pub/dinner-party debate, e.g. 'How dare you insult the good name of Def Leppard, sir? If you'd care to step outside, you ill-natured rogue, I will have my redress.' (At least that's my experience . . . as memory serves, that party didn't end well.)

So it follows that the music/artists I guard most ferociously now are the ones I fell in love with at school. In this case, St Bruce of Springsteen, who we've already heard from, the Smiths, the Housemartins and, most of all, the Pogues.

Joe got me into the Smiths during the hours of GCSE English coursework (as I've explained, so much opportunity for distraction . . .); it might also explain why I failed. *The Queen Is Dead* was out around that time, and Joe, being the more cerebral of the two of us, was lapping it up. He taped it for me, and before long I was lapping it up too. It was the sense of romance, tragedy and, most importantly, the sense of 'Why doesn't anyone understand me?' that any teenage boy/man in his forties would love/loves. But as much as I did love Morrissey, Marr and Co, I was always just a little too . . . happy (some might say simple) to be as devoted as my friend. I got on with my mam and dad, they *were* understanding, and I wasn't really bothered about relationships yet. Plus I was having far too much fun at school, so my heart wasn't in constant turmoil. It was more like occasional turmoil, and I had Springsteen for that.

Still, one day I found myself in Our Price, Colchester, with Joe, and there, staring at us was *The Queen Is Dead* – the empty cassette case. The staff in the shop had learnt from bitter experience not to leave the actual cassette in the case (though they were about to learn another cassette-sized lesson. Suckers!)

Sure, I already had the album (courtesy of Joe) and thievery wasn't really my thing, unless scrumping apples counted, in which case I was like one of the *Goodfellas* on the north Essex/ south Suffolk scrumping scene. But to have a taped copy of the album complemented with the original cover – well, I don't need to tell you what a coup that would have been.

Oh, yeah, I was deep into Temptation Land, but before I could think of the potential consequences (which, to be fair, would have only been making the security guard feel slightly miffed that he had to collar a couple of school kids for essentially stealing a bit of paper, and, if I was honest in Confession, a couple of acts of contrition and a Hail Mary or two) Joe had put said album inlay in my hand and legged it out of the shop.

There was no going back now; I was in too deep. There was no way I could put it back – put an inlay back in a cassette album? Crazy talk. It's a skill only a five-year-old and their tiny fingers can do with aplomb – certainly not a job for my Irish shovel hands – I'd get busted for sure. The only option was to high-tail it out of there. And so, with a deep breath, I followed Joe out into the veritable jungle that was the Red Lion shopping precinct.

As soon as I got out of the door, I ran with all my heart until I thought my lungs would burst. I ran until I realised . . . no one was following us, or cared, or was even aware that two fifteen-year-old kids had stolen some paper with words and pictures on it. The perfect crime was complete, and it was one that really did pay . . .

In the last couple of years I've interviewed Johnny Marr (nothing short of an absolute gentleman and genius, obvs; plus he hasn't aged at all) and he signed a copy of *The Queen Is Dead* as follows:

'Joe, give me my album cover back.'

Because, despite me doing all the legwork and taking all the risks, Joe ended up with the sacred cassette cover. With him being more the fan, and being the brains behind the op, it made sense. (See, crime doesn't actually pay, kids.)

I also loved the Housemartins. They're always talked about as a slightly more accessible Smiths, but that doesn't do them justice. *London 0 Hull 4* is a wonderful album that I always reach for when I'm heading down Nostalgia Lane. It was also one of my better Britannia purchases.

But this chapter is really about my love affair with one band: the Pogues.

I adore the Pogues. I can't tell you how ferociously I'll defend them from anyone who dismisses them as a 'shouty Irish band led by a drunk who can't string a sentence together' (argh, I'm feeling my blood boil even writing those words). I'm also one of those fans (the type I normally can't abide) who looks down on the weekend/Christmas-only Pogues fan . . . you know the ones I mean – the part-timers who like one or two tracks from the whole body of work of your favourite band and even then don't really know the words, putting together some hybrid version of the lyrics in their head. In the Pogues' case, it's normally their biggest hit: 'Fairytale Of New York'. I've lost count of the number of times I've shuddered as I've heard someone next to me at a Pogues concert bawling the line, 'The boys of the NYPD choir were singing "Galway Bay"' incorrectly, with something (usually) like, 'The boys of the New York city choir were singing on Christmas Day . . .'

To be fair, it's not too far off, but to a die-hard fan it is nothing short of an abomination.

There's nothing to make you feel smugger than making eye contact with another fan as you're singing along word-perfectly to an obscure B-side. It's as if you're saying, 'Yes, this is us. These others, they weren't there when it mattered. You and I – we're the real deal, no one else loves them like we do . . .' and other *Single White Female*/male-type sentiments.

The Pogues were the first band that us second-generation Irishers could call our own. After my Britannia Music Club and petrol station experiences, I was finally coming of regular-album-buying-age, and due to 'Fiesta' being a hit, and the fact I was Irish (it was kind of like a family law to like Irish bands). And the Pogues were tailor-made for me and those of my ilk.

Up until that point, the only Irish bands we had were the old-school legends such as the Dubliners (who were themselves very much the Pogues of their day), and bands most of you won't have heard of, like the Clancy Brothers and Tommy Makem. Real class acts, but that was the Irish music our parents listened to, so for obvious reasons we needed something different.

Out of nowhere (well, that's the way it seemed for me) came a group of both first- and second-generation Irish:

boys-about-town who had all that folk heritage, but who were also influenced and brought up on the Clash, on punk, on rock and roll, all chucked together with a healthy dose of Irish romanticism, heritage, tragedy and whisky. They were perfect.

They were also (when I first got into them) on tour, having just released their third album, *If I Should Fall From Grace With God*. It was added to my ever-growing, though still embarrassingly small collection, within days of it coming out, but for this album there would be no liberal parents sending their 15-year-old boy off to Brixton with a return train ticket in his hand and wishes that he should 'have a great time and don't do anything we wouldn't do'. Nada. There was no way I was seeing the Pogues yet.

However, sixth-form college was just around the corner, and that meant freedom . . . (in a way).

Colchester Sixth Form College was three (yes, three – I failed my GCSEs first time around. I won't mention it again if you don't) of the best years of my life. I went from a school that numbered 800 to a sixth-form college that was about 1,600 people, all the same age, with no uniform, and teachers you could call by their first name, e.g. 'Hey, Keith! He's my Communication Studies teacher, you know . . .' etc, etc.

After leaving school with two GCSEs (dammit, I've done it again), my normally pretty-chilled dad gave me an ultimatum: 'Get those GCSE retakes done, and then we'll see about A levels – if not, then out into the big wide world you shall go.'

It was all he needed to say: I was nowhere near big enough or wide enough for the place he was talking about. Of course, what it meant was no longer could I be distracted, like I had been at school, by what was going on when I saw two people talking in a corner (although I still afforded them the occasional glance). Anyway, with new, improved, hard-working(ish) Dermot in place, I had also finally reached the age of gigging.

It started small. The first band I ever saw was the Dubious Brothers at the Colchester Arts Centre. Two of their number were dressed as surgeons, and they had had local hits with 'South America Welcomes the Nazis' ('and Austria Welcomes Them Too Too Tototo!') and the equally catchy 'The Dog Ate My Poll Tax Form'. They'd have smashed it on *The X Factor*, if it had existed back then (all right, perhaps they'd only have made it to boot camp, but Louis would have said yes).

Other great Colchester venues included the Charles Dickens pub (God bless those crazy goths) and the Essex University Union, where my sister famously once saw Curiosity Killed the Cat – and never stopped banging on about it (she still goes on about it today). It was also about the time that Blur was starting out as a young band, but alas I never saw them.

Finally, though, I graduated to the Big Smoke. By now, the Pogues were on their fifth album, *Hell's Ditch*, and with my powers of concentration having recovered sufficiently to have got my necessary GCSEs and for my A-level studies to be going well, I was allowed to go to my first gig in London, to see the band I loved, in Brixton.

I can remember everything about it: the train journey up from Colchester on my own, drinking cans of what could have only been Kestrel, along with the teenage 'mothers' milk' – 20/20 (a fortified wine that only hardened alcoholics, graveyard dwellers and teenagers drank); meeting my friend, Tom Curry, who I'd been at sixth-form college with, and who was by then at university in London. He'd sorted the tickets, thus making him quite simply the coolest man on Earth. Then there was the pretence at nonchalance on the tube journey, like Brixton was somewhere I always went to see gigs, saying things really loudly like, 'Yeah, you know, I'm always up in London,' to try to make myself sound cool. (God, is this whole chapter actually about me really wanting to have been one of the cool kids?)

Now, if you've never been to see a band at the Brixton Academy . . . *go*. If you've never seen the Pogues at Brixton Academy, GO!

It was a terrifying experience. For a first-timer, going to see the Pogues at Brixton was like mainlining music: it was that dark orange glow as we came out of the tube station that only a British city can give you in winter time; it was the smell of the venue – the smoke, the sweat, the alcohol; it was the demographic of the Pogues' audience, which has always been so diverse – rockers, bikers, young drunks and punks, nationalists, old folkers and romantics. No one judging; no one looking out of place. It was overwhelming.

Like any good concert, if you are under thirty it's practically a prerequisite to spend some of it 'down the front'. In a Pogues concert, however, this means that you have to be prepared to kiss your friends, your drinks and sometimes your shirt good-bye. Being at the front at a Pogues concert essentially means that you are picked up at the start and put down at the end. Where? Well, you're not entirely sure yourself. Suffice to say that I didn't see Tom for the rest of the night. The first song the Pogues often play is a track called 'Streams of Whiskey'. It's one of the band's classics, and a real crowd favourite. The title would lead you to believe that it's somewhat of a drinking song, and you'd be right. My last and abiding memory of the gig is cuddling up with a biker and crying into a pint of God knows what as the Pogues finished the night with one of their weepies: 'Summer in Siam'.

I had arrived . . . in Brixton, and I belonged. To whom, I wasn't sure, or for how long, but as a music fan, those precious few minutes you share with each other – or with a biker you've only just met – are enough to earn a lifetime of loyalty. Apart from playing sport, it's the closest thing you have to a family outside your own.

Since that night I've seen so many other concerts. I've seen the Pogues play many times again, seen Shane collapse drunk and be carried off (which at the time seemed fun, but was actually very sad). I've even seen the God that was Joe Strummer play with them. But the first cut really is the deepest. So thank you, or *go raibh maith agaibh*, Shane and the boys. I don't know where I'd be without you (though I do know that, nine times out of ten, I'd have been a lot less hung-over).

SOUNDTRACK

7

'November Rain'

by Guns N' Roses (and a nod to Bob Marley)

So far, with the possible exception of the Boss, I think it's fair to say that my soundtrack choices haven't exactly been mainstream (I'm not sure what stream Brendan Shine was in, but it certainly wasn't main – more of a tributary).

Now, though, we find our hero (me) about to embark on a journey that would find him (still me) staring squarely in the face of two classic tunes that stalked me around an entire continent.

We all remember the first big trip we ventured on without our parents, for many reasons. For me, and in no particular order, those standout reasons are:

1. Having to actually pay for stuff. (You know, those pre-adult luxuries like food, board and travel.) A terrible shock to the system.

2. Existing almost entirely on bread and cheese, pretty much wherever we (I'll come back to who made up the other part of

the 'we' later) went. For the record, Vienna utterly rules when it comes to an early morning bakery.

3. Early morning, bleary-eyed arrivals at Eastern European railway stations, which meant roaming cold, deserted streets for hours on end until an equally cold, deserted hostel opened its doors.

4. An Egyptian man having nightmares and screaming all night in a hostel in Prague as I was throwing my guts up thanks to food poisoning – yes, that old classic . . . it lasted a week! (A particularly fond, vivid memory.)

5. And, finally, awful, awful music in Euro cafés. For the most part this involved covers of Bob Marley tunes. Actually, I'm lying – it *always* involved Bob Marley tunes. Specifically, 'One Love' and 'No Woman No Cry'.

In fact, no matter what café/bar/themed Irish pub you went into, if live music was being played, you could guarantee poor Bob Marley was getting murdered by well-meaning but limited musicians/barmen in bands with names I can't quite remember, but, for the purposes of this chapter, let's call Vladimir and the Impalers. (That's actually quite good.) Paris, Basel, Montreux, Venice, Vienna, Budapest, Prague, Berlin, Amsterdam, Rotter-bloody-dam, and then home, all played their part in ruining reggae's greatest ever exponent for me. Nowhere was safe. I know that the poor man's life was a spiritual one, but I'd wager even Jah himself wouldn't have objected to Marley getting a

◀ Me, Nicola and Dad, my dad's penchant for a 70s Afro in early evidence

▲ Me and my first love, you don't need to point out that nothing's actually on the TV ... stupid child

◀ Practising my first 'Blue Steel' or, more likely, going for the 'Train Driver' look

▼ The Family O'Leary, complete with Dad dressed as Travolta/70s Mafia Kingpin

▲ Me with Nicola, note her thousand yard stare as if already contemplating future vinyl robbery

◄ My first day at school, my poor sister seemingly oblivious to an impending lifetime of having to say 'please don't beat him up, he's my brother'

▼ Boys' Brigade: Nice club, itchy uniform, me second from right

► Cuddled up with Mum in 1983. Mum hugs, can't beat them

▼ Taking an early interest in history, whilst also sporting quite a camp pose in 1984

▲ Gap in teeth and unkempt hair, school pic standard

◄ Christmas Day at home in 1985, where Mum's love of Piesporter Michelsberg was first born

▼ Me, all dark and brooding about some such, and Mum in Turkey

▲ The Britannia Music club gang: Post water fight, endless summers, obvs. Myself second from right, Neil Butler, the Grand Wizard of the scheme to my right

▲ Me and Nicola, (me aged 16) getting ready for a night on the town in Colchester, in my case, bracing myself for a night of getting asked for ID

◄ Me and James Brown getting early hugging practice in at American Football camp with the legendary Walter Payton, July 1991

◀ The Tottenham home I shared with Anne and Sid, mischief on his mind

▼ Rob Morgan, epic man, and creator of epic mixtapes

◀ InterRailing with Glen Rayner in Venice, bum bags obviously not saying 'Please rob us' to any passing crook

▼ The 'wild man, with er, stick look' America in 1995 . . .

▲ My first taste of hosting live TV. *T4* with my first TV wife/sister Margherita Taylor

▲ On the cover of *Attitude* magazine in 2000

▶ Hosting a Madonna special for Channel 4 and trying hard not to think . . . 'Christ, I'm stood next to Madonna'

▲ The start of seven happy years hosting *Big Brother's Little Brother* on Channel 4

◀ ▼ Myself and Davina, the best of times, with the best of people

▲ Big decisions, but luckily an even bigger seafood platter at SXSW in Austin, Texas, 2007

▼ Being briefed by Sid, my producer and dear friend on the good ship X

▼ My team 'The Glam Squad' Tom and Sarah. Getting the show pony ready

▲ The first *National Television Awards* with myself and the team for X *Factor*

▲ Getting ready for showtime . . . with my hands in my pockets, slacker!

▲ Backstage with Britney in 2008, work it!

◀ Judges houses with Cheryl. Hellish I know

▼ With Katy Perry on the X, always a great fun guest

▲ 'Is the teleprompter on?', 'What?'. Me and Michael Jackson on stage at the O2 for his comeback concert, 2009

▼ Play the *Pipes of Peace*. The main man. McCartney after performing on the X *Factor* final in 2009

▶ See, he does smile. Me and Simon at the NTAs in 2010

little Old Testament on some of the Euro musicians I had to endure in the summer of '91. (Incidentally, the final nail in the very specific coffin marked 'Dermot Enjoys Listening to Bob Marley's Music' was when I learnt to dive in Dahab, Egypt. The Marley bands were so bad you couldn't wait to get back underwater.

To set the scene, I was in sixth-form college, doing A levels in Politics, Communications and English – proof for my dad that I could concentrate on something (anything) for more than five minutes. (As Timbuk 3 would have said, 'I'm doing all right, getting good grades, the future's so bright, I gotta wear shades,' etc, etc.) In fact, things were going so well that my friends and I decided to go InterRailing across Europe for the summer.

If memory serves me correctly, InterRailing involved getting a rail pass that granted unlimited rail travel across Europe for a month or two, so long as it was off-peak, on a really, really slow train (unless you were in Germany, where such things simply don't exist) and you didn't mind getting woken up four times a night by grumpy train guards demanding to see your passport; even though, more often than not, you were still in the same country as you were in when they last asked to see your passport, two hours before.

For a chap whose sole experience of travel without his parents prior to this had been trips back to Ireland to see family, this was nothing short of a winning lottery ticket. I was off to see different cultures, off to eat different foods, off to make a hash of trying to speak different languages, off to meet and largely get knocked back by exotic foreign girls, off to see the wizard – you name it, I was off to see it. There was, however, just one tiny little problem for my friends and I. Cashish. (Just to be clear, that's *cash*ish, not hashish – this isn't going to end in some *Midnight Express* horror story).

To be honest, this wasn't the worst problem in the world for me. I had a steady weekend job at Colchester Leisure World, thanks to my mam, who now worked on reception there. (I know, bloody nepotism, my sister worked there too – the Irish and their families were taking over . . . it was like New York in the 1800s with the police; only it was Colchester in the 1990s, in the sports centre industry). My job at CLW was classic dogs-body: it involved everything from being a lifeguard/dogsbody in the sauna complex (those post-sauna plunge pools could be lethal you know, and the less said about cleaning out the saunas after the ill-fated 'Men only' night, the better) to bar work – juice bar work (an entirely different thing. Tricky mistress, the juice bar, largely because of, well, *juice*) and running a kids' club on the weekend, part of which involved dressing up in an enormous costume as I played the part of 'Wilf the Whale', a character that was supposed to promote water safety but was mainly an excuse for eight-year-old kids to beat the living shit out of me. There was supposed to be some kind of Wilf the Whale rota system, but somehow I always ended up doing it. It wasn't the best look, especially to any Leisure World girls that I hoped to court. 'Fancy going to get some krill?' doesn't really cut it.

But, the upside was that whilst Mummy's little darlings were exacting all sorts of pain on my be-costumed shins, I was at least earning, which meant my ass was going to Europe. My friends' combined asses, however . . . not so much.

My old buddy Joe was by now with his long-term girlfriend (now wife), Jenny (or Jenny Ling Plastic Gothic, to give her her correct title – she loved the Cure, but wasn't really a goth. Made sense to us at the time). Many of my other mates had girlfriends too: Big Mike and the lovely Sam; Matt Mackman with the beautiful Jenny; and if they wanted to keep them (and they did), it meant no boys' trips away. I, on the other hand, didn't have a girlfriend, so that left the following motley crew from my group of sixth-form friends: Tom Le Her, Adam Wright, Rodney Appleyard and James Brown (great diverse names, well, apart from Adam, whose surname, as you've read, was only Wright).

The problem, however, was as follows: this group of pals who, incidentally, is still very tight to this day, weren't really interested in doing anything over the summer that didn't involve smoking, drinking and kicking a ball around/getting a tan in Colchester's Castle Park. Now, don't get me wrong, just writing those words down has made me nostalgic for being back there and having days where doing nothing was actually an option. But, be that as it may, if I was to get this gang heading Europe-wards, I needed to gee them up a little bit. And I do mean only a little bit – they were all up for it, they just weren't that umphy.

Rodney was half-British, half-Jamaican, and played on the opposite wing to me on the college rugby team, with a love for life and an attitude of 'just letting the river carry me there'. He threw one of the great sixth-form house parties of modern times, by which I mean, one of the *first* house parties for our sixth-form, which obviously went into legend pretty quickly, but in the midst of the party had got busted by his parents. (I honestly thought that only happened in the movies.) His mam had gone tonto at this betrayal, and Rodney had been put under house arrest to the point that he wasn't even allowed a key to his parent's house (something that is still the case to this day – genuinely – and he's now forty).

Adam was your olive skinned man-mountain/male-model type – he made it to the heady heights of the regional heats of a Levi modelling competition to be the next Nick Kamen – and he was also in the rugby team. A great man (apart from the fact he set me on fire once), but an insomniac, and so unlikely to get a job because, frankly, he slept all day.

OK, very quick detour alert – if you were wondering how and why Adam set me on fire, here goes: post-pub, we often used to head down to one of Essex's or Suffolk's many beautiful beaches, start a fire, swim, fish and stay the night. One night, however, the wind was up and the wood was wet, so some genius got the idea to siphon petrol off his car to light the fire. The same genius freaked out when the desired fire started and dropped the petrol can. Adam and I both instinctively went to kick the can out of the way, Adam getting there first. He kicked the petrol can out of the fire and no doubt thought, 'Disaster averted . . .' Well, not quite. I'm not entirely sure what Adam was on that night, but he was the God of hellfire and he brought me . . . fire. He inexplicably kicked the petrol can back and forth through the fire several times until it created a fireball – beautiful, but deadly, as the contents of said petrol can landed on me. My leg suddenly burst into flames and I turned to run towards the sea to find a) the tide out and b) Adam clinging on to my other leg screaming, 'It's out, the fire's out!' The only problem was, it wasn't. Thankfully, James Brown, who wasn't on whatever Adam was on, stepped into the breach by rugby-tackling me to the ground and properly putting my burning leg out in a kind of stunt-man-dampening-down-flames kind of way. (This incident sums up Adam in a nutshell: he'd take a bullet for you, but just as likely be the one to accidentally shoot you.)

Tom was, and still is, a languid, Celtic, Jarvis Cocker type. A passionate Scot and like a brother to Adam, they largely kept the same hours.

That left James: half-Irish, half-Jamaican and a more than formidable running back on my American football team . . . (I know it's weird, but at the time we lived for that sport. Go Dolphins!) He also had a sergeant major for a dad. No, really, his father was an actual sergeant major, so discipline and home-work were a big priority. On top of all that, he was also going through his 'Fight the Power' stage (we bonded over our Irish/black 'Fight the Power'/no one understands us, short-lived ethos) so doing shitty jobs for 'The Man' to raise money to travel wasn't exactly in his remit of righting injustice. (It wasn't really in mine either, but I was a little less committed to the cause.)

These guys were like brothers to me, but they weren't exactly the get-up-and-go crowd. So, although they were still on the team sheet in terms of travelling companions, the net would need to be cast further afield.

My salvation came in the shape of Glen Rayner (doesn't it always!). He was in my Communications class at college. He had lovely, curly blond hair and, judging by his array of slogan T-shirts (No Nukes man!), he also had a healthy social conscience. In short, he was a catch. We'd bonded over making a video for PWEI's 'Def Con One' as a piece of GCSE coursework (which, as I've just re-watched the original, wasn't actually that bad in comparison). Anyhow, Glen was perfect: he was a lovely guy who actually had a job, so he could save up money; yes, he had a girlfriend, which to most of my single friends meant he was deeply suspect, but she was the under-standing type (you know, best to let him spread his wings/if you really love someone let them go, etc, etc); and if you could over-look his faults, i.e. the stability in his love life, then he was perfecto.

As it turned out/could see it coming a mile off, the other boys never did get the cash together (this was to happen several times in the years that followed) so it was down to Glen and me to conquer Europe (in a good way, mind, not in a Third Reich/ Ottoman Empire/Austro-Hungarian Empire way).

The plan was simple: to get to Istanbul. It was daring (we'd been brought up with the aforementioned *Midnight Express*); it was ambitious; but it was also complete and utter balls.

As any muppet, and maybe even the actual Muppets, will tell you, if you are going to go InterRailing on a budget, you need to get your sweet ass out of Western Europe as fast as possible. It drained our money. It's like Las Vegas, only the size of half a continent and with no chance of hitting the jackpot. It was so expensive that by the time we'd seen Paris (starting in Paris – genius), we were broke and seriously needed to change our plans, and quickly.

To be fair, even before we'd got to Paris there were signs that things weren't going to go all that smoothly, proving, if proof be needed, that we weren't exactly the brightest tools in the box. After saving for the whole summer to go *InterRailing*, the first thing we did when we got to Calais was to try to *hitchhike* to Paris, half-hoping some *Betty Blue*-type would pick us up on the way. As it turned out, even surly French and Belgian truckers didn't want to know – an insult to what we imagined were our irresistible, boyish good looks.

So after wasting all our cash on God knows what in the 'City of Lights' (probably one *baguette avec fromage* too many, and a couple of Pastis in a bar in the Gare du Nord, such was the tightness of our budget and the expensiveness of Paris), we needed to get somewhere more affordable, somewhere we could live like kings. In short, somewhere only recently turned post-communist, and very soon.

So, a whistle-stop tour of really expensive Western European countries followed: Switzerland – where Glen had family (all I remember is swimming in the Rhine, and having my first taste of pumpernickel – earthy); Venice – incredible, the most romantic city in the world, though somehow it's not the same when you're with a man; Vienna – great bread, grumpy bakers . . . To be honest, I'm not sure we even stopped in any of them long enough for a whistle, before we headed off to Budapest with the few remaining funds we had.

And this is where G N' R and their bandanas enter the story. Guns N' Roses were played *everywhere* that summer: between Budapest and Prague (as it turned out, the only two major cities we could afford to stay in), they were second only to poor old Bob Marley in music played.

This was 1991 and the height of Guns N' Roses' fame. The track – 'November Rain' – is from their *Use Your Illusion I* album, and weighs in at a meaty eight minutes and fifty-seven seconds long. I love long tracks, when bands decide they are, to all intents and purposes, going to fit two to three songs into one. Even by my standards this is a biggy.

I have no idea if its popularity was because the Cold War was coming to an end (the Berlin Wall had only come down two years earlier), but those Eastern European guys *loved* this tune. They played it everywhere: bad fast-food restaurants, 'November Rain'; hostel reception areas, 'November Rain'; Jewish resistance museums, 'November Rain'. (Not sure about the last one, but it *was* pretty ubiquitous.) It was as if the Czechs were lapping up MTV like Coca-Cola.

Now, I liked the song, but the reason it's on my soundtrack is down to pure earworm. I can't think about travelling in Europe without it buzzing wildly around my head.

As things transpired, we had to leave Budapest pretty sharpish due to the attentions of a young Korean chap called Won-Jay who we'd befriended along the way. The night after we'd taken him out (in a friendly way, not a contract-killer way), a piece of graffiti appeared on the wall outside our hostel room that said, 'I really like you a lot.' And so did we, honestly – we did like Won-Jay a lot . . . but not that much, and clearly, not as much as he liked us. So, with a knowing look to each other in a corridor that morning, Glen and I knew what had to be done. (Looking back, we could have just changed hostels, as running away to Prague might have been a tad overdramatic, but you live and learn.)

After we'd got to Prague and seen the sights (more 'November Rain'), we hooked up with some Scottish chaps from Port Glasgow and . . . well, to be honest, I can't remember much after that. But I recall waking up in a gymnasium-style hostel (or quite possibly an actual gymnasium), with the friendly Egyptian chap I mentioned earlier midnight-serenading us by screaming, at which point my belly and I suddenly realised I was about to be in for a fun night on, or certainly near, the toilet.

I don't know whether it was the food or the drink we had that night, but something made Glen and me very ill, for a *week* . . . though, to be honest, if you're going to be unwell for that length of time, Prague isn't such a bad place to be. As I recovered from my bout first, I took the role of head nurse and left our sick beds to get provisions. And so, for rest of the time we were there convalescing, I got an extra few days' worth of 'November Rain'.

By now the song was in too deep . . . I was institutionalised.

Finally, though, we were ready to say goodbye to the Czech capital and head on to our final destination: the great city of Istanbul. There was only one, well, actually *three*, problems: we'd pretty much blown our cash by then, and in those pre-Eastern-European-countries-joining-the-European-Union times, you needed visas to get through Romania and Bulgaria. Who'd have thought? Well, not us. Also, and probably most importantly, by this point Glen and I were beginning to get on each other's nerves. We'd fallen foul of that obvious and inevitable travel curse of spending too much time together, watching each other puke for a week and nursing each other back to health. As we weren't brothers, or lovers, this was quite a big ask. (We really should have heeded what GN'F+R were telling us – 'Do you need some time on your own? Do you need some time all alone? Everybody needs some time on their own. Don't you know you need some time all alone?' The answers to all those questions should have been 'yes', but maybe by then we'd heard it so many times we just weren't listening.)

Oh, I'm sure I was a pain in the arse as well, but it had got to the stage where even the way Glen smoked was getting on my wick – really short, shallow drags. Just take a big bloody lug of it – it won't kill you! (At least not right there and then.) You know it's all over when you reach that point – it's just a short step from there to the point where hearing them breathe makes you want to strangle them.

We'd realised we'd run our course. We'd come up short for Istanbul – not enough cash, not enough team spirit, too much vomit. Plus Glen was missing his girlfriend (I *knew* there was something suspect about him) and he'd agreed to meet her in Copenhagen. (Didn't mention *that* before we left, did you, Glen?) So we made the call to call it a day.

And as we sat there, awkwardly, trying to be all grown-up and sensible about it, what was playing on MTV in the bar . . .? Well, exactly.

So, I returned to Leisure World four weeks later to resume my next Wilf the Whale shift, feeling like I was Hannibal having crossed the Alps, though with fewer (for which read no) elephants. Glen and I kind of lost touch after that, but whenever I hear that song I'm back there, in Eastern Europe, eating food from a questionable source and watching Glen smoking those bloody cigarettes as Axl, Slash and Co save the world from communism, and plunge it headlong into free-market capitalism . . . whoop dee doo.

So, whilst this chapter was more about Guns N' Roses contributing to the fall of the Iron Curtain in Eastern Europe (or was that President Reagan? One or the other), it would be remiss of me not to include those Marley murderers – which I have done now, so let's move on. R.I.P. Bob. Actually, don't. Come back and haunt them, till they can at least do half-decent cover versions.

8

'Gimme Shelter'

by the Rolling Stones

So, with sixth-form college behind me (and an A in A level Politics, if you don't mind), I had squeezed through academia and was off to university. (Only just, as it happens. The place I went to – see below – had just become a university. It had previously been a polytechnic but, frankly, there was no real difference – it was a rebranding exercise along the lines of ITV becoming ITV1, and then back to ITV . . . I'm on the channel, and I'm *still* confused.) This was just before New Labour came to power, so just before everyone in the country went to university, but, make no mistake – I was aware I was a lucky boy.

I'd loved sixth form and, to be honest, wasn't overly looking forward to going to uni. I loved my friends, my family, had grown to love my studies and, on top of all that, I was in love with a girl – the wonderful and wonderfully enigmatic Gaby Butcher (blondish, slight, bit surfery, loved her music a lot and, I thought, me – but never enough). She was a year below me in sixth form and we never really got together in a boyfriend–girlfriend way, but sort of did, almost did, then didn't, then did, then didn't, for two years. And as we know, that kind of constant heartbreak makes the music all the more special – cue a lot of Springsteen, a fair bit of Morrissey, a sprinkling of the Levellers and even a little Dire Straits chucked in for good measure.

All told, despite the heartbreak, I loved my endless last summer and I loved the lack of any responsibility. So why go to university? Well, for two main reasons: a) we're now talking '92, so at the time uni was free (big caveat) – the only debts we incurred (to cover our living expenses) were in the shape of an early nineties student loan (about a grand a year) which, when introduced, was greeted with such outrage that you would have thought we were modern-day Chartists (in the fullness of time, however, compared to how hard undergraduates have it today, it appears we had it pretty easy); and b) most of our parents had been born post-war and more often than not hadn't been to university themselves. My dad, for instance, worked on building sites in London when he first emigrated from Ireland, before getting his job at British Telecom, during which time he studied for and got his degree and a Masters (I did tell you he's hard-working). So, for our parents to send their kids to university was a big deal, as I'm sure it still is; but, back then, it felt that if we had the opportunity, then there was no question that we weren't going to take it.

So, with an A in Politics, a B in English and a d (lower case, makes the shame even greater) in Communications Studies (I know, I know), I was off to, well, the short and only answer was London.

For as long as I can remember I've been in love with London. Some of my earliest and fondest memories involve being in the capital with either my Aunty Angela and Uncle Frank, the pubs of the North London Irish community around which my dad played hurling for a team of Wexford immigrants called the Father Murphys, or down in South London with my Aunty Geraldine and Uncle Michelle. Geraldine educated me about good wine ('Beaujolais, lovely tipple, drink as much as you like . . . it's pretty much just fruit juice, and therefore doesn't really count,' being one of her classics). She's my dad's sister who ran away from home (well, left) in her teens to go to study hospitality in Switzerland (which, at that time in Ireland, was the equivalent to running away to the Democratic Republic of Congo). A beautiful, tiny woman (at my wedding, she was convinced my wife's Norwegian brothers thought she and my Aunty Anne were actually midgets) but who was always the height of glamour, Geraldine met Michelle (French) in Switzerland and together they moved to . . . South London! (Fewer cuckoo clocks, but more cuckoos.) He set up a restaurant (French) which, as a kid, and even now when I think back, I found exciting (although the less said about turtle soup, the better – different times and all that). It also means that when I think of Croydon I think of good, home-cooked French food. Doesn't everyone?

So, as far as I was concerned, there was only one place to go and further my education. But my parents who, bless them, were willing to help out with me going to university, were rightly freaking out about me going to live in one of the most expensive cities in the world. So, even though I knew it was never going to happen, to appease them I agreed to go and see the most out-of-the-way university I could find: the College of Mark and John in Plymouth (I assume it was named after the saints, as opposed to two over achieving guys in Plymouth called Mark and John, but you never know).

I took the trip down there with a tiny quiet Chinese girl called Min who was in my English class at sixth form. After a six-hour train journey we, along with a number of other potential students, boarded a coach from Plymouth station eager to see what the next three years might hold for us. Looking around, we were slightly perturbed by the weird looks we were getting from everyone else on the coach, all of whom looked late teens (fine), white (slightly strange) and with the same close-cropped haircut (strangest of all, especially when you think that this was the early nineties and a Levellers-style dread-look was very much in – not least in that part of the country).

The disconcertment was further heightened when a scary-looking college-admissions type got on the bus and started barking out a register that we weren't on. As all eyes turned to the short kid in the Brendan Behan (a legendary Irish writer who was, shall we say, a touch revolutionary) T-shirt and his even shorter Chinese companion, I began to think that maybe we weren't on the right bus: a fear confirmed when the admissions guy asked us if we were sure we wanted to join the Navy.

Well, as it goes, I wouldn't have minded some time at sea, and the discipline does appeal, but at that point in my life it wasn't at the top of my to-do list, so we made our excuses and rapidly exited stage right, without so much as a hornpipe.

And that was my experience of the provinces and what they had to offer, further-education-wise; and so, much to my parents' dismay, I was London-bound, specifically to Middlesex University, née Polytechnic.

To be fair, it didn't scream 'bright lights, big city'; it actually screamed 'Tottenham', which as a lifelong Arsenal fan didn't exactly sit well. There was, however, another more pressing problem. As I lived in Colchester, I didn't qualify for halls of residence – they were reserved for students from such far-flung places as Manchester and Leeds. And at the crucial time of needing to find somewhere to live, I was rocking out with Glen Rayner to 'November Rain' in a Euro bar somewhere in Czechoslovakia. So, in my absence, it was down to my dad to find me somewhere to stay. Which, to his credit, he did.

In a house with a landlady.

I was off on the adventure of a lifetime. I was terrified, I was excited, I was eager, I was . . . in Tottenham and, as it turned out, I was in a version of the classic British sitcom, *Man About The House*, starring my landlady, Anne, and a dog called Sid.

Anne, an old-school Londoner, could have been a gangster's moll back in the day ('Those Krays, lovely people, never hurt their own') – she has the looks, the sass, the pure Babs Windsor. For £60 a week she would make me (her only tenant) breakfast and dinner (mainly a generic meat pie) five days a week. This was the place I was going to call home for the next year.

Whilst it wasn't the student halls of residence (and therefore I was not meeting girls), on the plus side I got to listen to a lot of John Peel on the radio in my room; Anne was lovely (although not overly keen on the 'Stiff Little Fingers' Peel Session recordings); and the dog was similarly lovely. So much so, that the three of us would often end up going to the pub together, with her lady friends (I turned into quite the player with the over-sixties in Haringey). All in all I was, actually, and surprisingly, happy. These were enlightening times, even if it wasn't exactly the free love, Ban the Bomb and 'The Student Union Rules OK' experience that I had been (kind of) expecting.

As it turned out, I didn't stay at Anne's for the full year. A family friend from Colchester, Polly (whose brother Tyrone, or to give him his Greek name, Thrassyvoulous, was a good mate of mine) was up at Middlesex too. After a small, internal debate with myself over whether to stay with a sixty-year-old woman and her dog, or go and live round the corner with people my own age, I moved in with her.

Polly was second-generation Greek/Irish, so I ate like a king – though mainly potatoes, salads and kebabs – which helped me cope with the slight sadness at leaving that little haven in Tottenham. But, in fact, the move was not before time as Sid the dog had turned out to be, well . . . a bit racist.

To give Sid his day in doggy court, this was only because Anne had been mugged a year before whilst out walking him, unfortunately by someone of Afro-Caribbean origin. Anne had lived in Tottenham all her life and she wasn't an idiot, she held no prejudices either before or after the event, she just went on with her life – it's just that no one explained that to Sid.

When I moved in with Anne, take one guess as to who innocently volunteered for walking duty . . . I walked Sid every night, and as Anne lived next to the Broadwater Farm Estate (which, due to the riots in 1985, had a terrible reputation), our route took us right past it. Now, the people and the community were never anything other than incredibly friendly and welcoming; Sid, however, had other ideas. Every time we passed a young man of Afro-Caribbean origin, he would scowl and growl.

Naturally, they would look at me as if to say, 'Are you racist?', at which point I'd look really apologetic and non-verbally try and convey: 'God, no, *I'm* not racist – the *dog* is racist! Look, it's a long story, but my landlady was mugged . . .' etc, etc. Which, as you can imagine, is quite hard to convey using just your eyes.

Walking the dog, eating meat pies, and at last meeting people who were actually my own age, were my extra-curricular activities. I was there to study Politics with a minor in Media, or Culture, or Communications (I can't quite remember what it was called, exactly). Middlesex was a weird and wonderful place, with the university a sort of academic equivalent of the Silk Road: all cultures and all countries were there. It specialised in and attracted mature students, which on paper (even though they never actually told us that on paper), sounded like a nightmare, plus it didn't exactly make it easy to get a girlfriend, but what I actually discovered was a whole group of people from different cultures, with different opinions and, most importantly for our current concern, into different music. The folk I met there were people like Sean Sutton, a prince of a man, who at the grand age of thirty seemed to me incredibly suave and sophisticated – it was like being friends with Omar Sharif (if Omar Sharif was from Liverpool); Rob Morgan, a wiry chap from Portsmouth with trouble in his eyes who just oozed fun and mischief in equal measure; Gavin Andrews, a dance-music junkie who became my flatmate and one of my best mates . . . they all brought something different to the party.

So, whilst I wasn't having the conventional university experience that most of my friends were having – blank faces would greet me when I'd return to Colchester and tell my friends about some avant-garde jazz band I'd seen – I was soaking it up. All of a sudden, I was listening to music I'd never heard before, and because the students were older (if not actually more mature), I was getting an education in music history too. It was a bit like taking a subsidiary course in Modern Music, with its own subsidiary of History of Music. Sure, I'd heard of some of the acts/band before, and listened to a track here or there on the radio, but I'd never properly heard albums by Johnny Cash ('Hello, I'm Johnny Cash,' and a group of cons in San Quentin go mental . . .), the Rolling Stones, early Bowie and many others.

This introduction to a whole new world of music came predominantly via the mix tape. This was the last great era of the mix tape (the CD's dominance was upon us) and it was/is the greatest gift you could give a friend or, more importantly, a young lady you were trying to impress. (It could go one of two ways: it could make you a hero, 'You like that!' or a loser, 'Oh, you like *that*.')

So, during my academic career, my greatest musical influ-ence came via my friends and their mix tapes. And the one album that shines out from that period is one that was recorded onto a TDK ninety-minute cassette I'm currently holding in my hand: it has the Rolling Stones' *Let It Bleed* on one side and Big Audio Dynamite's *This Is Big Audio Dynamite* on the other. It was made for me by Rob Morgan and, looking at it now, even the writing on the cassette makes me smile, not least because I hero-worshipped Rob. He was never not funny and was the kind of guy that would never say no (although his libertarian ethos did almost get us into a spot of bother once in the Marathon Kebab House in Camden, when an older man who claimed to be a composer of TV themes suggested he indulge himself in certain drugs off our – at the time – young bodies – shudder. Thankfully, Rob did say no on that occasion.) Rob was also a fierce intellect and a ferocious reader. He got me into Charles Bukowski, Hunter S. Thompson, Ginsberg, Kerouac, Chomsky and others of that ilk. He was one of those people who you always felt good to be around; and when they weren't around, you missed. I think Rob is up north now – we lost touch for a while but I saw him a couple of years ago, when I bumped into him on a street in Soho – I saw him from the back and recognised him straight away from his trouble-is-just-around-the-corner gait. We had coffee, and he still had the fire in his eyes . . .

No offence to Big Audio Dynamite, but Rob's legacy to me will always be the Stones' *Let it Bleed* and, in particular, 'Gimme Shelter'. It's not just because 'Gimme Shelter' is the anthemic song it is; it's because of the passion, love and intelligence of the friend that introduced me to it – you must have had that moment in your life when someone converts you to their favourite band/song/food by the sheer love of how they talk about it. That was Morgan and *Let It Bleed* and, more specifically, 'Gimme Shelter'.

If you're over, say, twenty-five, I'm thinking you should already know this track; if you're under twenty-five, go and listen to it immediately and report back ASAP.

Are you back? It's quite something, isn't it?

The problem was, however, that even though I was getting to hear this – to me – new and exciting music, and even though I was in one of the most exciting cities in the world, apart from the odd gig at the student union (a Ned's Atomic Dustbin here or there), I couldn't go and see any of it.

Once again, the old problem of cashish had reared its ugly and, frankly annoying, head.

My salvation came in the shape of the most inappropriately named company ever christened: Class Caterers. My friend from sixth form, Mike (Big Mike), had got a job recruiting undergraduate friends of his to work on short-term catering contracts at various different events. It was seemingly easy money, too good to be true . . . which, as we've all discovered, often turns out to be the case.

Mike (who, by the way, is still one of my best friends today – I'm godfather to his son) was essentially nothing more than a glorified catering slave trader. I had played rugby with this guy – he was my 'O, Captain, My Captain', and how was that love and trust repaid . . .? I, along with any other unfortunates he'd roped in, would get picked up and loaded into the back of some van, then driven to an unnamed location where, with no training whatsoever, we'd cook, serve and make fast food for whoever the unlucky recipients happened to be, all for below minimum wage (if such a thing existed back then). Worse still, Mike's boss wasn't exactly speedy on the old payments, so you'd be chasing him for your wages for about six months until, eventually, the money came.

Notable jobs included working in a burger van at Wembley Stadium (or 'Poisoning Northerners' as Rob called it); bar work at the Royal Albert Hall when Elton John played; serving champagne at the launch of a new fire engine ('Please welcome the fc-648!' or something equally thrilling like that); working behind the members' bar at Lords cricket ground the day they let women serve (not 'in', just serve), which consisted of me telling a group of incredulous old MCC members queuing solely in front of me for their pint of Directors that the ladies were happy to serve them as well; managing the bar at the Nigel Benn/ Gerald McClellan fight, one of the most brutal nights in the history of boxing; and a stint at the Three Counties Show, where thirty or so people stayed in the same tent for a week with the couple next to us (in the same tent) having sex every night . . . not nice. (Although at the same show my friend bumped into the legendary actor and hero of ours, Richard Harris, and asked to have a beer with him, which he did! So not all bad news).

All told, the work was varied, low-paid and hard, but if it meant I would finally get to see some of these bands I was being introduced to, it was worth it.

And I did. With my *hard*-earned cash I got to see the likes of the Levellers (crusty, but musty); Battle for the Planet (the Levellers on crack); the Stereo MCs (nice!); and Sneaker Pimps (Gav and I were in love with the lead singer). But, unfortunately, despite putting in the long hours at Class Caterers, I never earned quite enough to see the Stones, as a student.

One of the weirder perversions of doing the job I do now is that when you're on the way up, no one knows who you are, you haven't got any money and, unsurprisingly, no one wants to give you anything; but when you're earning and can actually afford the things you want, you get sent free stuff aplenty. And while it's odd, to be honest I'm not complaining. (It's kind of like the show-business version of the MP expenses system, just without any of the public responsibility.) Being a DJ and working on music shows, that free stuff sometimes comes in the way of gig tickets, and so, years after my days of slaving for Class Caterers, when the Stones played a one-off gig in London's Astoria, I snaffled a pair.

The Astoria was an incredible venue. It held a few thousand, had a terrific atmosphere, and the Stones were doing everyone a favour playing there. It's not that unusual, though – quite often a truly world-renowned band will go back to their roots and play somewhere small. I've seen the Chili Peppers play the Garage, Coldplay play Dingwalls and Elbow play the Barfly in Camden – all tiny. There really is something special about being there when a huge band plays a relatively intimate venue.

As I've said, I'm lucky now in that I get to see a lot of gigs, but I'll never forget the Stones. As soon as Jagger ran on stage, the place went nuts. He spread his arms out to soak up the acclaim, and it was as if an albatross had taken flight, his wing-span (or armspan, to be precise) seemed enormous (like a rock 'n' roll Mr Tickle) – it filled the stage. They didn't disappoint, playing hit after hit including, obviously, 'Gimme Shelter'.

I've seen the Stones a couple of times since then, but it's always been at a festival in a field somewhere that will be forever England . . . much as I love festivals (for the most part), but seeing live music in an intimate venue is something else.

Sadly, the Astoria isn't there any more: it's been knocked down to make way for the Crossrail project, so that people who are in a hurry can get to somewhere faster . . . That's going to bleed for a very long time – thanks a bunch, progress!

SOUNDTRACK

9

'Protection'

by Massive Attack (featuring Tracey Thorn)

I graduated from university with a 2:2 – what I like to call a gentleman's degree. I wasn't smart enough to get a first, should have got a 2:1, but still not lazy enough to get a third. Truth be told, I was actually a little disappointed not to get a 2:1 (Jim, who shared a house with Gav and me, also got a 2:2, primarily due to the fact that he refused to get an important piece of coursework in on time because it was Bob Marley's birthday, and he had to commemorate it. I was told I was a couple of per cent off a 2:1 (although pretty much everyone I went to college with who got a 2:2 was told that, so it was probably a load of old shit).

By the time I left Middlesex, politics had become a love of mine, but it was never something I considered as a potential career. I was never a fervent supporter of any one party in particular – I'd always loved certain politicians rather than believed in any one party's doctrines. I saw so many great politicians speak whilst studying: Tony Benn, John Smith, Robin Cook, Edward Heath, Michael Heseltine – all largely due to the passion with which they spoke – stirred my juices and made me want to wave some white paper in the air and shout, 'Hear, hear,' a great deal, but just not for a living.

If you pushed me, I'd say I was a shade to the left of centre, with a certain penchant for a bit of thirties protectionism (ah, those heady days . . .), a sympathy for the small, family-owned business, and a belief that the people alone should own their own natural resources, i.e. water, gas, etc. But I still like a cuddly Tory or two (Hezza was a brilliant speaker, and had time for everyone). I know – so old-fashioned. So whilst politics was a thing, it wasn't 'my thing'. Na, I picked an industry with the power, but *none* of the responsibility. Woo hoo!

I was by then utterly convinced that I wanted to work in television/radio. Christ knew doing what, but I'd never managed to shift the bug that I'd been bitten by at the BBC Television Theatre when I was eight. And it was now pushing me on to go and do work experience for . . . wait for it . . . BBC Radio Essex, on their sports show.

As is the way of these things, actually getting the job involved politics. Specifically, in this instance, my sixth-form college Politics teacher Neil Kenny (always with the politics), who knew someone who knew someone (Essex, the hotbed of nepotism), and who got me a job as a runner there (I'll explain all the roles in TV/radio later, but suffice to say, the runner is, as you'd imagine, the very, very bottom rung of the ladder).

I did this for a year or so every Saturday, for £10 expenses a week (high-roller). It essentially involved making tea, and, well, running. As I always tell runners now, it's a verb, not a noun . . .

Runner (verb): To take a tape (I know kids, a tape! What is this? The 1900s?) from a cutting room to a studio.

Exciting stuff . . .

Actually, it was. The BBC Radio Essex sports show was a live show, and exciting things happened. Admittedly, those things were largely to do with lower-league football, but because it was live, it was changeable, it was fluid – you had to chuck the script out of the window if a goal had gone in during a Premiership game that would then have to be crossed to live. It was seat of your pants stuff, and for me, it was catnip.

After running for about six months or so, my boss, a guy called Jonathan Overend, a really gifted live broadcaster who's gone on to do really well at BBC Radio 5 live, asked me what I wanted to do. I sheepishly said I fancied giving 'on air' a go, at which point a brick of a mobile phone and the keys to a Peugeot 205 were thrown at me and I was off to cover the 3 p.m. Essex Senior League match between Heybridge Swifts and Grays. Not exactly big league, but definitely league.

So began my short-lived stint on local radio. Much to my – but no one else's – surprise, I wasn't exactly what you'd call a natural. Quite apart from the actual broadcasting, I kept getting lost on the way to the grounds (pre-satnav), which meant that my first link – 'We're crossing live to Dermot O'Leary now, pitchside, with all the team news from Heybridge' – was delivered from the hard shoulder of the A12, pretending to be at the game: 'Well, Jonathan, there's a heady atmosphere here at the ground . . .' (I made it just about generic enough not to get busted).

The one piece of advice I was given was to script everything – which I, of course, totally ignored. As far as I was concerned, to script would be tantamount to giving in and not relying on my (hilarious) ad-libbing qualities. However, if *I* can now give any young broadcasters out there a piece of advice (and please don't follow my example and ignore it), when someone who's been in radio for twenty-odd years tries to help you . . . let them. I was awful! The chasm between hanging out and riffing with your friends and, well, being on the radio, even the local radio, is pretty big. My nadir came on my very first post-match broadcast when, after the teams had trudged off to the riotous applause of the thirty-seven people who were there, I had to go out to the middle of the pitch to get a mobile signal, some-where on the banks of the Thames in deepest Essex, on a very cold December evening. Just as Jonathan was crossing to me from the studio, the piece of paper containing my notes (not script, mark you – just some 'gold', names of players etc., I'd noted down to wax to Jonathan about) was caught by a gust of wind and thrown mercilessly into the Thames, leaving me to busk it about players I didn't really know the names of and a score I could only just remember.

Can I just say, if you played non-league football, or indeed listened to local radio in Essex circa 1995, I am truly, truly sorry.

Despite my failings, however, I was loving doing my work experience on radio (clearly loving it more than it was loving me). But I needed a full-time job, as in a career-type job.

Before I could get cracking though, I had my last student

loan to spend as, in a remarkable act of economic sanity, I'd managed to save most of it during my last year at university. I had an autumn in which to do it.

So it was that I made the decision to leave BBC Radio Essex (they were devastated) and travel again. This time, America was the place to which I was headed.

It is hardly a revelation, O'Leary leaves on the Mayflower, or off the beaten track, but I'd loved anything American since I was a kid – still do. When I was young, it was the cop shows: *The Rockford Files* (R.I.P. James Garner, whilst we're here), *The A-Team*, *The Dukes of Hazzard* (were they racist? Maybe not, but how did they have no black friends? In Georgia? What gives?); and, later, and a wee bit darker, *Hill Street Blues* ('Let's be careful out there'). Now, I probably love the actual place even more. Having worked there loads, I love the East Coast sense of humour, the West Coast laid-back ethos, and I like the actual sincerity of the rest of the place, how they want people to do well . . . it's refreshing. OK, *we* couldn't be *that* happy – it's not in our DNA – but we could learn a thing or two from our colonial cousins.

America it was, then, but although it was now four years on, I was still reeling from my experiences with Glen and Guns N' Roses whilst InterRailing around Europe (I know, but it takes time to get over these things . . .). so I wasn't about to jump back into the travelling merry-go-round with just anyone. Oh no, I was heading out, post-uni, on my own.

Now, I know there's always something a bit 'social pariah' about going away without a travelling companion, and most of my conversations about it with my friends at that time went something like:

'Hey, I hear you're off round America!'

'Yeah, really looking forward to going. Can't wait.'

'I bet you can't wait, I wish I was going with you. Who are you going with, by the way?'

'Oh, I'm actually going on my own.'

(*Dermot begins to sense that this might be the wrong thing to say, so then, quickly . . .*) 'You know, you guys couldn't get your act together, and I just thought I'd go myself. I'm sure I'll meet loads of people, though; in fact, I doubt I'll be on my own at all really . . .' etc, etc.

'Oh, right, well, good luck, enjoy.'

(*Dermot's friend looks down at drink, and slowly moves away to join another group of people.*)

I got it. People think you're insane when you go away on your own. Not in a 'He's such a crazy-do-his-own-thing guy' way, just a little, you know . . . *odd*. The idea being that why would you want to spend all that time on your own?

I've never really understood that. I was, to all intents and purposes, forced to go away on my own by virtue of the fact my friends, as I had discovered four years earlier, were just a bit shit at organising anything. (Apart from Glen Rayner, though obviously he was a bit shit at the telling-me-he-was-going-to-meet-his-girlfriend part.) But, actually, I was quite happy to be going away on my own and I found I loved it, with the exception of the first day/night, most of which I spent crying silently to myself in a communal shower in Harlem (a great look, straight outta *Shawshank*). Travelling on your own is terrifying, but rewarding. It forces you to meet people, people that had you been with your friends you'd never have met. OK, admittedly, sometimes that might not be such a great thing, but the key for me was that you never had to compromise, and that is an all too rare and wonderful feeling.

I didn't want a year out as I was keen to get a job – I just wanted to get away for a couple of months. So I took my student loan and decided to cross America in the shape of the letter 'W' by train. (In case you're wondering, there was no 'W'-based master plan to that, by the way. It just meant starting in New York, and ending up in Seattle. If your geography is any good, you can probably work out the places in between.)

I didn't have that much cashish, just my loan and a little Wilf the Whale action to supplement it. My sister had worked out (I'm not sure why I couldn't have done it myself, but the night before leaving I was probably freaking out, so thanks all the same, Nicky) that I had something like $26 to live on per day, which even then wasn't exactly a great deal but, hey, all part of the fun/poverty. So long as I stuck to food that was cheap and really bad for me, I'd be doing just fine (financially, not gastro-nomically . . . or nutritionally . . . or healthwise).

On my flight to New York I was expecting, well, I'm not entirely sure what I was expecting, but I ended up in between two people in their late eighties. Not a problem – always been a fan of the silver surfer and the stories they can tell (WW2 and all that), only in this instance one didn't speak a word of English and the other had barely the strength to lift the dinner tray. So my first experi-ence of the glamour of long-haul air travel involved me as a kind of long-distance Nerys Hughes from *The District Nurse*.

Having survived the flight (that's all three of us), I checked into my hostel on the Upper West Side. Naturally, my first port of call was to head to Times Square (tourist – of course it was). Now this was before Mayor Giuliani had cleaned up/sanitised the place with his zero-tolerance approach, so a walk anywhere could be a little, let's say, punchy. As Denis Leary says in *No Cure For Cancer*, on a walk through New York you go through 'good block, bad block, good block . . . crack block'. Undeterred, though, and obviously keen to shake off the internal 'District Nurse' tag, I decided to go double denim (jacket *and* trousers . . . what *was* I thinking?) and strut the streets.

About ten minutes into my walk, a local drunk/homeless gent (all lean and lithe, and not in a good way) asked me for change. I, being jet-lagged, broke and, frankly, a little scared, said nothing, popped the collar on my denim jacket and kept on walking. This might have been a mistake. In fact, it definitely was. My new friend proceeded to follow me for about ten blocks screaming, 'You think you're a rebel? You wearing denim, you think you're a rebel? You ain't no rebel!' etc, etc. Not a dignified sight for him or me. (We still keep in touch, and you'll be happy to know Crazy Motherfucker Joe and his family are doing fine – and for fine read, they're down to just three vials of crystal meth a day.)

Despite that first experience of the States, I loved it there. I loved the history, the food, the people, and I especially loved travelling by train. Over there it was like seeing a movie set every day, the vistas were . . . *bueno*.

Rail travel in America is unique, and so are the people that use it. The only thing is that us Europeans are used to travelling by train; in Britain, it's been part of the fabric of our lives since the Industrial Revolution. In the US, however, while the railway opened up the American West, it's just that they've embraced the motor car and the airplane in quite a big way, so the only people who travel long distances by train over there are . . . a bit different, shall we say.

It's not that I don't like to talk; I do – so much so, I do it for a living! – but (some of) our colonial cousins I met kind of didn't have the capacity for internal thought (the sort of internal thought which might say something like, 'Maybe I'll keep quiet now and give this guy a break') which, when you're on a forty-four-hour train journey from New Orleans to Los Angeles, can make having a good natter kind of lose its appeal pretty early on.

My companion, who I was seated next to on this particular epic encounter, decided that, to jazz up the journey, as well as talking, he'd play his radio and try to tune into any local radio stations we might find along the way. Now, I know that this book is my love letter to music, but *every now and again*, you can kind of fall out of love with it . . . in a big way. And spending a forty-four-hour train journey with this radio ham was definitely one of the bigger ways.

I can't recall his name – I'd have a better chance remember-ing the 20,000 Country and Western radio stations we listened to along the way – but he was exactly how you'd expect Lassie's human friend to look: a traveller with a small knapsack, more than happy to help you out of a well, a bit down at heel, but with a good heart. His party piece was to wait until we stopped in the middle of nowhere (which was quite often as we were pulling in to . . . the middle of nowhere) and run to the centre of town and back before the train would leave. I went with him a couple of times, while on many others, I'd simply *will* him not to make it back.

He wasn't a bad fella, and I'd rather hear some music than no music – just, for the most part, not all the time (and definitely not at three in the morning). So, I had a problem. However, some salvation was on hand in the form of my – rather heavy – CD Discman.

Remember, this is in the days before iPods, iPhones or laptops, and the idea of a Discman now seems so archaic. A Walkman kind of made sense: cassettes were a portable medium, so a portable cassette player fitted the bill, but ever since *Tomorrow's World* lied to us back in the eighties by telling us CDs were indestructible – at which point every school kid in CDT class tried to hammer their own Beastie Boys CD to death – we've always had a slightly distrustful relationship with CDs and their players. A Discman was an extension of that.

But my Discman (or a selection of redneck radio stations) was all I had, along with the five or so CDs I'd brought with me. Not a huge collection, and as I was limited to $26 a day, it meant I wasn't really in the market for CD shopping (unless I just wanted the fries and not the burger), so I was stuck with what I'd brought with me. And even though I loved some of those albums . . . three months + five albums = you're going to get bored out of your mind.

There are, however, exceptions to that rule, and 'Protection' by Massive Attack featuring Tracey Thorn is one of them. It's a six minute and thirty-three second beauty, a really simple, and yet not simple at all, anthem of its time about love and sacrifice. The video is pure *Rear Window*, with Thorn killing you with those sad eyes and stunning voice. Go and give it a gander . . . https://www.youtube.com/watch?v=Epgo8ixX6Wo

I had it on for three months from New York to Seattle, and never, ever got bored of it. I listened to it everywhere – it was my go-to tune. I listened to it after Crazy Motherfucker Joe had questioned my rebellious qualities and who I might have fought for in the civil war; I listened to it the first time I saw the Pacific, coming off *that* train journey from New Orleans to Los Angeles; I listened to it when I got lost and found myself having to walk back on a gang-infested beach from Venice Beach to Hermosa – 'Stay off the beach at night,' they said (yes, a really easy thing to do when it's your only way home); I listened to it after I sat next to a Korean war veteran I tried to engage in friendly banter about Korean food (didn't go down well); I listened to it after taking a midnight piss whilst camping in what turned out to be prime tourist-eating bear country in Yosemite National Park; and I listened to it as the Discman itself was giving up the ghost and I was sitting in a café in Seattle really quite worried as to what exactly to do with the rest of my life . . . or even next.

SOUNDTRACK

10

'The Macarena'
by Los Del Rio (I'm so very sorry)

Right, I'm just going to come right out and say it: this is the first song I have to truly apologise for. It's a dreadful piece of work, pure nonsense. It's not because it's pop – I love pop, and I can't abide people that dismiss it. It's not even that it's a novelty song – there's a (very definite) time and place for that too. I'll always have a soft spot for a Joe Dolce or a Renée and Renato, and I'll even allow a touch of Glenn Medeiros into my heart, but when it comes to this slice of Costa del Sol, Brits-abroad pap, even I have to hold my hands up and say mea culpa. I'm sorry.

It's not even Los Del Rio's fault. Apparently, they wrote it as a homage to a Venezuelan dancer who reminded them of Mary Magdalene. (Deep stuff, right up my papist alley.) It's just that in the mid-nineties, if some dance producer somewhere, anywhere – but mainly somewhere in mainland Europe – could take an old track and make a sampled, half-arsed, up-to-date version of it, and in so doing grab some easy cash, they did so, and that, subsequently, meant that a whole load of nonsense ended up on our radios and, in turn, in our brains.

So, apologies again (enough now?) but for me, this song is firmly entrenched *deep* in my head as the tune that was playing again and again, and AGAIN, when I got my first break in television. And therefore (and I can't quite believe I'm writing this) it has a special place in my heart (argh, I need a wash!), and deserves its place on my soundtrack.

Man, writing that was like chewing nettles.

So, I arrived back in the UK from my travels at the start of December '95 realising that, frankly, I was in the shit. I might have had a great time travelling, but I had no job and no prospect of a job. Even Wilf the Whale had been supplanted by a younger, faster, Wilfier whale. (It happens to us all – you know the story; no one values fish-based experience any more.) Also, it wasn't just about getting a job; this was career time. So, unless I wanted a career in that graduate staple – media sales – I had to get my act together.

On the plus side, I was suffering from terrible jet lag. This might not sound like such a positive, but the thing about jet lag is that for about a week or so, you sit bolt upright at five in the morning wide awake and, in my case, incredibly focused. (I've been lucky enough to travel a lot with my current job, and it's always the same. When I'm jet-lagged I'm always up in the middle of the night, either working on whatever I'm working on, or my body kids me into believing I'm Mo Farah, and I just want to run as fast as I can, for as far as I can, then eat as much as I can. Thanks a bunch long-haul.) So I decided to use the time wisely.

I was, like most of my friends post-university, living back with my parents. This was quite a daunting prospect, not because I didn't enjoy being with Mam and Dad (I drifted pretty easily back into life at home, and whilst we were hardly *The Good Life*, we were a pretty muck-in family, so I didn't need to be cleaned or cooked for) but because, for the first time in my life, I had no *exact* idea of what I was going to do next. Pretty scary that. I knew what I wanted to do and, sure, I could say I wanted to work in television, but if you're not actually doing it, it's like telling folks you want to work in deep-sea exploration or space or be a footballer: people ask you what you're up to, and . . . well, you've kind of got no real answer, other than the old fudging-it classic of telling them you're sending your CV out. Always a trifle awkward. For their part, Mam and Dad were very supportive as, like I said, I was at least busting my chops trying to get a gig, not sitting around in my pants, eating cereal and watching my mam's VHS copies of *M.A.S.H.* (Well, OK, there was *a bit* of that.)

So, for me, using my time wisely meant getting up at 5 a.m. and doing exactly that: sending out CVs. One downside to my switched-on early starts was that we had a noisy house. I don't mean raucous, I mean, you know, how some houses are just loud. My home now is like that – every step you take on a stair or floor wakes someone up, making you the bad guy for just going to get a glass of water. So for about four weeks – it was a very bad case of jet lag – my poor dad was woken every morning at 5 a.m. thinking we were being burgled as I shuffled around the house, freaking out about not having a job.

Looking back, it would be quite interesting to find out what my CV contained. (Christ knows where the copious and varying drafts are now – probably somewhere in the attic next to a pile of toy cars missing their tyres and an electric guitar I didn't have the patience or talent for.) I'm not sure how dressing up as a whale, bar work, the occasional stint on local radio and, let's be honest, a distinctly average degree reads. I probably should have dressed up dressing up as a whale as: 'Detailed marine mammal research.' You live and learn.

This was also the dark ages of pre-internet (it sounds so long ago just saying it), so sending CVs out involved a bit more of a scattergun approach – kind of hit and hope, which proved incredibly frustrating. You had no real way of following up on a letter apart from picking up the phone, and calling the same HR person again and again and . . . (you get the picture) – and NO ONE in TV (or any industry, I'm sure) wants to be *that* person who doesn't stop badgering someone for a job. There's a fine line between being that young, go-getting type and simply a big pain in the arse.

So whilst I was sending CVs out to as many production companies as I could get addresses for (and scouring the Monday edition of the *Guardian*'s Media section for jobs, itself a hilariously futile act, i.e. 'Deputy Editor of *Newsnight*? Well, why not – who's to say I'm not *exactly* what they are looking for?' *Dear Sir, even though I have no experience in live news and current affairs, I do have a 2:2 degree from Middlesex in politics and I really believe I can bring something quite special to the team . . .* etc, etc), I did kind of feel like I was essentially sticking my head out the window and just shouting my CV to passers-by for all the good it did me.

Day by day the rejections mounted and, you know what? *Good*. I know it's easy to say that now, but I was the same then – I can't bear a martyr: it's part of life, and I'm weirdly glad it happened – it fires you up and thickens the skin. I also felt for the person getting the hundreds of letters and CVs from the likes of me every day . . . what do you say? Well, I can tell you quite precisely because, in my case, they all said the same thing – no vacancies at the moment, will keep your file on record, wish you best of luck in the future. In short, I'm really quite busy, so, without meaning to sound unsympathetic, please leave me alone.

Now, much as rejection always hurts a bit, in the TV industry of the late nineties, you could handle it from just about anywhere but rejection from one particular company was more than you could bear. Anyone who wanted to work in entertainment TV at the time wanted to work for Bob Geldof's company, Planet 24, and, in particular, their graduate training scheme, which was like the TV equivalent of getting recruited into the Cambridge spy ring (kind of). If you met someone who'd somehow got into it, it was like they'd made it through SAS training, and wore it (quite rightly) as a badge of honour. Planet 24 was the Mecca at the time. Who didn't come home from the pub and stare blankly at a screen watching *The Word*, wondering why they were staring at a screen watching *The Word*? *The Big Breakfast*, however, was a different matter – a game changer in TV and for me a thing of beauty. For those who weren't around for it, it was a revolution in breakfast television, all filmed in a cottage in East London. If you look at it now, it might seem dated but it really isn't, and a lot of entertainment TV that has been made in the last twenty years has been inspired by it.

All I've really ever wanted to do was to host live TV and radio (at least, that's what I thought then, and luckily still think now). There's nothing like it, and in the mid-nineties it was seen as a tour of duty to work on *The Big Breakfast* – something to have survived and been proud of. This was largely due to the hours – hideous; the location – in the middle of nowhere; and the pretty alpha atmosphere. Also, for me as an aspiring host, Chris Evans, and later Johnny Vaughan, were top of their game, live broadcasters that I could learn from/stalk, so naturally I wanted a job at Planet.

Of course I got rejected straight away. Though they did say they'd keep my details on file. Yeah, thanks!

I sent out close to 300 letters in all, and I promptly got 290 rejections which, let me assure you, is rare for television: not the rejection, the promptness. As a rule rejection and nos in TV are usually strung out over six months and normally work like this: you pitch an idea, if they like it you might get some development money, after which you pitch it again, several people try to make a decision, then, if it's anytime approximating the summer, some go on holiday, then some leave, then they can't really afford it, then the boss leaves, then no one's there to champion your idea, then you wait another six months, then you pitch a version of the same idea again, then they get a focus group to consider it, etc, etc.

However, I *also* got seven or eight not-outright-nos – they were sort of nos but the kind of answer that told you: 'If we are really desperate and all our runners are ill or get killed, we *might* give you a call . . . but we're not promising anything, so don't get your hopes up.' So, not yeses either. But, remarkably, I got two yeses: one from a film company for work experience that my old friend Tom Curry of Pogues gig fame helped me get, and the other – try to contain your excitement – an interview for an actual job.

The job was to be a runner for a big, well-known documentary company called Barraclough Carey. The founder was a chap called George Carey – he'd helped create *Newsnight* (and, as such, had probably been involved in rejecting my previous application via the *Guardian* to be deputy editor . . . was he mad?). He was a heavyweight producer who didn't suffer fools gladly, but was adored by his staff and was rightly regarded as godlike.

Naturally, I was pretty nervous – this was, after all, my only interview from 300 letters, so it was kind of a big deal. I put on my best (only) decent shirt – a natty, blue button-down Ted Baker number that I'd bought for my graduation – and it was off to the interview, at the tender age of twenty-two, to the glamorous media hub of . . . Hammersmith.

In my – slightly simple – head, I was expecting all TV companies to be what I imagined Planet 24 was like. We're talking Soho, bright colours, young people with headsets looking and being important, table football in reception, girls with clipboards telling people to do things, black coffee in cafetières, and maybe beer after work from a branded fridge. Similarly, I also expected my interview to go like this: everyone falling about laughing at everything I said and excitedly beckoning their colleagues to come in: 'You have to come and listen to this guy! He might be the most hilarious and original person we've ever interviewed! He came in for the runner's job, but let's get him on TV right now – hell, let's give him his own show! Get the

CEO, and get Channel 4 on the phone! We've found him, the saviour of television!'

Well, it didn't go *quite* like that. The office was beige, it was sombre; it was oblivious to my existence. When I walked in, it felt as if someone had died, something that in my smart-arse, 'try to say something, anything, you idiot/I'm afraid of silence' way, I was about to comment on when my prospective employer came in and told me that, tragically, someone *had* died.

My interview was with George's office enforcer and *caporegime* called Sheila. I was terrified of her immediately and, in fact, would be for the following eighteen months – pretty much as long as I worked there. She was, however, one of the fairest, most meritocratic and, after a period of thawing, warmest bosses I've ever had. A real mensch. (Look it up.)

As it turns out, getting a runner's job isn't too difficult if only you can get your foot through the door, which thankfully I did. The key then is to make yourself indispensable, and the only way to do that is through honest hard work and intuition (so, no getting by on 'just being a bit jammy'. Drat.)

And so, 3 January 1996 saw me back up in London, starting work as a runner. And that, my friends, was living the dream – if the dream involves making coffee, answering phones, photo-copying, lunch runs, sorting out the recycling, going to the bank, dropping off dry cleaning, picking up dry cleaning, making sure 'the talent's' dinner is the right temperature, ordering cabs, putting people in cabs, clearing out dusty old cupboards, filing away tapes, filing away CVs (they actually did keep them on file! Who'd have known?), answering letters, finding venues for parties, serving drinks at said parties, staying late at shoots and edits, scrubbing – in one instance – cobbles at 2 a.m. on a cold February night in Leadenhall Market to make them shine on camera, and clearing up after everyone.

I loved every single minute of it. My direct boss was a dream, a guy called Dave Winchester who I've lost touch with. Dead pan humour, deputy dog features and pure of heart. He made life really easy for me and I'll never forget him for it.

As I said, it's a make-yourself-indispensable type of job. Make sure they can't live without you, but don't be cynical about it – you have to want to do it. It's some of the hardest graft I've ever done. It was also the most important apprenticeship I could ever have served, and it's the one thing I tell people who want to know how to get into TV now, either in front of the camera or behind the scenes: get thee behind the camera and be a runner.

I'm not saying that London was easy. I was living in north-west London (gravitating back to the old London Irish haunts), in a flatshare with my uni friend, Gav, and a couple of other guys. I was on £9,500 a year (for two years), at a time when all my other friends coming out of uni were getting jobs that weren't necessarily their passions, but which were helping to pay off their loans, buy cars and leave them with a nice, disposable income. It was almost like an extension of school: I didn't have time or money to have a girlfriend, but what I did have was fire in my belly. A hungry belly, but a fiery one.

I was fully prepared for, and looking forward to, learning the trade and becoming a producer. Of course I wanted a career as a host then, but I just couldn't see where that would come from. Also there was another problem: the one thing no one in television likes is when they ask you what you want to do and you tell them you want to be a presenter. I'm not sure why – well, I am in some cases, as it attracts the type that wants to be famous, simply because they want to be famous. And so, as such, it's the thing you don't say in TV, even if it's the thing you want most. But after hanging around for six months, working hard, proving to people that you're not a wrong 'un, it's the question that they, being the people you work with and for, always ask, and it's a difficult one to answer. So, unintentionally, I always answered in a kind of Hugh Grant-style, 'Ooh, that is to say, if possible, I'd like to, maybe, if the opportunity should arise, perhaps, well, you know, how should I put it, ah, erm, give presenting a go . . .?'

Anyway, cut to six months in and Freddie Nottage, a film researcher – a specialist job where you have to find archive of old films, etc – at Barraclough Carey, and one of the many people I owe my career to, asked me what I wanted to do.

Big dilemma . . . This was from the guy who, when he saw me drinking a can of Coke, would berate me for the empty calories I was putting into my body. He was a man so cynical, he wrote in my birthday card that year: 'Gravity always brings you down in the end.' To tell Freddie you wanted to be front of camera was sure to invite at best, derision, and at worst, total humiliation.

Inexplicably, however, when I confessed all to Freddie, he simply sort of smiled (well, he didn't sneer) and then, a day or two later, he told me about a screen test going on at a company called Chapter One he worked with sometimes. If I could get a showreel together, or at least a letter and a picture, he couldn't promise anything, but he'd try to make it land on the right desk.

That's TV when it's at its best – just people wanting to help each other out and going out of their way to do that. Thanks, Freddie, you magnanimous, grumpy old sod.

Of course I had no showreel; I didn't really know what a showreel was. As we know, I had a CV, and was told to send a picture of myself in the post. The post! (this sounds like a story from the 1800s.) All I knew about the actual job was that it was a pilot (a one-off test show) for a new Friday-night, Channel 4 post-pub show called *Seaside Special*. Yes, looking back now, it does sound dreadful – in fact, about six months later it didn't sound too great either – but at the time it sounded like a dream. (Going from runner to presenting the sort of late-night show that Planet 24 would make? Are you crazy? I'm *in*!!!)

So I sent in the picture and CV, along with a covering letter in which I was just honest and said that this was what I wanted to do, but that I had no idea if I could and I'd appreciate a screen test, whilst dropping Freddie's name not so subtly (in fact, if I'm being frank, very heavily).

Well, it must have been a slow day in the office, or possibly the 'Let's pick one application at random and give them a screen test for a laugh' day, as they got in touch and asked me to come in. They did, however, repeatedly remind me it was just a screen test – hardly instilling a motivational, get-up-and-go-for-it, mission statement, can-do-style attitude, but I figured I'd take anything I could get.

So, two weeks later, not quite knowing what to expect (they'd given me nothing to prep for), I bounded out of bed with that classic I've-got-an-exam-today-like head on, sort of ready for my big day. I put on my most late-nineties, TV-presenter style clothes – a short-sleeved navy shirt from Gap (move over, Chris Evans) – and I was off.

Except I wasn't, because there was a tube strike on. And whilst no one respects the right for a worker to withdraw his (or her) labour as a form of protest more than me . . . do they have to do it on the day I've got a bloody screen test? I ended up – along with half of London – queuing for a bus for hours, and eventually arrived for my screen test just in time, only because I'd reverted back to my fourteen-year-old self on the way to an exam and set off three hours too early, having not slept the night before. The perfect preparation for the biggest audition of your life.

After a couple of bright young things with clipboards had acknowledged my arrival, and given my natty short-sleeved shirt the once-over (I'm pretty sure they were impressed), I was ushered into a nondescript office that looked anything but a glamorous TV studio.

Sitting behind a desk were three or four people – the *Daily Mail* might describe them as 'Soho telly types', but to you and me, they just looked like people. Amongst them was a guy called Phil Parsons, the series producer, who I still credit with properly giving me my first chance front of camera (blame him). They pretty much all had the same look on their face, which was a mixture of a) boredom and b) I hope this guy knows this is just a screen test (yeah, I got it!) . . .

Tough room!

Unperturbed (actually, quite perturbed), I chucked myself into the screen test, which involved three or four pretty basic pieces to camera that were classic late 90s TV hyperbolic fare, i.e. 'Hi, and welcome to a brand-new Channel 4 show, where anything can happen!' in an upbeat, late-night, Channel 4, pseudo-dangerous manner.

Then they hit me with the big test and asked me to ad-lib a piece about my perfect day on the beach. Now, slight problem – my perfect day was, and probably still is, me aged eight with my parents and sister on Curracloe Beach in Wexford in Ireland eating banana sandwiches, and as I wasn't entirely sure if this was quite right for late-night Channel 4, I thought it might be slightly wiser to tell them a more up-to-date anecdote. So, rather than talk about a perfect day on the beach, I opted to bring the old Adam-Wright-setting-me-on-fire story out of the locker.

Through rose-tinted spectacles (mine) and the passage of time, I believe they might have found it quite funny, but the truth was I had no real idea what they thought of it. And over the next week, whilst I was certain I hadn't got the job, I was happy that, for a first attempt, it hadn't felt too shabby.

When the call came, I was expecting a close, but no cigar. What I got, though, was a close, but no cigar – yet. And a, 'Fancy coming in for another crack, only this time with autocue?'

So, after another trip to Gap – short-sleeved white shirt this time – I pitched up at what I (obviously) thought was North London's version of Burbank Studios – the Business Design Centre in Islington.

Now, whilst my first audition had been a Got-nothing-to-lose-gung-ho-if-they-don't-get-me-they're-just-squares type of approach, this was a bit more serious, i.e. a bit more Blimey-actually-I-hope-they-do-get-me-after-all-as-I-might-be-in-with-a-shout-here style of approach. This was evident from the fact that, this time, along with the producers, people from 'the channel' were also there. Traditionally, when they turn up, it means either a) decisions are about to be made and cheques about to be signed or b) (worst case scenario, as I've learnt over the years) oh shit, they want to change everything last minute.

Amongst the party was a wild-looking, raven-haired assistant commissioning editor from Ireland called Jo Wallace, who I hit it off with immediately. Being Irish, I thought she'd give me the job there and then, but it wasn't quite that simple (bloody mer-itocratic system)! She did, though, become a real champion in my early career.

In actuality, however, I looked around the room as the auditions got started and thought I was in deep doo-doo. My competition included Tug from *Home and Away* who was, it must be said, quite the beefcake, and Steve McDonald from *Corrie*, who was knocking his screen test out of the park (apolo-gies for X *Factor*-related analogy – a hard habit to break). All I was thinking was, 'I haven't got a chance.'

I'd never used autocue before, and you learn pretty early on whether you can use it or not. If you can, well, you can – it just looks like you're talking out loud (the mystery of telly). However, if you *can't* it's obvious to all, and a painful experi-ence for both the viewer and – trust me – the broadcaster. It essentially looks as if you're suffering a demonic possession as your eyes dance and flicker from side to side, and then sink back into your head.

As it turned out, I *could* use autocue (yay, go me for being able to read words on a screen out loud) and it went pretty well. Once again, though, they told me it was *only a screen test* and I *didn't have the job.*

By now, I'd got the message, and to be frank was starting to feel a little paranoid.

Obviously by this point, the possibilities of the situation had begun to mean something to me and so, over the next week, despite myself, I started to believe that maybe, just maybe, I could be in with a chance of actually getting this job. Every time the phone rang at my desk at work, or the fax machine started to buzz (remember how exciting it was to get a fax?), I was thinking, 'Could this be it?'

And, one day, incredibly, it was. I had the job.

When I got the call, it was more surreal than overwhelming. I thought both screen tests had gone well, but I honestly thought they'd give it to someone well known, or just known. Plus, I remember, I took the call in an edit suite at work and whilst the enormity of it – i.e. 'This is what I want to do and I've got a chance to do it for my career, if I get it right' – was swimming around the back of my head, at the front of my head I was thinking runnery things like, 'I must get the editor's lunch from Pret and the recycling needs doing . . .'

So began the weirdest month of my life. Sheila and all at Barraclough Carey were brilliant, and generously gave me time off, which meant I went from being a runner – the least-noticed but most under pressure member of a production – to being the most noticed and equally under pressure person on a production: the host.

In my experience, there are two sorts of host: one who wants to be involved from the outset and be an active member of the production – even if the production doesn't always want you to be – and the other, who just turns up on the day and tries to style it out. Right from the start, I wanted to be the former, so at the first opportunity I was in the *Seaside Special* production office, badgering, annoying, pestering, ingratiating and generally getting in the way. Which was fine, however, on the first day of what's known as pre-production, there wasn't that much for me to do, unless I wanted to help out with ordering some props.

Pretty soon, though, it got busy and I had work to do. It was a summer-based (which is where the 'seaside' bit came in – I know, revolutionary), late-night entertainment programme with guests, bands and games, which in turn meant there were scripts to write, people to research and co-hosts to meet.

My co-host was a beautiful Dutch Buddhist called Bear van Beers, which I believe directly translated means, 'The bear, the little bear'. She was a Dutch starlet who was presenting *Top of the Pops* at the time, so I was very much a junior partner. When I first met her she took me to a Buddhist restaurant in Soho. She was everything you'd expect a Dutch Buddhist to be: completely Zen, with a libertarian streak and a slightly comedy accent.

Whilst meeting Bear was lovely, I was anything but Zen in the week leading up to the recording of the show. It was terrifying: photocopying during the day, rehearsing lines at night. Kind of a boring superhero with a double life, whose special gift is the ability to . . . talk. I was waking up with that pre-exam sink-ing feeling in the pit of the stomach, thinking, 'It's OK, there's no need to worry, there's four days to go . . . three days to go . . . two days . . . one day . . . Oh God, it's here! *Don't be shit!*'

The actual night of the recording is something of a blur. Lovely as Bear was, we did have one small problem in that, inexplicably for a Dutch person, she didn't speak *great* English, and my Dutch was at best shaky or, as they say on the mean streets of Rotterdam, *beverig*. So, come the night of the show, a lot of ad-libbed lines that I considered to be pure gold were kind of lost on her. I know I have a dusty VHS tape of it somewhere and I know if I watched it back I'd be mortified about the awful linen clothes, doing links next to scantily clad models, terrible innuendoes in the script and eating bulls' testicles. On the night, though, I a) thought I was great and b) realised categor-ically that hosting in a studio, being able to ad-lib, having fun with an audience and everything else that goes with the job, was definitely what I wanted to do for a living. In fact, what I really learnt from that night was simple: TV is really a people-based medium. I know that sounds pretty basic, but if you like spending time with, and getting to know, people, the chances are you'll like working in TV.

That should be the abiding memory of the night. However, like most TV pilots, if you've only got one shot at it, the director and producer will want to get it right. And this involves doing pretty much everything again and again. And again. And that includes the music – in particular – The Macarena.

I should have woken up the next morning with a sense of pride, satisfaction and, if the late-nineties TV etiquette had been observed, one of the scantily clad models. Instead, I woke up alone with one thing in my head: the Maca-bloody-rena. I'd heard it several hundred times the night before as the music guests booked for the pilot were, of course, Los Del Rio. Time and time again they closed the show, and then closed it again, and again . . . It really is one of those Duracell bunny, wood-pecker-pounding-on-your-head kind of songs that worm their way into your mind and take root there. And so that day, cycling to work (back as a runner – there's a comedown for you), when I should have been thinking, 'What's next? Where do I go from here? Will it be commissioned?' in fact, I was actually thinking about how when she dances they all call her Macarena. And now, having written this chapter, when I should be think-ing, 'What happy memories of a lovely first day at work,' I'm actually thinking . . . well, you know what I'm thinking. A-hai!

11

'Frozen'

by Madonna

'It's Freezing'

by Mel and Sue

Really, if I was going to choose any Madonna track for my soundtrack, it should be 'Hung Up'. I've been lucky enough to interview Madonna for a Channel 4 special, and it was around that time period. She was, as you'd imagine, Queen of Pop-like, without being at all Queen of Pop-like; meaning, I guess, that whilst 'the presence' was there, i.e. when she walked in she was the epitome of 'owning the room' but she also, like most true stars, had time for everyone, and was interested in people, in a pretty alpha, 'you'd better not be bullshitting me' kind of way. So, all in all pretty hardcore. During the interview, she asked what kind of cocktails the hotel in which we were filming did, and that we should have one afterwards, which I took to be interviewee banter. But when the interview finished, sure enough, she asked, 'So, what kind of cocktails *do* they do here?', followed by myself, my producer (who was beside himself) and a couple of slightly awkward, bemused, understandably intimidated, North Face-clad (as always) but no less in-awe camera/soundmen, very enjoyably but quite surreally sharing a mojito or two with, well, the Queen of Pop.

So, that *should* be the track, but a far more significant signpost in my life was accompanied by an earlier incarnation of Madge in the shape of 'Frozen'. But even *that* isn't really the track I've chosen. Mine's more a hybrid of that song, and a well-intentioned pastiche by two comedians to whom I'll be forever indebted.

Right, back to the late nineties and, as the months ticked on, it became obvious to all involved (apart from me) that the pilot – this passport to me doing what I wanted to do – wasn't getting picked up. Were these people mad?! It had Los del Rio in it! And it was called *Seaside Special*! ('No,' is the answer to the question, incidentally.)

So, I was back running, doing a bit of researching at Barraclough Carey and thinking that every time the phone went it would be Channel 4 telling me to hand in my notice and get ready for the bright lights. (Instead, more often not, it was someone very much not from Channel 4 asking me to change a light bulb or the toner cartridge on the printer.)

However, about six months later, just as I was giving up hope, the call came. Kind of. They'd commissioned a second pilot, and wanted me to host, only now with Melanie Sykes as my co-host. Which, as you can imagine, was a tough/hellish gig.

This time I insisted that I worked as a researcher as well as the host, which meant I *really* could go into the office and order props during pre-production (it's all glamour, you know). Obviously this meant leaving Barraclough Carey, which I was sad to do – but I couldn't be a runner any more. My time there had been invaluable and I'll always be grateful to them.

The second pilot wasn't all that different to the first, but working with Melanie was a treat. She's a really smart, charming person and a natural at live telly, mainly because she never tries to be anything other than herself (which is always the first rule to hosting). Plus, actually working there as a researcher as well meant a step up in the industry I'd fallen in love with.

As it turned out, the second pilot didn't get picked up (in retrospect, I *do* blame the Macarena) and I was out on my ear, as when the production finished, so too did my researcher's job. It meant I had a massive problem: I was neither one thing nor t'other; on one hand, 'Well, I'm a TV host/presenter/broadcaster now, right?' and on the other, 'No, you're not. You're a researcher at best, who got lucky, and now you're sort of in the shit, aren't you, as you haven't got a job doing either.'

Both of these devil/angel-on-the-shoulder scenarios were correct. I *was* a host – I had the showreel to prove it: 'See? There's me! Yes, ignore the linen clothes . . . that's me, right there, on that tape . . .' But then, if you're not *actually* hosting anything, and you've *never really* hosted anything that's *actually* gone out on telly, can you call yourself a host? Well, no, not really. It's not like acting, where you can say you went to Guildhall or RADA; it's not even like being a musician, as you can't unlearn how to play a guitar (although I'm sure I could give it a crack). With my job, you're either doing it, or you're not. And I . . . just wasn't.

So, it was back to sending my CV out, only this time things weren't quite so simple. I was going for researcher jobs that I really wanted and needed, but because I'd cobbled together (with the help of a friend/boss from my old Barraclough Carey days, Dave Winchester) a showreel, I was also sending that out to agents and production companies in the hope of getting hosting work. The problem was that, often, both CV and showreel were going to the same company, so more than once I was interviewed for a researcher's job by someone who recognised me as the same person who'd been in a couple of months previously peddling his wares as a presenter. That kind of has the potential to make you a laughing stock.

Worse still, I was by now broke, and whilst I've never shied away from hard graft, I was forced to go on the dole for a few months as I looked for relevant work.

Having been there, I do find it hard to believe that anyone is actually happy to be on the dole. That might sound naïve, but I just don't think it's in our make-up. OK, so I've met *some* people who loved being on the dole – mainly due to a non-existent work ethic, and a penchant for recreational drugs – but for me, it was the most degrading, embarrassing, introspective, self-doubting time of my life. I wouldn't wish it on anyone, but for the impact it had on me, I wouldn't change a minute of it.

What it also did for me was to give me the sick-to-the-stomach feeling that I woke up with every day, which told me I was broke, and reliant on someone/anyone else to pay my way. I told no one about it. It was the shame I felt going to sign on every two weeks, and the look of resignation on the faces around me. You could argue that for a graduate to be there for a few months was benefit tourism, and I did feel a bit ashamed to be there, but I was no less broke, and felt no less despair, than most of the other people in there. It was, thankfully, only for a short time, but in many ways it was one of the most formative periods of my life.

To ensure that the whole presenting thing wasn't just a blip, whilst I was trying to find a gig researching I endeavoured to get myself an agent. Chapter One, the company I'd made *Seaside Special* for, had encouraged me to approach an agent called Vivienne Clore, a heavyweight in entertainment with a fearsome reputation, who looked after Johnny Vaughan (as I've intimated, a TV hero of mine from *The Big Breakfast* days) and the brilliant, and very much up-and-coming at the time, Mel Giedroyc and Sue Perkins (currently of *Bake Off* fame). Chapter One had also expressly warned me off another agent called John Noel, who was apparently sniffing around. 'Not sure about him,' was the message. 'A bit weird. Shifty.'

Before I had a chance to go and see Vivienne (and, coincidentally, as soon as it was clear the second pilot wasn't going to get picked up), she understandably decided to pass on me, which meant I was off to see Mr 'Weirdly Shifty'.

I first met John in a coffee shop in Primrose Hill. It's renowned as a genteel, village-like neighbourhood that is friendly but pretty quiet; John, as I was to discover, is the antithesis of all of these things. He'd called me, and although I'd had the warnings ringing in my ears, he was a big agent, having managed Davina McCall, and was soon to be looking after the likes of Leigh Francis (Keith Lemon) and turn the life of the mercurially talented Russell Brand around. So, of course I was going to meet him. Besides, it was *a meeting*, and it was then, and still is now, my policy to take one when it's offered.

So – and it's important to reiterate that *he* called *me* here, having seen my showreel – when I chained up my bike and went into a café in sleepy Primmers, I was expecting to get the hard sell: 'Come on board, we'll look after you . . .' etc. Instead, what I got was a man not really making eye contact and looking out of the café window whilst occasionally asking me questions in a gruff Lancastrian accent.

John sort of looks a bit crazy, in that dancing eyes kind of way: if someone told you to cross the road to avoid him, you wouldn't question their logic. He just looks like he's dangerous, which, in fact, he is. In all the time I've known him, he's been thrown out of his *own* party (twice. Once for throwing a dead rat around!), insulted people I've worked with and for, and started food fights and actual fights, including at my own wedding, where security was going to throw him out because they thought he looked shifty enough to be a paparazzi who'd wormed his way into the church. He's also one of the most loyal, intelligent, TV and radio-savvy, street-smart friends I have. That's why he's been my manager, counsel and friend for fifteen years.

But that was all to come. At the time I just thought he was a nut job, never looking at me, just out of the window, with a thousand-yard stare and those dancing, piercing eyes of his. At the end of the meeting, I honestly thought it had been a disaster. I'd done all the talking, most of it nonsensical babble – as you do in any interview when you don't know what to say. My whole 'Play it cool, don't say too much, let him do the running' plan had gone to pot in . . . oh, let's say, about thirty seconds or so. He'd also left abruptly (as he's done at every meeting since), and I was left thinking I'd messed up one of the most important chances of my life.

I got the call pretty much the next day. He'd loved our special time together and the way we'd gelled, and said that he'd take me on. Extraordinary man.

So, I had an agent, but I needed a job. Of course I wanted to be front of camera, but I also wanted to learn a trade and find out what went on behind the cameras so that when the time came, I could be a better presenter. So, whilst John and his team looked at getting me worldwide stardom (at least, that's what I understood the deal to be), I went back to getting the by now trusty, and somewhat dusty, CV back out there.

My salvation/education came in the shape of the best job I've ever had (bar actually being on the box). Princess Productions was a company formed out of the ashes of those who had worked on *The Big Breakfast* and for Planet 24. They had recently had a show commissioned by Channel 4 called *Light Lunch*. It was a live entertainment show hosted by two very clever, self-effacing Oxbridge comedians, Mel and Sue. I'd applied for a researcher's job there and got the nod to come in for a chat with the bosses, Henrietta Conrad and Sebastian Scott.

For the most part, the interview went well. I was asked questions about popular culture: who was number one? (Hanson, with 'MMMBop', if memory serves me correctly – classic); who was top of the league? . . . All pretty standard stuff. Then, towards the end, just as I thought it was going a bit too well, they asked me: 'So, how many guests have you booked on a live entertainment show?'

Excuse me? All I could do was frantically search the filing cabinet in my brain to try to remember WHAT THE HELL I'd put in my CV for them to ask me that.

(Internal dialogue): '*Look*, you idiot!'

'That doesn't matter, they are asking you *now*! So come up with an answer!'

In a situation such as this, do you . . .

a) Think: 'This is going well, so busk it, Dermot. Just tell them you've done it loads of times – it'll be fine and you'll be off the dole, easy!'

or:

b) Tell them the truth (you fool!) because whatever is on your CV, you'll last about thirty minutes on the first day of the job when they find out the only person you've ever booked is the guy who brings sandwiches to the office.

After a debate in my head that seemed to last for ever, but was probably only about two and a half seconds, I went with option b). They looked at each other, laughed, and thanked me for my time.

This was a big deal for me and I'd clearly fucked it.

By the time I got home I had two answering-machine messages waiting for me. The first was from Princess saying that they liked me and wanted me to be a researcher on *Light Lunch*, along with the money they were offering. The second, about thirty minutes later, was from Princess saying that they admired the fact I was playing hardball, and that they were willing to up my rate by £50 a week.

It had obviously gone very well! As tempting as it was to continue to do nothing and see if my seemingly razor-sharp negotiating skills could get me any more money, I accepted the job/bit their hand off there and then.

Princess Productions was where I really fell in love with live TV. Working on any live TV show is the closest thing us pampered media types will ever get to being in the army. It is, of course, *nothing* like being in the army, but doing live TV gives, or should give, when it's done right, a sense of camaraderie, togetherness and team spirit. *Light Lunch* was exactly like that: from the runners right through to the executive producers, it felt as if we were in it together – 'it' not being the Falklands, of course, more a lunchtime cookery/entertainment hybrid show, but one that definitely had a follow-us-over-the-top-style esprit de corps. The group of friends I made there are still some of my best friends today, including a chap called Drew Pearce who was instrumental in me meeting my wife, and who was later my best man.

What I loved was the working culture: early mornings, in for 7 a.m., walking through the scene dock doors of London Studios in Waterloo in the cold of the morning, where the burly and pretty salty stagehands would be moving sets and props from studio to studio; on air at lunch, then working on the next day's show for the rest of the day until 6 or 7 p.m. Then a true 'weekenders' Friday night, where the whole staff would get battered together, sleeping it off on the weekend before starting all over again on Monday. It was exciting, exhilarating, exhausting and exactly where I wanted to be.

My job was audience researcher. On *Light Lunch* we had an audience segment where Mel or Sue would lunge into the audience to check out what certain punters had brought in to eat for their own lunch, live on air. That meant I had to find 'characters' in the audience: the type of person who wanted to be on TV (easy); wanted to eat on TV (trickier); who had brought with them a TV-worthy lunch, e.g. cookies with Mel and Sue's faces on them; and, crucially and trickiest of all, the type of people who weren't mad. By which I mean insane.

My job also involved answering Mel and Sue's mail. Given that the internet and email were in their infancy, and camera phones a glint in Steve Jobs' eye, this meant they were inundated with requests for signed photos. The problem was that Mel and Sue, understandably, wanted to get out of the office pretty much after their post-show meetings were done . . . so, if you received a Mel and Sue signed autograph circa 1998, I'm sorry, as you probably received a signed Dermot-O'Leary-in-the-guise-of-Mel-and-Sue autograph card. (Doesn't have the same ring to it, I know.)

The job also meant finding an audience full of whomever the producers wanted on the show the next day, which normally went something like this:

'Dermot, we need a group of fishermen from Norfolk or Suffolk, but preferably Norfolk.'

'OK, I'll try my best but the problem is that they might be, you know, out at sea . . .'

The key to being a pre-mass-media/internet researcher was to be a charmer on the phone, which predominantly involved lying to whoever you were speaking to by mainly telling them that you worked for the BBC, as it was the only broadcaster most of the country trusted. (To this day I have friends whose mothers wouldn't let them watch ITV, as it was seen as commercial, and therefore not in the spirit of television.) I worried about the fallout from this fib/white lie later, if at all. (No one sued.)

As well as the energy and immediacy of live television, watching Mel and Sue work every day was truly inspirational. They sort of/not really stuck to the script, and always embraced the live element, revelling in it when stuff went wrong. If being a researcher on *Light Lunch* was the formative gig behind the camera, then Mel and Sue played a big part in my education in front of the camera.

Like any great live telly, the show had an 'anything can happen' feel to it. TV often makes this claim but for the most part, when it's claimed on a show that 'anything can happen', it normally means the people making the show really *don't* want anything to happen. *Light Lunch*, and latterly, *Late Lunch*, was different. It genuinely encouraged things to happen, and happily went with them when they did. It was, above all, a flexible show: it could turn on a sixpence, it could adapt and even flourish when it had to.

Which brings us to Madonna.

Light Lunch had an incredible booking team that punched way above their weight. For a lunchtime show that was competing for guests with the big prime-time talk shows on other channels, we got some massive names: Kylie, Matthew Modine, the ladies from *Ab Fab* – Jennifer Saunders and Joanna Lumley – Ricki Lake – all came, chatted, and felt slightly awkward to be eating live on telly. So when we got offered Madonna, as a team we were beside ourselves.

It was the biggest guest/coup we'd ever had and we wisely decided to name the show in honour of her, to wit: *Madonna Meets Mel And Sue*. The only problem was, twenty-four hours before the show, Madonna dropped out.

Now, having the world's biggest pop star pull out on you, especially after you've been relentlessly plugging the show for the previous month, is not, as you might imagine, a good thing. But, somehow, the team turned it around by a) booking one of the biggest actresses in the world, Gwyneth Paltrow, to replace Madonna, and b) in a matter of hours, shooting a parody of 'Frozen', the very track Madge was meant to be on to promote.

Take a look at this link – http://www.youtube.com/watch?v=N7NofU7cT5Q – at four minutes in . . .

Now, at the time, the *actual* 'Frozen' was about to be number one and was all over the radio and TV but for me, in the bubble of a quite niche Channel 4 show, this parody, rather than the song itself, is what I associate most with one of the most exciting times of my life – being part of a great team, properly falling in love with live TV and watching two masters of their craft at work.

As enjoyable as it was, that first month at *Light Lunch* was terrifying; it was a real case of sink or swim. Live TV is one of those industries where no one actually tells you how to do your job, largely because they haven't got time to and they're too worried about not screwing up themselves. So, about six weeks in, I was understandably 'concerned' when I got summoned to Henrietta and Sebastian's office (actually, it wasn't much of an office as we were in an open-plan-type setting – this being TV in the nineties – which meant everyone would be able to hear if you were getting a bollocking, which was what I assumed I was in for). However, to my, and possibly their, shock, they informed me that they had sacked the warm-up guy (who presumably *did* get a bollocking), and effectively told me the job was now mine, even though I hadn't asked for it.

I was flattered, speechless, intimidated and also thinking to myself, 'How much was he on?' I also thought, 'If I stand here long enough, then my already rewarding bargaining technique will come good again and I'll be making out like a bandit . . .' Unfortunately, this didn't quite come to fruition – instead, as they dismissed me, they asked me to put the kettle on. Showbiz.

The first day of my new job as the researcher-cum-warm-up guy was absolutely nerve-wracking, far more so than doing the *Seaside Special* pilot. I'm not quite sure why this was because all I had to do was talk to the audience, which, as audience researcher, was what I did for a living anyway. To try and quell my fears, I penned what I considered to be a couple of cheeky gags (but which, more likely than not, were just awful), and learnt quite quickly that the best form of warm-up was just talking to the audience, and that reactive humour was a better fit. (That tape, by the way, if it existed at all, is at the bottom of the Thames.)

In fact, the couple of series working on *Light Lunch*, doing both warm-up and learning from Mel and Sue, was the best apprenticeship I could have wished for. I learnt an awful lot.

Such as:

1) Wherever you are, whatever 'gig' you're doing, always play to the room. If the people in the room are having a good time, there's every chance that it will translate to the people watching at home.

2) Similarly, it's important to treat every job with respect. It doesn't matter if you're hosting to 200 people in a small venue or playing to ten million on *The X Factor*, it's a job and you're lucky to have it.

3) If you let the nerves get to you, you do yourself a disservice. 'Channelling' those nerves – using them and the energy they provide – helps you do a better job. It's the same today as it was back then: people often say to me, 'Aren't you scared doing *The X Factor*?' My answer is, 'Yes, I am, but you channel the nerves and, like any job, you get used to it.'

Right, telly titbits over, let's get back to the other stuff.

As with Barraclough Carey before them, Princess Productions was also great with me and my other prospective career. From the start, I'd told them that I wanted to be front of camera, so they'd agreed to let me take an hour or two here and there to go to auditions.

The reality of going to auditions (got for me by old shark-eyes himself, John Noel) while working was quite mental. I'd leave work when *Light Lunch* came off air and leg it across town in time for a full audition for some show, which usually meant having to learn the script or preparing whatever they wanted you to do – a mock interview or some such – en route. Once I got there, I had to sell myself and do a good audition, then get back to work before I was deemed to be taking the piss. It meant everything was going at a hundred miles an hour.

The worst example of this was an audition I did for a Channel 4 show called *Dinners*. After the audition, which I thought had gone quite well, I was just about to put my foot on the (metaphorical) accelerator and set off back to work, when they reminded me that I hadn't finished my coffee. Now at the time, I had an aversion/reaction to lukewarm coffee whereby if I drank it, I threw it back up again but, in the circumstances, it seemed rude not to. So, with the adrenalin still pumping, I quickly downed the very-much lukewarm coffee and made to head off, back to the *Light Lunch* office. Unfortunately, at this point, the producer of *Dinners* came over to shake my hand, whereupon I realised that said coffee was going to make a reappearance and that it might not be the best impression for me to leave my impression all over his shirt. (Though on some level, given that it was a show called *Dinners*, maybe bringing mine up wouldn't have been such a bad idea . . . ?) After a hurried handshake he stared after me, bemused, as my walk rapidly turned into a run . . . I made it around the corner, out of eyeshot, just in time to deposit the coffee next to a phone box, out of which, moments later, a terrified old Indian lady emerged, berating me for being drunk halfway through the day.

I didn't get that job.

After umpteen auditions, not all involving throwing up, and countless runs across town, I suppose it's ironic that my next break came pretty much on my doorstep, out of the *Light Lunch* office.

We filmed *Light Lunch* at London Studios, the home of ITV, and at the time Andi Peters was working there. He's someone who most of the country probably thinks of as the pleasant children's television presenter they grew up watching with Ed the Duck, and whilst this is true, he's also a brilliant producer. At the time, Andi was just about to be put in charge of a youth TV strand on Channel 4 called *T4*. Somehow, he had heard about my warm-ups – which, I'm glad to say, had got a lot better since the first day – and had come along to see how to whip an audience into a frenzy when it comes to eating lunch. (It's a specialist gig.)

Later, Andi called me into his office and uttered the immortal words: 'I don't have a job for you, but what I do have is a few screen tests. Would you be interested?'

To which I replied, 'Nah, not really.' (I didn't. I replied, 'Yes, please.')

12

'Stolen Car'

by Beth Orton

Once again it was dilemma time: did I leave a job that I loved, was learning from, and was getting paid for, to do a job that I knew I'd love more, wasn't as hard (come on, let's face it, we do live a blessed life, camera side) but – and this is *quite* crucial – didn't actually *have*? As the series of *Light Lunch* was drawing to a close, however, circumstance forced my hand. I knew I had to make the call – I couldn't be going for both researcher and presenter jobs.

On the plus side I had an agent who was getting me screen tests, and a bit of work here and there. John – and Jan, who worked for John, and who was looking after me at the time (rumours of him only employing people whose name began with the letter 'J' were rife in the industry) – had got me a day or two working on a Saturday morning show for the BBC in Scotland called *Fully Booked*. It was hosted by Gail Porter who, at the time, was enjoying/not really enjoying her 'naked on the side of the Houses of Parliament period', and involved a couple of nice trips to America: one a cheerleading piece for a new Disney theme park which was based on Africa (the animals looked worryingly tired/sedated); the other was a not too shabby gig in LA, a junket for the movie of the old TV series *Lost in Space*, starring Gary Oldman and Matt LeBlanc.

Now, it might sound great, and it was, but a junket is a bloody minefield for a presenter. It's essentially a series of rolling interviews in hotel rooms whereby actors promote a movie. The interviewers line up in a corridor and you are then each given a time slot and a set amount of time with the actors. It's a bit like waiting in a doctor's surgery to have an appointment with a doctor where you'll be asking all the questions, and the doctor is really famous, and at times a bit bored and tired. It's also the nearest I've come to actually being on a conveyor belt (. . . cuddly toy . . . Teasmade . . . presenter . . .).

The process seems simple enough, but it is fraught with potential difficulties. To start with, the floor manager, who is in charge of making the whole day go smoothly and, vitally as far as they're concerned, *to time*, runs their ship like a prison guard – not those nice, cuddly Tom Hanksy ones in *The Green Mile*, these guys are pure *Shawshank* – which means if you engage in even the smallest of small talk before the actual interview starts, you can well eat up a couple of precious minutes without even knowing it. Then there are the publicists, who are usually watching from the shadows, like snipers. They want to ensure that pretty much all you talk about is the film, which is fine – I was never one for tabloid-style gossip, but you always want your interview to stand out so you have to ask some other questions – curve balls, if you will – thereby risking incurring the wrath of Mr or Mrs Publicist. (The alternative is asking the same questions that everyone else asks.)

Then (at last) you've got the actors themselves. My friends who are actors dread the junket precisely because they *are* asked the same questions over and over again (see above), so when someone comes in with something different they normally jump at the chance to have some fun (putting them, but mainly really you, on a collision course with the publicist).

On top of which, more often that not, most actors are exhausted. The promo tour for a film is the (far better paid) modern-day equivalent of one of those dance marathons from the Depression era. They might take place in nice hotels and involve first-class flights, but a long day is a long day, and the publicity tour for many is an intense, and at times monotonous, lurgy-inducing experience.

Years ago, I interviewed Heath Ledger on a junket for a knockabout medieval film called *A Knight's Tale*. It went terribly. He mumbled all the way through (although in his defence, as it turns out, he did actually mumble a lot anyway), looked uncomfortable and couldn't wait for it to be over. As you grow in experience you learn how to deal with these situations, but at the time I was mortified. As soon as the interview finished, however, he was up on his feet, all sweetness and light and really apologetic, saying that he'd got the flu and was sorry he'd been short with me, but he felt so rough. He then went on to quiz me about the best places to go in London (proving it must have been man flu, not actual flu). The point being that most actors are a) actors, so they'd rather be pretending to be someone else, anyone else, rather than themselves and b) if you *do* do a junket, don't get too close, even to your idols as, far from being on a glamorous, international carousel, they're actually on a glamorous, international Spanish-flu-spreading mission.

That said, for the most part my junket experiences have been fine. It's not an ideal situation to be interviewing someone whilst an overprotective publicist is in your eyeline, scowling at you for eating up precious minutes of their day, but if you can get a decent interview out of it then everyone usually comes out happy.

So, I was dipping my toes into the world of presenting, but while a couple of *Fully Booked* reports here or there was a start, it was nothing concrete, and by concrete I mean, something that I could buy food with. That said, it was what I wanted to do so I took the plunge (again), and decided I was now a presenter.

There, simple. No more researcher jobs for me, OK? (Well, maybe just a couple . . .) Actually, there really were no more researcher jobs, because by now I'd got to assistant producer level (lah-di-dah!) and whilst I was screen testing/auditioning like a good 'un, I was also doing short contracts here and there behind the camera, on the production side.

I'd pretty much given myself/could afford a year or two of working like this before I'd have to have a quiet word with myself and go back, full-time, to learning my trade as a TV producer (hopefully of live television) with my tail between my legs and a 'I coulda been a contender' speech stuffed in my back pocket ready for a drunken night out. I am, however, a lucky boy (or a lucky punk, if you're jive talking).

When asked, I always say that success in the TV world is in equal parts down to luck, talent and hard work. There are scores of my contemporaries who have all three, but not in equal measure.

Firstly, you have to work hard at presenting. It honestly drives me nuts when I meet young presenters who think the job finishes when they *get* the job, and you do meet loads of them with that attitude. Worse still is when you meet reality-TV stars, or fading pop star/actor types, who just think they'll give it a go. It's a bit like me thinking I could walk in and be a hat maker. Don't get me wrong, presenting television is not brain surgery; nor, indeed, is it hat making. It's not an art, but it is a craft, and to do it well takes hard work. (Note: hard work in the telly world, not hard work in the real world – totally separate things.)

Secondly, you have to have talent, or at least you should have, but that's for others to judge.

So, thirdly, you HAVE to be lucky. There are loads of people I know in the industry that are so good, but just haven't had the luck of the draw – I'm sure it's the same in any walk of life. In TV, radio or film, the distinction between success and failure is small, and yet cavernous. I've had friends who have taken jobs that have *cost* them money, just so they could be in work. The perception is that when you have a job you've made it, but when you've been out of work for a while, the money dries up very quickly and you'll take anything to keep going. Pride has never been an issue for me, and I'd rather be doing something, anything, than nothing, and most people in my trade are the same.

I can remember one instance, when I was coming back from a short skiing trip with an actor friend. He was practically broke, but had taken on some gardening jobs and really saved up so he could afford to come. We'd flown easyJet and as we were getting our luggage from the carousel to go back home, he was recognised by someone who asked him what he was doing on a budget airline and why he hadn't flown first class on Concorde. (The fact that Concorde had been out of service for some years and, to the best of my knowledge, never flew to Austria, would probably have been lost on our new acquaintance, so I chose not to point it out.) This exchange had a terrible effect on my friend, who'd saved up for a year for a lift pass and a cheap, bucket-shop plane ticket. Luck. He was/is a good actor, just an unlucky one, and with better luck could easily have afforded the trip; though to the guy who'd met us, he was an actor, on the telly, and therefore had made it.

So it was luck (which, admittedly, you make a lot of yourself) that got Andi Peters to meet me, and that then got me the screen tests/auditions for *T4*.

The screen tests went well and to start with, I bagged a reporter's job on a show called *Buzz* (I was in Ireland with my auntie Angela when I got the call. I'll never forget the feeling of relief. Let me tell you, some dairy was consumed that night!) it was here I met the host of the show, Leigh Francis (also at the time being looked after by John Noel). Leigh, of course, went on to be 'Keith Lemon'. You couldn't wish to meet a nicer or more private, family-orientated guy, the one frustration with him being that early on in our friendship, if I'd call him up, he'd always answer in character. This went on *forever* before we could actually just have a regular guy-to-guy conversation (which, as any man will tell you, isn't the deepest of affairs at the best of times). So . . .

Me: 'Oh, hi, Leigh.'

Keith: 'Hello, Dermot, how are you?' (Followed by some unprintable, smutty Keith-like line).

Me: 'Keith, may I speak to Leigh, please?'

Keith: 'Yeah, I'll just go and get him. See ya.'

Pause *Which goes on for ever, even though he's standing by the phone.*

Leigh: 'All right, mate? How are you?'

Funny? Yes, well, kind of, but after a while (twice), you actually want to kill your friend.

Leigh and I started out together, and I've always had a soft spot for him. He has grafted to get where he is. In the early days, he'd routinely get banned from London restaurants as he'd turn up for a meeting with a producer or commissioner (set up by our agent, John), and all would be going fine until, in between courses, he'd go and get changed in the toilet, coming out for the main course dressed and acting like someone totally different, much to the confusion of his dinner guest – and the whole restaurant. (John found it very amusing, but remember that this is the man who gets thrown out of his own parties.)

That's weird enough, but he'd also interrupt/gatecrash other diners. On one occasion he decided to audition for the film director, Alan Parker (who happened to be on the next table), by singing songs from *The Commitments*, dressed as Keith Lemon. Understandably, 'Mustang Sally' sung by an odd bloke with a bandage on his arm isn't the greatest accompaniment when you're trying to eat your sea bream.

Off the back of working with Leigh, Andi Peters paired me up with a Capital Radio DJ called Margherita Taylor for a new sports magazine show called *No Balls Allowed*.

This woman is an angel – I don't know where I would have been in the first few years of my career . . . I owe Margherita a great deal. Whilst I had been taking my job seriously up to then, Margherita had a puritanical work ethic to my, let's say more Catholic, approach. She was *so* thorough in her prep. But whilst I prepped a lot, I've always seen questions in interviews as more of a starting point to a conversation. On the surface she was pretty strait-laced and didn't drink too much, while I kind of did/do, but underneath she could party with the best of them. And she was and is an intensely private person (I'm private but in a different way and can be prised open without too much persuasion). We were pretty much opposites in every way but, somehow, we just gelled, and a lot of how seriously she took her job rubbed off on me.

After a couple of series of *No Balls Allowed*, Andi promoted us and we got the opportunity to do our first live show on *T4*, joining the then host, Ben Shepherd – a fine gent, built like a wall, who has gone on to have a great career. Only, we didn't join him. Luckily for Ben, he was away at a wedding the week we started, which meant our first live broadcast was on our own . . . Yikes doesn't begin to cover it.

Prep or no prep, I (and, to be honest, Margherita) was absolutely, well . . . *terrified*. This was it, all I'd wanted. I was now about to host live TV, with someone I'd been working with for the last six months. We were a team, we were keen, we . . . didn't know what the hell we were doing.

Live TV presenting is like no other. You feel like a circus ringmaster and the driver of a passenger train that could go out of control at any minute, crossed with an air traffic controller.

And at the heart of it . . . is you. There are no second takes; no, 'Sorry, could I try that again?' No. It's you and your ass on your sodding own. And if it doesn't work, and something goes wrong, even if it's not your fault (which for the most part it is), no one remembers the name of the producer, the director or the cameraman. No. Everyone remembers that it was on your watch – Dermot O'Leary's watch: 'He's the guy that screwed up, him over there, take him away in showbiz handcuffs . . .' It's a pressure like no other I've ever felt. And you can either handle it or you can't.

Central to all this is being able to do your job with at least three to four people in the control room, or gallery as it's called, talking in your ear at any given time through the earpiece you see presenters wearing. If you use what's called 'open talkback' (which I always do) i.e. you hear everyone and everything, as opposed to 'closed' or 'switched', which only allows you to hear people when they push a button to speak to you, then through your earpiece whilst you're talking live on air you can hear the following:

1) Your producer telling you which part of the programme to go to next (or in some cases, just where to go).

2) Your PA, or script supervisor (the hardest and least-heralded job in TV), telling you exactly how long you've got left on any given item. Or how long you have left before we go to a break/fall off air. (Note: these are sometimes known as 'hard counts', meaning that you have no choice but to stop talking by the time your PA has counted you down from a minute or so to the 'stopping talking' point. For example, when I'm doing *The X Factor*, what (I hope) you're thinking towards the end is, 'That

was a good show, what's on next?', whereas what's going through my head/ear is: 'Stop talking in 10, 9, 8, 7, 6, 5, 4, 3, 2 ,1 . . . and we're off air.'

3) Next to the PA (physically – they sit next to each other) is the director, who's telling me what camera I'm on, and where I'm headed next, although some of the more fanciful ones for example my director on *The X Factor*, Phil – lion of a man with a penchant for a bit of brawn, chuck in a couple of cheeky gags with it – sort of like your very own director's commentary, live.

4) Then there is also the bevvy of other people such as a vision mixer, graphics op, and a couple of people who, in fifteen years of doing live TV, I still haven't *quite* worked out what their job is (although it does look very important), whose voices drift in and out of the quagmire of sound going on in your ears.

5) And then finally, behind the front desk of the gallery, you've always got a group of executive producers and some people from the channel, all of whom have opinions (if they're reading this – very worthwhile, but *loud* opinions), and some-times even the occasional family member, including once someone's mum who, as I was being hard-counted to coming off air, looked in to tell her son (my PA) – and me, as it turned out – that she was just 'popping up west to Oxford Street'.

You get the picture. It's pretty much a fly-by-the-seat-of-your-pants kind of scenario, but it's something you learn to harness. (For the first six months of my career, I just repeated whatever anyone said in my ear in a Pavlovian way, most of which was nothing to do with what I was supposed to be talking about, e.g. 'We've got about three minutes left on today's show, then we're off for some lunch!') But, like any job, you learn and get better with experience. I drive my wife mad (in many ways, but this one in particular) when she's trying to talk to me and I'm watching or listening to something else, as it's the only form of multitasking I'm good at: she'll ask me what she's just said, and I'll be able to tell her word for word along with what's on the TV/radio/stereo/and, at times, what the couple sitting fifteen yards away from us in the restaurant are talking about. (Be warned if you ever eat near us.)

But all that is further down the line. For now, Margherita and I had our first live TV show to do.

Our first live show was a debutant's nightmare. Girl group Cleopatra was making an appearance – so far, so Sunday morning telly – along with Beth Orton, who I was kind of in love with in every way, but who I'd heard had recently had an attack of nerves that had sent her blind for a week which, urban myth or not, meant that live TV might not be exactly the best place for me to do my first chat with her. Also on the show that day was the cast of a new Channel 4 drama called *Queer As Folk*, a brilliant but pretty graphic depiction of the Manchester gay scene. In the week before our first broadcast, the Channel 4 lawyer (who we got to know *pretty* well over the next two years) came to the office and gave us a stern talking to about being sensitive to our viewers on the subject-matter depicted in *Queer As Folk* and, with our time of transmission being early on a Sunday, about taking into account the fact that there might be children watching. That was all well and good, and no one wants to offend for the sake of offence, but *Queer As Folk* was kind of famous for how honest its portrayal of the gay scene was, and that included . . . sex.

So it was with some trepidation (meaning spending most of the night before on the phone to each other, trying to hold it together) that MT and I entered into our first live weekend.

For a short while before that first live Sunday morning show on *T4*, and for the six months that followed, you could find me in the toilet most days throwing up my breakfast. It's weird – it wasn't like I wasn't enjoying presenting the show; I was loving it, every second when I was actually doing it! I just couldn't stop throwing up beforehand.

As it turned out, we had the time of our lives: Cleopatra, as their song 'Comin' Atcha!' suggested, did indeed come at us; the boys from *Queer As Folk* didn't go too off-message, although I did get a scowl from the lawyer when I innocently asked them all how they came to get the job; and Beth, well, Beth was, of course, nothing short of magical.

She was on the show to perform her new single, 'Stolen Car'. I love that track, and whenever I hear it now, it reminds me of that first weekend of live telly. It's all strings and minors, which I've always been a sucker for, and it was just so exciting to be in a TV studio seeing an artist who I'd listened to at home playing live. It was the first big gig of my life . . . not a prime-time gig, and a youth TV show that hadn't yet found its feet – but it was my first live gig and the song always sticks in my head because of it.

In fact, *T4* was great for that: if we personally liked a band, we booked them. Sure, for the most part we played pop (some of it great, and some from bands that you didn't end up hearing too much more from, to the point where we played, and still play, a game called 'Who booked *them*?'), but we all had a say.

Just before we went on air, Beth told us that she'd just come back from recording in America. She also told us that she was terrified of live TV (that made two of us) and so would like to see the questions we were going to ask her. This, today, is not my policy. I loath any form of media training that a lot of pop stars, footballers and others in the public eye do, whereby they have pre-prepared answers for pre-planned questions. Normally, even on *The X Factor*, I refuse to say what I'm going to ask our guests, though given that it's, frustratingly, usually in no more than sixty seconds, they should be able to work it out (single/ tour, etc). Back then though, because it was my first live TV show and because it was Beth, who was beautiful, talented, the kind of girl who wouldn't look at me at school, and who, over-whelmingly, I didn't want to go blind, I acquiesced.

So, having shown her the questions, and seemingly having helped her relax a little, we get on air to our live interview. And I find myself thinking, before we get to the planned opening question, that I'll chip in with the following, just to make her feel even more at ease:

'So, Beth, you've just got back from the States . . .'

Beth (*with look of terror, as this was not the question she thought was going to be asked*): 'No . . .'

Me: 'Oh . . .'

Uncomfortable silence until MT picks up the slack.

MT: 'Thanks, Beth.' *Cue 'Stolen Car'.*

Admittedly not the greatest start to an interviewer's career. But at least it was a start.

13 (the middle eight)

'We Will Rock You'

by 5ive (featuring . . . er, me)

'Fear'

by Ian Brown

This chapter is kind of what you'd call my middle eight. This is, for those not in the know (and, if I'm honest, I'll admit to being one of those, so I believe/hope I'm right in saying), the bit in the middle of a song where someone says something like, 'Break it down,' or 'Take it to the bridge,' and the band know to play something a bit chorusy and a bit versey.

So, mine features Made in London (you won't have heard of them), LFO (you probably won't have heard of them, either), and a menagerie of acts you will have heard of, but not in the same sentence: 5ive, Steps, Brian May and Roger Taylor (sort of) and Ian Brown. To be honest, it's more of a medley based on my time at *T4* and will, no doubt, be a montage when the film of this book comes out. (Negotiations are ongoing – in my head: Ryan Gosling is playing the lead, although he's playing hardball. Wants too much back end.)

Working on *T4* was brilliant. We weren't watched by millions – well, maybe 'a' million or two (if we wanted to flatter ourselves), but it felt as if we were doing something new and fresh . . . ish. From the outset, Andi Peters had total faith in the team which, in retrospect, might have not been the best of calls, but he effectively told us (a group of twenty-something aspiring TV producers, directors and hosts) the following: 'Listen, I don't drink so have no real idea what a hangover is. You lot, however, seem to, and you want to continue to do so whilst also wanting to work in telly, so how about I teach you how to make TV and not pay you very much, and you get much-needed experience, and make some TV?'

That might have not been the exact dialogue, but you get the gist, and that was the unwritten contract of *T4*. (I'm not sure what the written one was, but it probably wasn't far off that.) I'm sure I'm probably looking at this through rose-tinted spectacles. The show wasn't *that* big; *T4* didn't change the way TV was made (it was essentially a continuity programme done in a slightly irreverent way); it was never going to win any BAFTAs; and, before Andi had a budget to buy and pepper the schedule with heavy-hitters like *Dawson's Creek*, we essentially just played whatever Channel 4 had in the locker that they had to put out – more often than not, the folksy and charming show that was *The Waltons*. But, somehow, God knows how, despite playing out John Boy and Co to hung-over students, it all seemed to come together. We were encouraged to gently, but always without irony, take the mick/piss out of elements of the shows we had on *T4* – shonky *Hollyoaks* plotline anyone? (See, gentle, not ironic.) Simply put, we just had to reflect the reactions and views, and ask the questions, that our audience would be asking at home. That, in my view, has always been the key to authenticity when you're on television – don't pretend to be anything that you're not. It's pretty simple really, but stick a camera in front of some people's faces and it's extraordinary how they behave.

Andi was incredible. As I said, most of you will either be too young to know who I'm talking about or, if not, will remember him as a – it has to be said – slightly squeaky-voiced (sorry, boss) TV presenter on children's TV in the late eighties and early nineties, where he spent his time in a broom cupboard with Ed the Duck. (More recently, you might know him from *Good Morning Britain* as the roving reporter who travels around the country giving away money.) But we all have skeletons in our closets or, in his case, ducks in our broom cupboards, and as well as being a presenter, he is also a gifted producer, director and commissioner of programmes. I owe him a great deal, and will be forever thankful for everything he's done for me; as I will be to the entire *T4* team who, to this day, remain some of my best friends, and comprised most of my ushers at my wedding (although the less said about the 5 a.m. finish the night before the wedding, the better).

Andi insisted that his presenters used 'open talkback' which, as I've explained, means you can hear everything that's going on in the gallery (the television control room from where I hear the voices in my ear) . . . which, reading back, sounds just about as scary as it is in practice. This is something that, undoubtedly, makes you a better live presenter. He also had some slightly weirder rules, including: no chewing gum (OK); no swearing, ever (hard, as who doesn't love a curse from time to time?); and (weirdest of all), no wearing black. To this day, I feel like I'm about to be gently but firmly scolded if I do the triple whammy of these on any studio floor.

I guess the biggest deal for me with *T4* was that it had a small but dedicated following, which, when you are making a TV show, gives you a real boost: the fact is, you're not making TV that you know only your parents are watching (and even that's out of duty)! For the first time in my life, I was working on a show that people I met outside TV had actually heard of, and when asked what I did, my reply was no longer met with a blank stare and a look as if to say, 'Is he making this up?'

This I put to the test about a year into my time on *T4*, when we were away in the French Alps doing a ski special (such were the budgets in TV at the time, no one actually questioned the point of this: '*Hollyoaks* goes alpine?' 'Of course it makes sense.') On the last night, whilst a little worse for wear in a bar, I bumped into a chap in the toilet who asked if I was the 'guy off the telly'. Not being sure if he was going to be a bit 'punchy' or not, I put on my best norf Landan accent and told him that I got that all the time, and I was actually a plumber from Kilburn. At which point his eyes lit up and he told me he was a builder in Kilburn and was looking for a good plumber. At which point, I (now looking a bit stupid) told him that I was indeed the 'guy off the telly'. At which point, he in turn, rightly looked a little disappointed and thought I was a bit of a knob . . . Which I was.

Getting recognised was, and still is, a strange and surreal

experience. OK, admittedly, this is an odd one: on the one hand, it's what you've always wanted from the time you started out in the business, by which I don't mean people following you down the street chanting your name like you're Muhammad Ali – I mean people recognising you for the work you do and getting the occasional pat on the back rather than them wanting to smash your face in. It's a small victory, but a significant one (and I'm only half joking about the last point). On the other hand, it's very much a 'be careful what you wish for' scenario. I've been lucky: the fame or recognition that I have has come to me gradually, as I've gone from show to show. I started on TV when I was about twenty-four, I'm now in my forties, so you learn and grow with the experience (either that, or you finish maturing the age you start to get recognised, and emotionally stay stunted for the rest of your life, becoming an egotistical monster . . . one or the other, I can't quite remember which).

To be honest, and this still happens now, when people recognise me, my first reaction isn't that they know me from the telly, it's that we must have met before, so I usually end up asking them questions to gauge where and when (usually leaving them looking a bit bemused, as they'd only come over to ask for a selfie).

A little, and it is just a little, part of me feels sorry for some people coming into the industry today. Actually, that's not right. It's a terrific industry to work in, so I have no sympathy for people who moan about it. All I mean is that with social media the way it is, and how immediate any feedback/abuse can be, you need a pretty thick skin for it not to affect you. Luckily I have developed exactly that over the years, and reconcile any 'trolling' with the fact that there's a *fairly* good chance I might

Andi was also obsessed with the clothing label Abercrombie & Fitch (which is essentially a younger version of Gap, which in turn has been supplanted by Hollister, a younger version of Abercrombie . . . and so it goes on). You know these clothes stores are no longer for you when: a) there are model/extra types at the door wearing clothes that make you want to put a blanket around them and ask them if they want some cocoa, and b) the changing rooms in their stores are so dark that even though you can't really see what you're wearing, you get all in a fluster and buy the garment anyway, only to find, when you get home, it's a completely different colour/item of clothing than you thought you'd bought. Andi's obsession with Abercrombie went as far as booking a band called LFO, which I think (and bear with me here) stood for the Lyte Funkie Ones. They were booked solely because they namechecked Abercrombie & Fitch in one of their songs, I believe rhyming it with the line: 'Chinese food makes me sick.' May the god of music (Apollo, BTW) forgive us.

As the show became more successful, the bands got bigger. At the height of their fame, the band 5ive were regulars, although to be honest you were never sure who would turn up, as quite often they were fighting on the way in (and on the way out) – it was kind of like someone had emptied a bunch of feral tomcats into a TV studio. Perfectly nice boys . . . just not to each other. They were a bit of a breath of fresh air, though; at the time, pop was dominated by bands like Steps – again, all perfectly nice but musically (and I know I'm not exactly the demographic they were aiming for) it was all wrinkles of the nose to camera and high fives. So to get a band actually brawling as they walked into a studio was quite refreshing (if a bit odd), and quite rock and roll, even if you weren't sure they'd stay together for the time it took them to perform.

I'm not sure how it happened, or why they agreed to it, but when 5ive came in to do their cover of 'We Will Rock You', somehow both myself and MT ended up playing the parts of Brian May and Roger Taylor respectively (almost certainly because we couldn't book the actual Brian May and Roger Taylor). So my two years on *T4* and part of my middle eight chapter can be summed up by the following . . . apologies! (http://www.youtube.com/watch?v=KCWLi5-HWiE) And if that wasn't enough, check out the skinny little fella who appears at about 2.27 amongst the baggy pants in *this* little gem: http://www.youtube.com/watch?v=QsqsAxfM0aE

Worse was to come, however. And by worse, I mean a guest almost walking (as in walking off, not taking a little stroll) and coming close to punching me thirty seconds before going live. To make matters even *worse*, it was my fault.

When I found out we'd booked Ian Brown, I was, naturally – being one of the tribe of aforementioned shoe-gazing indie types – beside myself. Anyone who liked the music that indie kids liked LOVED the Stone Roses. They were royalty, and whilst I wasn't from Manchester, and Blur was kind of our local band (coming at least in part from Colchester), it was still a big deal that the Monkey Man himself was paying us a visit on *T4*.

At the time my producer was a guy who has since become one of my best friends, called Neil, a.k.a the Moonman – an unfortunate moniker given to him solely because, in his early life, he had a face shaped like a moon, something he grew out of (so much so that my own mother has a frankly unhealthy obsession with him now). But a nickname is a nickname, and once you've got one, it's pretty hard to shift. He's also one of the more eccentric of my friends, the type that always says 'yes' – which is always a healthy attitude – but he says 'yes' to everything . . . *everything*. For example, whilst we were doing *T4* together, he declared that he wanted to sleep outside in every royal park in London so that he could experience what it was like to sleep al fresco. On his first night under the stars, he was moved on by the police, who thought he was genuinely homeless. (Why wouldn't they?) At which point, he decided that as it was about 4 a.m., he'd go in to work and sleep under the desk . . . which was doubly odd when the rest of us turned up for work the next morning.

By this point in my *T4* escapade (I can't use the word 'journey' – heard it far too many times), Moon and I were in charge of the script, and penned what we thought was a nice little pre-break tease for our guest Ian, which featured the line: '. . . everyone's favourite scally, Ian Brown.'

Now, this is where me not being from Manchester comes into play. At the time, I honestly thought 'scally' was a term of endearment that my mother (when not asking after the Moonman) would use for me when I was a kid, i.e. 'You little scallywag.' Genuinely, I thought it was just the word 'scallywag' without the, you know, 'wag' bit. Well, it turns out that it isn't, at all. It is, in fact, really offensive, in particular to anyone from the north-west of England. You live and learn and, in my case, I was about to do so live on national television.

As I delivered the seemingly innocuous line, 'Coming up after the break, everyone's favourite scally, Ian Brown,' what I heard from across the studio is: 'I'm not a fucking scally. Who are you calling a fucking scally?' (I'm not sure of the exact details, but the F word featured heavily.)

As you can imagine, this makes you feel like a million dollars, and a bit scared. Cut to the three minutes of the break . . .

It was probably the longest three minutes of my life. Ian was (rightly) livid. At first, I thought he was going to lamp me one and, being still a little unclear as to why this was about to happen, tried to make peace (whilst I also tried to work out how I'd just offended a musical hero). Ian's manager then came up to me and started giving me a hard time: 'You're well out of order!' etc, etc – all really helpful stuff, which I could under-stand as he was just looking after his act, but by then I wanted to lamp him, especially as, as far as I was concerned, I was trying to make things better . . . Plus I'd got the gallery, which was two floors beneath me, asking if everything was OK and counting (always bloody counting) me back from the break, at which point I was supposed to be intro-ing Ian, who was supposed to be doing a performance, which, as the precious few seconds dragged by, looked very much as if it was not going to happen. Moon then finally piped up in my ear, '*Is* everything OK up there?', having finally worked out that something *was* up. It was bloody Scallywag-gate, and it was 50 per cent his fault . . . (and, OK, 50 per cent mine).

All I could do was apologise, again and again, and once more for good measure. Ian, being the gent he is, accepted, performed and was a star.

The following week, I wrote to him – innocent mistake or no, I had to do it (hangover from a Catholic upbringing – I don't like offending anyone, least of all one of my musical heroes) – and Ian, true to form, wrote back accepting my apology, since when I've always enjoyed a sheepish smile and the occasional hug whenever I've bumped into him.

So, Monkey Man, this one's for you. Thanks for the lesson: always do your homework.

14

'Newborn'

by Elbow

First things first – a warning: this is actually quite a sad song . . . (no surprises there). It's also, on face value, got nothing to do with this chapter, which is a chapter about me getting other TV work in the early noughties. (Racy stuff.) The song is a seven-minute epic about unconditional love that kind of morphs into another song halfway through and gives a nod to Elbow's love of prog rock . . . hang on a minute, this isn't the greatest sell. OK, don't skip to the next chapter just yet – bear with me, and see where we go with this.

Elbow is pretty much my favourite band of my adult (post-eighteen-ish) life. Now, I should point out that there's some vested interest here as I've known them long enough to consider them friends, so I'm not the most objective of music lovers in this instance, but I adore everything about them. And it's not just the music, which is emotionally intelligent (and actually just intelligent), melancholic but uplifting, with a slightly hung-over/lapsed-Catholic tinge to it. It's also because success has come quite late to the boys, and they're grafters. The music-al equivalent of marines. So, in other words, I consider them saints (my petition to have them canonised will be off to Pope Francis soon – he'd be mad to turn them down).

So I was now 'on the telly', meaning I was one stage up from being a hand-to-mouth presenter (something which, I suppose, can be described as, 'not really on the telly'). There are two upshots of doing a show that is relatively well known: 1) cab drivers recognise you and for the most part tell you their wives watch the show but that *they* think it's a bit shit (this is an immutable truth that has held fast for the fourteen years I've been working, regardless of the show – unless it's a show about the SAS), and 2) you get offered more work, anything, stuff that you *might* not be best suited for, but you get offered it anyway because . . . well, because you're there. It's an age-old fact: the more successful you appear, the more work you get offered. There's not much more sense to it other than that. It's TV Darwinism, kids.

The reason for this is that TV commissioners are, for the most part, busy people. They are the people in TV who work for the channel and decide what shows and ideas – pitched to them by various production companies – will get the go-ahead and actually be made. Some people in TV like to think commission-ers have an easy life, and whilst the lunch expense account is, of course, a sweet little perk – a sweet, *sweet* perk – it's actually a pressured gig. They essentially have to decide where and whether shareholders'/license fee payers' money gets spent, which, to all intents and purposes means they are gambling . . .

which in turn means that often their ass is pretty much tied to the success of a show. (I know the feeling.) So, I have a fair bit of empathy for them, especially the ones who have previously worked as producers. It's a busy enough job without also having to worry about trawling through CVs and showreel after showreel, so if someone is already doing a fair/not entirely awful job (if I may say so myself) on telly, and they're in the earlyish stages of their career, the chances are they'll get their next job on the basis that, 'He'll do.'

In an ideal world, you'd always stick to your guns as a host and only do shows that you think are right for you and really pique your interest. The people watching aren't idiots and know all too well when someone is 'phoning it in', especially if they are, indeed, on the phone (that show is most likely to be on radio, to be honest). For my part, I've always tried to take gigs that I'm interested in, even early in my career, plus anything that's live has always floated my boat. I once got offered a magic show on BBC One, and even though it would have helped my career – which was a big temptation – I had to ask myself a) would I watch a magic show myself, and b) am I that passionate about magic? (A 'no' to both.) Pretty simple answers really, which in turn made the choice pretty easy for me – I turned it down. (and ended up being told by the commissioner who had offered it to me that I wouldn't work again for the BBC while they were there. Naturally, this put the fear of God into me, and I had to be held back by my nearest and dearest from dashing to the phone to call said commissioning editor with a Paul Daniel's magic set in hand and a 'Hey presto!' at the ready.)

I've always tried to stick to those rules for TV work. Ask your-self the questions: would you watch it? Do you care about it? Would you be proud of it? (The last one's always debatable, especially mid-project.) If the answer is 'yes', then go for it. If not, don't. And if the show doesn't work out, hey ho, so long as the failure was born out of conviction. But you've got to stick to your guns. (Note: this doesn't apply to corporate or commercial work . . . ever.)

So, stick to your guns . . . high ideals, indeed. I've tried to do that, but in truth there are always a couple of jobs that *just might* fall through the cracks.

I know this is contradictory, but try telling that to the kid fourteen years ago who didn't really own any guns (just the odd knuckleduster). Luckily for me, and pretty much by virtue of the fact that I could nod my head in time when a band came on *T4*, I was offered primarily music shows.

On paper, this sounds great. 'Music! Music! I love music, and you want me to host it on the television? I'm in!' Job done. The difficulty was, however, that the commissioners and programme-makers weren't exactly choosy about what music shows they were offering to me. Basically – and I must stress that this had nothing to do with talent, more necessity of sched-ule and budget – somehow I was getting offered any/all of them.

The conversation in Channel 4 towers probably went some-thing like this:

'Dermot, he likes music, doesn't he?'

'Who?'

'That bloke that does *T4*.'

'Never seen it . . .'

'You know – the show that's filmed in the basement on Sunday and shows *The Waltons*.'

'No idea. Anyway, what kind of music does he like?'

'Search me. Shall we give him the job?'

'Not fussed.'

That's probably a slightly damning indictment/dramatised account of how television channels choose hosts, but in my case, probably in the ballpark of what happened.

It was the time in my career where I was making my way and was terrified that every gig would be my last. In truth, all the most successful presenters never really get out of this mindset. (Fear is a wonderful motivator.) Some of the jobs were brilliant, and ideally suited to me, à la *The Barfly Sessions*, where the song for this chapter comes from.

The Barfly Sessions was a late-night Channel 4 show from the early noughties that profiled up-and-coming bands. For a gigging indie kid, I was in gigging indie kid heaven. It meant touring the country on the coat-tails of bands, interviewing them in tiny clubs pre-gig, then downing tools and enjoying the gig like a paying punter. Sweet! (I must look into why that job isn't still going.) I was also lucky enough to get a musical vintage worthy of a Grand cru, as starting out on their careers when I was doing the show were the likes of Coldplay, Muse and Elbow.

So far, so career path. However, another music show I took/ was press-ganged into taking (OK, not really, but it makes me feel better when I'm recounting the story) that probably wasn't *quite* as good a fit, was the Channel 4 late-night dance-music show called, and bear with me here, *The Dog's Balearics*. (Yes, it's a pun.)

I'd like to go on record now and say (with the greatest respect to anyone else who worked on the show), that if any of you out there in Readerland saw it in the heady summer of 2000, please take this as my formal apology.

Even in my era of, 'I'm still a bit broke, I can't really say no to work if I'm offered it,' I had my reservations about this show. I got the whole 'weekender' thing about dance/house music, and some of it I loved, especially with strings (love strings) – but hard-core dance music as a whole has never really pushed my buttons. I did keep telling them this when they offered me the gig, but they just wanted me/anyone to do it and needed me/ anyone to do it, so . . . off to the Balearics I went. Or, to be more precise, the dance Mecca of the universe: Ibiza.

I did insist on one caveat when I took the job. I was assured that, and I quote, 'You'll only be interviewing characters in Ibiza and getting a taste of the real Ibizan lifestyle, history and culture . . .' rather than having to feign an interest in hard-core dance music.

And that was indeed the case . . . for a week, until I turned up for the second show to find, 'Interview Danny Tenaglia about "Global Underground" for eight minutes,' in my script. All memory of any assurances I had been given had apparently disappeared from the producers' minds, without trace.

I had two co-hosts: one was Jayne Middlemiss, who was at the height of her fame. Jayne was really good at her job: smart, always lovely, and in my humble opinion, not seen enough on TV nowadays; the other host was legendary club DJ Brandon Block – he of the Brit Awards ruckus fame. (If you don't know what I'm talking about, check out the following link, at around

2.23, but before you do, it's important to stress that they gave him the job of co-presenter AFTER this had happened.) It's also worth pointing out that Brandon a) is actually a lovely chap – he was then and is now – and b) was a VERY different person back then. But none of that helped me back in the year of Our Lord 2000 . . . http://www.youtube.com/watch?v=vmuZ1tadluw

Just to reiterate, he got the job *after* that.

So, for two to three months, I flew out to Ibiza every week for three days, which sounds great, but it isn't, well it is, but it isn't . . . if only because it doesn't give you enough time in one place to do anything. I loved Ibiza – I just wanted to love it my way: take me to a bar, let's have some dinner, chat about anything, maybe take in a gig, and then more drinks – perfect; I just wasn't that keen on the 'go to a club, can't hear what you're saying, yes, I guess I'll have another water, but no, no, I'm not a drug dealer [shaven headed at the time, I got that a lot], no, I'm not mad keen on having one of those pills, no, I don't really dance, and this music isn't exactly floating my boat, oh, the sun's come up, I'm sober, you're all high and we can't get a cab, great' experience.

Strangely, Brandon and I got on like a house of fire – we had some great times together, even though we were chalk and cheese, with my chalkiness being that I sort of knew when to call it a night versus his cheesiness of never, ever calling it a night. I'm not a turn-up-for-work-drunk sort of person: hungover sure, but not actually drunk. Brandon on the other hand, had slightly more . . . libertarian tastes.

In fact, the only problem with us getting on so well was that I quickly became the 'You have a word with him, Dermot' guy, which actually meant, 'Wake him up, get him coffee and, yes, if needs be, another drink, but mainly get him on side and on set.'

We filmed the show in a bar (great, especially when your co-host, as you may have surmised, likes a drink) in the less salubrious side of San Antonio, which in turn is the less salubrious side of Ibiza. Our green room-cum-dressing room was a room at the back of the bar which quickly became Brandon's 'Wake me up when they need me' room. So, my abiding memory of that summer is waking Brandon up and essentially getting him ready for school; making sure he was compos mentis enough to do an interview with Carl Cox or Tall Paul, whilst all the time thinking, 'This isn't what I was offered in that meeting six months ago.'

This short-lived show ('No!' I hear you exclaim) also coincided with me being offered my first radio gig with XFM.

XFM began as an independent radio station in London that specialised in rock/alternative music. It was taken over by the Capital Group after a while, who, whilst keeping with its indie roots, wanted it to be a little more the MOR side of indie and, more importantly, wanted to make it more commercial, or 'Capitally' (which really meant, understandably, that they wanted it to make, or at least not lose, money).

In charge was Richard Park (of *Fame Academy* fame) who was keen to try out more TV faces, and had obviously heard about my legendary match commentary from BBC Radio Essex back in the late nineties . . . or, maybe, had heard that I'd fancied giving radio a go from Margherita, who was herself a cut-me-and-I'll-bleed-Capital DJ. One or the other.

So I was asked to come in and do a couple of pilots, which, before I knew it, had swiftly turned into my own show on a

Saturday morning . . . (I know! I'm not entirely sure how that came about. Like I said, work begets work!)

Once again, on paper it sounded great, and of course it was. It's just that 'great' came with some provisos. So, after high-fiving my good luck at getting the gig, the questions went as follows:

'When is it?'

'First thing Saturday morning.'

'How long is it?'

'Three and a half hours.'

'Can I play some of the music I like?'

'No. We have a strict playlist policy that is decided in a meeting that you're not in, so you won't like some of the songs you're playing and what's more, you might have to play some of them twice on the same show, due to our heavy rotation policy.'

'Right . . . Do I get to choose any music at all? It's just that if I play a song twice in one show, I might look a little, you know, silly?'

'No.'

'Right. Um, do I get a producer?'

'No, but we'll teach you how to drive the desk . . . in half an hour.'

'Great, where do I sign?'

This no producer/engineer thing really wasn't a great idea, as SO much can go wrong when you're on air. It's essentially like putting an apprentice in charge of steering an oil tanker, only with less environmental, but more creative, risk. Even with my half-hour masterclass I could barely operate the desk. If you accidentally flicked the mic open just a tad, it meant that all other sound, including the music you were playing, went mute in the studio, which in my novice-like head meant that I'd crashed the radio station off air. So, several times early on in my XFM days, I ran down five flights of stairs to the snoozing Capital engineers to get help before my three minutes and thirty second Blink-182 track had finished, only to drag some poor chap from his weekend slumber up five flights of stairs so he could look at me with something approximating disgust as he averted my panic by simply tweaking the mic.

Still, at the time, XFM was a really exciting place to work. Loads of the people that worked there were truly gifted and went on to do great things: Zane Lowe, Christian O'Connell, Ricky Gervais, Karl Pilkington . . . Karl was the nearest thing there was to a producer, though he was more someone that popped their head in from time to time to give me a gruff, northern, 'All right?' then accompany me to lunch, where he'd be classically Karl.

He's a true pal. I don't see him as much as I'd like to nowadays, largely because he doesn't like seeing anyone that much. When I tell people I used to work with him, I'm always asked if he's '. . . that stupid.' He's not stupid at all; he's one of the most intelligent people I know, he just has a unique world view that's governed by common sense but precious little tact. He tells the truth, and he's also famously blunt. When Gail Porter came in to do a pilot, Karl was the obvious – but in many ways worst – choice to be her producer that night. She came off air and in that lovely, sparkly way she had about her, said, 'How was that?' to which Karl said, 'Well, it isn't going to win any awards, love.' She burst into tears and kind of . . .

never came back. (A tad oversensitive? Maybe, but I wouldn't want him being my GP.)

Ricky Gervais and Stephen Merchant had the show that followed mine. They were on the cusp of *The Office* getting big, and making Karl a star, but you could tell they were destined for big things. So there was a lot of talent at XFM, but you always got the impression that it was a creative place in spite of, rather than because of, the management, who were, well, slightly too safe. I'll elaborate . . .

There was a little white phone in the studio. If it rang while you were on air, you knew either the Queen Mum had passed, or you were in a lot of trouble for saying something you shouldn't have. Now, I wasn't used to the world of spon-sorship – it was early days in TV and radio for that sort of thing. So, for example, when Fosters sponsored my show for a little while, and by little while, I mean a show – one single, solitary show – I had no idea that ad-libbing, 'Fosters, the lager it's OK to drink with lime,' wouldn't go down so well with them, or the management.

Cue little white phone.

Who'd have thought Australian lager could be so touchy?

So, music-wise and work-wise, I was a happy boy. I'd bought my first flat in Queens Park, and was living with my old university friend, Gavin. I was loving doing XFM (even with the draconian playlist restrictions) and *The Barfly Sessions* at the same time, while *T4* was still bubbling along.

One rainy Friday I travelled up to Liverpool for *The Barfly Sessions* to do an interview with a band I'd never really heard before, called Elbow.

The Barfly Sessions were notoriously eclectic. For example, we'd previously had a band on the show called Clinic, who routinely dressed up as surgeons, so I had no idea where Elbow would feature on the 'out there' spectrum. The little I did know of them was that they'd been together for a while, had changed their name (they had been called Mr Soft), and had been dropped a couple of times. So it wasn't that I wasn't holding out much hope, just that I didn't know what to expect.

I turned up to a tiny little club in Liverpool, walked in and met the band. Immediately I could tell I was going to like them as people; the kind of guys who gently rib each other whilst always having an underlying respect and love. But when they played I heard seven minutes and thirty-six seconds of possibly the most beautiful song I'd ever heard in my life. It was 'Newborn', and it was one of those moments that, as a music lover, you always count yourself incredibly lucky to experience: a band playing a small gig, on the cusp of something quite special and, frankly, beautiful.

If you've been to this sort of gig, you'll know what I mean, as you exchange a glance and a nod with the other (mostly single) lucky punters. Externally you're trying to keep it cool, just nodding the head; internally, you're saying/screaming, 'Oh my God! This is brilliant, I can't wait to tell people about this; in fact, I'm going to be boring the ass off people about this for years to come. Even writing about it in a book!' I ended up having a good night with the boys, bonding on Catholic upbringings (I swear we can sniff each other out) and they also got re-signed that night, so there was cause for celebration all round.

I couldn't wait to get back to the radio the next day to play 'Newborn' on the wireless and be that unbearable DJ who bangs on about seeing a new band in concert, and how great they were and how '. . . you have to check them out!' etc, etc. However, to my horror, I found out that even though XFM had put it on the playlist – which was a good thing – the version they'd gone for was the radio edit. Tsk!

This is one of the few things that drives me nuts about radio. If an artist or group has gone to the trouble of writing a song, and the radio station has decided to play it, that should be that. But somewhere along the line, someone decided that the people listening couldn't possibly have an attention span long enough for anything that's over five minutes long, so the poor band have to butcher their own song so that we all get a nice three minute and thirty second version . . . all because of the (entirely ir-rational) fear that those listeners might go and make a cup of tea instead, even though radio is a blind medium! (Exclamation mark – that's how strongly I feel about this.)

With this beautiful Elbow track weighing in at an admittedly portly 7.36, the choices were either don't play it, or play it but at least credit the listener with some intelligence because, maybe every now and again, they might want to hear something that *is* over three and a half minutes long.

What did I do? I fought the power, kids. I said, 'No, middle management, not on my watch. This is my act of subversion – I might not go on marches against cuts and wars, but I'm going to play the full seven minutes and thirty-six seconds version.' And, as no one was there and therefore I could do what I wanted . . . I did what I wanted.

Of course, as soon as the song finished, and even though it was 9.30 on a Saturday morning, the little white phone went.

(God, their quality control was good, I'll give them that.) But this was my *Shawshank* moment (as in the moment when Andy Dufresne was playing Mozart). Yeah, I knew I was going to end up in the hole; yeah, I knew I was going to end up in musical solitary and wouldn't ever get that drive-time gig; and yeah, obviously I folded like a cheap stack of cards and promised not to do it again . . . but inside, and for a very short period of time (7.36 to be precise), we'd stuck it to the Man. (Kind of.)

Elbow was always very grateful. But I find that it's weird when bands say thanks for your help, especially when you played them early on, because, lovely as it is to hear, you don't really feel as if you deserve it. All you've done is play their stuff on the radio, and given them a session. Nonetheless, there's always a sense of pride when you see a band go on and do great things, and the first time I saw Elbow play an arena, the O2, I had a lump in my throat. Well, maybe a lumpette.

I've gone on to see them so many times since, like a proud cousin, and watched them soar. Guy is a perfect front man, part poet, part stand-up, and the rest of the boys are his perfect foil, like loving, indulgent brothers, which I suppose is what they are. And I've had some great nights with them. Moon and I almost ended up overnighting on their tour bus heading to the northern leg of the V Festival one year, a feat the Moonman repeated successfully with Athlete only last year . . . but that's all to come.

However, despite the many times I've seen them over the years, nothing compares to the rainy night in a small club in Liverpool. Always nice when good things to happen to good people.

15

'Somewhere Only We Know'
by Keane

OK, this song is a biggy on the soundtrack as it was the first track that I remember from my time on *Big Brother*, a show I worked on for seven years.

Anyone familiar with reality-show parley will know the term 'Best Bits'. These are the highlights (or lowlights) you play to a leaving contestant as they are weeping away about getting booted out of the house/contest. Some of these best bits contain wonderful, uplifting moments, whether it's an unlikely perform-ance in a studio, or a moment of compassion or courage shown in adversarial circumstance in a house or jungle. Others include a young lady shoving a wine bottle up her fanny. Reality, it's a mixed bag.

So this choice on the soundtrack comes from my first best bits of what, in many ways, has been the most important job of my life, on *Big Brother's Little Brother*. It was a song that was played to accompany a housemate's highlights package during my first year on the production and, from the housemates' point of view, it perfectly summed up their time there. (Keane were three public-school boys from Battle, in East Sussex, and there was an unfair whiff of inverted snobbery about them. They were a band that came to the height of their success as I was getting into XFM and *T4*, so I met them a few times and always loved their music. They've written some timeless, beautiful tracks and always credit their fans with a lot of intelligence. 'Somewhere Only We Know' has really stood the test of time, with Lilly Allen taking it to number one last Christmas nine years after it was first released).

Getting a job on *Big Brother* was a total fluke. I started *BBLB* in the second year of *Big Brother* and at first, no one I knew really thought *BB* was going to last more than a year or two. Of course, the first year was brilliant, everyone knew that, but the genie was out of the bottle, wasn't it? How could it be replicated? Any housemate that went into *Big Brother* after the first year would surely know how to play to the camera, and therefore the whole thing was a busted flush after year one, right?

Well, no – as it turned out it was an unstoppable phenomenon. The house itself had this weird, claustrophobic effect that meant people couldn't play a game and always ended up being themselves. It brought out the best and worst in people, which invariably meant it played on people's pride, and I'm sure you *know* how people can be when they're proud.

It was easily the most divisive show I'll ever work on, and any form of competence I have today as a live broadcaster (refrain from comment, if you please) came from six days a week for seven years hosting and producing *Big Brother's Little Brother*.

▼ My new radio home. *The Dermot O'Leary Show* on Radio 2

▶ We're lucky to have such brilliant guests on the show, here I am with Elton John and with that old smoothie himself, Morrissey

▶ The hallowed turf of Maida Vale, we've had many a great session there

▼ A winning night at the Sony Radio Academy Awards with my producers Ben and Simon

▶ Launching *The Saturday Sessions* with Athlete in 2010

◄*Big Brother* alumni. Quite the most gifted man I know, Russell in LA in 2010

▲ Backstage with good friend Leigh Francis, thankfully not in character

◄ The start of the journey. Me with some unknown *X Factor* band . . .

▼ Blushing Brides! Yep. With Richard Curtis, a great man. Saint

▶ A cause close to my heart. Trekking across the Kaisut Desert, in north Kenya, for Comic Relief in 2011, with human dynamo, Olly Murs

◀ The team and some well-placed graffiti. Ok, I did that

▼ With Sherzy in the Rovers, filming for the *X Factor* final. Like I said, constitution of a sailor

◀ The Dermot dancers, Dermarettes, as they like to be known (or at least that's what I call them)

▼ Brave new world, our first year without Simon.
Not quite knowing if we could pull it off

▲ Chris Martin of Coldplay, just
the loveliest, pure of heart band

◄ Just me and Clooney
exchanging style tips while
presenting the coverage of
the BAFTA Awards for E!
Seriously, no biggy

► With Nicole
and Gary
on *The
Jonathan
Ross Show*

◄ Mum and Dad arriving at our wedding

▲ ◄ With my best friend, and thankfully also my beautiful bride Dee, at the ceremony and on stage with Athlete

▲ Trekking in Bhutan

◄ My best men and musical muses, Joe and Drew on my wedding day

▶ A regular who never disappoints, Rihanna in 2012

▼ Sharon and I at the wrap party in 2013 . . . God knows what time this was

▲ An incredible stripped back *X Factor* performance from Ed Sheeran in 2012

◀ Paying homage to The Man, The Legend. Me and Gary with Sir Terry Wogan for Children in Need

▼ DJing at Latitude Festival (at least putting one CD on after another)

◄ At home with Sharon. Judges houses with Robbie in 2013

▼ Me and the young King Harold, Harry Styles in 2013 (pork slice and Corona trade out of shot)

▲ Casual with a frog and rabbit backstage at Latitude. Me and my radio team . . . the goons

► Me and Leo on the red carpet for BAFTA

▲ As ambassador for the British Fashion Council (Men's week) at the Burberry show . . . still can't get that Blue Steel down pat though

▼ One of the newest additions to the O'Leary household, Silver

▲ *Live From Space*, 2014. Mission control with a true legend, the man who fixed, but also almost broke the Hubble Telescope, Astronaut Mike Massimino

▶ On holiday in France with my parents, Nicky, brother-in-law Sean, and niece Josette

▲ Me and Dee at Glastonbury, 2014

▶ Dee and I at a friend's wedding

I miss doing it (live TV every day), er, every day. It was my apprenticeship and I owe it, and the people who worked there, everything.

We began realising that there was something addictively more-ish about the first series of *Big Brother* when we were having our early morning script meeting on a Sunday at *T4* – there was no *BBLB* in the first year as we kind of fulfilled that role on *T4*. In the early days, there was no public access to the twenty-four-hour camera known as 'live streaming', but employees at Channel 4 could get access for work, so we'd asked our researcher Sam to keep an eye on the house to see if anything happened that night. At 7 a.m. the next morning, she walked into our script read-through looking as if she was dead to the world. She hadn't slept a wink, glued to the footage of *Big Brother*, essentially watching people doing nothing (maybe Nasty Nick being a bit nasty)! Crucially though, she had loved every minute of it.

You forget now how big and groundbreaking that first series of *BB* was. It was the first time modern TV had become democratised. We were able to vote for the one we liked and (shamefully, but more importantly) the one we didn't like. Think about how TV changed due to it, both in how it's made and how it's watched. *Big Brother* was the modern mother of all of that. When he left the house, Nasty Nick even (somehow) had his picture taken with Brad Pitt at a premiere. OK, Brad probably (definitely) had no idea who he was (at all) but it was splashed all over the front cover of the *Sun*, for Christ's sake! 'Hello,' we thought. 'We might be on to something here'.

After the first series, Andrew Newman, the guy then in charge of *BB* at Channel 4, together with Phil Edgar-Jones the exec producer of *BB*, called me and asked if I'd be interested in hosting a show devoted to *BB* six days a week, called *Big Brother's Little Brother*. To be honest, my first reaction was . . . 'Are you nuts? There's no way this kind of show will work! Who is ever going to watch a show about a show?' But he'd piqued my interest, especially when he said it was live, and as I was a fan of the main show, it seemed like a no-brainer.

One of the reasons why I was so proud of what *Little Brother* became was that it was the first of its kind. There had never really been a sister (or, brother) show before, especially one that was, at its heart, quite irreverent and wasn't afraid to poke fun at its older sibling.

You know, there are times when I'm watching *The Xtra Factor* do its thing, and I have to stop myself from interjecting with something along the lines of, 'You young things – you think you're so groundbreaking? Take a look at *BBLB* back in the day, that was irreverent, you have no idea . . .' etc, etc. (Along with all those other boring/mental things people who have been there, done that, say.)

Big Brother's Little Brother was simply the most fun; it was a pleasure to work on. We had pretty much the same production team for the seven years I was there, so it really was a compact, tight family that you saw . . . more than your own family. Not dissimilar to *T4* or *Light Lunch* we *were* a family: we ate, drank, partied, played football together; we had in-jokes that as a team we found hysterical, but like most in-jokes, to anyone else they were unfunny at best and unbearable at worst. Everyone from the executive producers to the stagehands, the lighting guys, the prop mistress and the runners – it just felt like we were all in it together. It was spit and sawdust stuff – I got changed in the toilet four minutes before the show started – but that sense of camaraderie never leaves you, and you try and replicate it at every job you go to afterwards.

After the first series I also started being a producer on the show, which ticked a big box for me. All in all, it was the first time since I'd started in television where I felt anything approximating a feeling of security (if such a thing exists in TV . . . which it doesn't).

It was such a tight team and such a special period of my life that when I left I made a (small, internal, and on the face of it, pointless) vow not to watch *Big Brother*. It wasn't supposed to be a statement (I'd be a little sad if that's what I decided to make a stand on: 'Never mind child poverty, or the two-state solution, don't watch *Big Brother* any more'), it was just that after I'd worked there for seven years, and seen every *Big Brother* episode in that time, it kind of takes over your life, so I figured if I'm watching it, why aren't I doing it?

OK, I *do* tune in from time to time, and try not to do that awful thing everyone does when they go back to their old workplace of 'It wasn't like that in my day,' but if I've started watching it's hard to stop. It's like light-entertainment crisps.

The phenomenon of *BB* has always fascinated me and, in particular, the criticism it attracts. I understood it, but I never really *got* it. For me, the viewer could always get as much or as little out of the show as they pleased, and our viewers did. You could be making your dinner and use it like radio, bubbling away in the background, or you could see it as a fascinating study of human behaviour (which changes every year with every housemate), and how people react to living in such close quarters with others, and how they deal with the knowledge that (at least then) a huge part of the country is watching them and forming judgements and opinions about them based on their behaviour.

And if you think that study of human behaviour stuff is a little lah-di-dah and highfalutin, well, one of the proudest moments for me on *Little Brother* was when, in one of the first couple of series, the show was getting beaten with the 'worst kind of TV to be made' stick by papers (all of whom neglected to ever do the maths to work out that *BB*'s profit probably helped fund a lot of the drama/documentaries on Channel 4 that we were accused of eroding), and the famous zoologist and ethnologist Desmond Morris wrote to me saying he really enjoyed our show and found the whole *BB* phenomenon a fascinating experiment in human behaviour . . . Cue smug faces all round in the office.

For me, *BB* was all of those things – that was the *point* of it, while much of the criticism of *BB* has always been related to the unintentional backwash of fame it created for its housemates and what that says about society going to the dogs. This is a weird one for me. I'm a martyr for all this meritocratic, working-class-boy-come-good, roll-up-your-sleeves, pack-up-your-troubles-in-your-old-kit-bag ethos (maybe not the last one) and, as such, I'm not the biggest fan of fame for fame's sake (which, to be fair, *is* what some of the *BB* housemates achieved). But no one on the show had any idea that these people would become as momentarily famous as they did (Brad Pitt, for God's sake – who would have predicted that!). It was never the intention for these people to be famous (but don't get me wrong – it never hurt the show) but the show never purported that they were talented; it was simply twelve people picked from all strains of modern, multicultural Britain, put into a confined, claustrophobic environment to see how they would handle it, and you vote for your favourite. Simple. It was never particularly cruel, never really exploitative, and the duty of care for the contestants was always prevalent and paramount, to the point where some of them are still being looked after, ten years down the line.

My co-hosts, or rather stablemates (as we never actually presented shows together on *BB*), were both important influences on me, and in completely different ways.

From the day I started, Davina McCall was like, well, a big sister to me. *Big Brother* was her show and, as is often the case, the mood that reigned on set and seeped into every aspect of production was dictated by the key talent on the show, i.e. her. That mood was an enormous pair of welcoming bosoms with a cheeky slap on your bum for good measure. Davina was and is one of the warmest, most naturally gifted and hardest-working presenters in the business; someone who has overcome a great deal to get to where she is and yet hasn't once shown an ounce of self-pity or ever traded on a past that could easily have been made into a movie. From the outset she was particularly warm and welcoming to me, and made me feel like I was part of the family. At the time she was looked after by John Noel, and the day she eventually left the agency, it felt as if we were losing a member of the family.

Russell Brand turned up to *BB* in a whirlwind. He was another of John's signings and I remember that when I was told that he was about to sign with the agency, I honestly thought John had gone nuts. The only thing I knew about him was from a friend of mine who'd been to see his stand-up show. Apparently, as the set hadn't been going as well as Russell had liked, he'd set fire to his own arm with a cigarette lighter. Oh, and there was also the fact that the day after 9/11, he'd turned up to work at MTV dressed as Osama Bin Laden. As lovely, warm and smart as I'd heard he was, how the hell was John going to get him any meaningful employment?

Well, true to form, John did find him work and, having sorted himself out and turned his life around, Russell is now one of the country's finest comedians, with a successful acting career to boot.

When Russell strutted onto the *BB* set to host the late-night post-eviction show, *Big Brother's Big Mouth*, it was as if a cross between Mick Jagger and Captain Jack Sparrow had landed. If I'm honest, my initial thought with Russell was that I was in trouble. This guy was good, really good. He was, well, he was who he is – Russell Brand: anarchic, surreal, quick, well read, warm and blisteringly funny. He could also do live TV . . . My first thought, Oh shitbags.

I liked him immediately, whilst also feeling a tad envious of the new boy coming onto my patch and (rightly) getting all the plaudits. Such ridiculous rutting-stag-like thoughts quickly gave way to genuine respect, admiration and a great deal of (I hope) mutual fondness. But what Russell did do (unintentionally, and I'm sure obliviously) was give me a good boot up the arse. I've never been a 'rest on your laurels' type, but when someone turns up to your workplace who is brilliant at *your* job, you can either cave in and wave the white flag or try a little harder. I went for the latter. I don't see either Davina or Russell enough these days, though to be honest, it wasn't like we ever hung out as such – it's pretty hard to get on the phone and see if your two addict friends want to meet for drinks – but both of them made my time on *Big Brother* all the better.

Back to my best bits. They could fill a whole chapter, but I'm going to narrow it down to a top three:

1) Alex Sibley, *Big Brother* 3, dancing to 'That's The Way I Like It'. Yes, a weird one, but this is the moment the wall came down (OK, maybe that's a tad overdramatic, but . . .). There's a party going on, so the song is being played into the house. As the rest of the housemates are looking for Alex, he hides behind a door, waits until the coast is clear and then starts singing and dancing along to the music, direct to camera. For us, it was like Truman realising he was on a TV show.

2) Nicky Grahame, *Big Brother* 7, best unintentional catch-phrase: 'Who is she?' Tricky one this, as there have been some great catchphrases down the line, and Jackie Stallone's 'Yeah, Jackie' and Michelle Bass's 'No naked Jacuzziness' come close. But it has to go to Nicky, who was one of the most memorable, infuriating but ultimately loveable of housemates. Her diary-room rant when threatened by . . . wait for it . . . another housemate having the temerity to join the house made her lose it, but gave us our first great catchphrase.

3) The audience/voting public. All we ever heard when we did the show was how 'lowest common denominator' it was, and

how the public watching were an angry, reactionary mob. And yet in my seven years on the show, winners included a gay man, a transsexual, and a mixed-race lad from Basildon. Hardly the UKIP-voting, pitch-fork brigade!

Those are three of my highlights, but if one person summed up everything positive and negative that *Big Brother* came to mean to me and, I guess, those watching, it was a twenty-one-year-old dental technician from Bermondsey whose audition tape back in 2002 consisted of her putting herself through an elastic band. Step forward and take a bow, Jade Goody.

Jade was a South London working-class girl who irritated, appalled, bemused, amused and, eventually through charm and a fair deal of endearing idiocy and warmth, won the heart of the nation. Or at least the *Big Brother*-watching public (which was a large part of the nation then), until her death from cervical cancer at the tragically young age of twenty-seven.

From the off she was a television gift, someone who we could poke fun at, but who was also able to laugh along with everyone else at how stupid she was. Only she wasn't stupid at all. She was ill-educated, sure, and she didn't know a lot. (Examples of 'Jadeisms' that kept us going on the show for weeks included her thinking East Anglia, or as she called it, 'East Angular', was 'abroad'; her belief that Sherlock Holmes invented toilets; and that her fellow *Big Brother* housemates were trying to use her as an 'escape goat'. She also ran the London Marathon later in life, only to collapse at mile twenty-one, saying later, 'I don't really understand miles. I didn't actually know how far it was going to be.' And yet, like I said, she wasn't stupid – she was street-smart and worldly-wise. She came from a really tough background – both her parents were addicts and she had had very little education – but it was her own self-awareness, work ethic, and nous that drove her to work hard, make quite an industry of herself and provide a good home for her two boys.

I know this kind of contradicts what I've been saying about people being famous for fame's sake, but the key to Jade's appeal, and her longevity in the public eye, was her charm. There was no master plan, no cold, calculated agenda to become famous for doing nothing, and you have to admire a worker, which is exactly what she was. Jade auditioned for *Big Brother* when it was still in its infancy, and had no real idea what she was doing or why she was doing it. She didn't have a clue that she could become famous off the back of the show, and probably expected nothing more than a few tabloid interviews and nightclub appearances. But (and you may have guessed something like this was coming), pretty soon after her appearance on *Big Brother* my agent John took her on (he can't resist a working-class underdog/recovering addict), and he helped shape her into the personality she became.

A few years later she went back into the house for a series of *Celebrity Big Brother*, which proved to be a disaster when she became embroiled in a row with Indian actress Shilpa Shetty, an impeccably well-mannered Bollywood star who was about as far away from Jade's Bermondsey estate as you could imagine. The media went crazy for the race element of this row, and whilst Jade did say some stupid and culturally ignorant things, others around her at the time made far, far worse comments, and were never seen to be reprimanded. Jade's part in all of it was, in my opinion, nothing to do with race, and everything to do with class. She was a working-class girl who felt intimidated and threatened by a well-educated, middle-class girl who happened to be Indian, so she ganged up on, and bullied, her. It was that simple.

Pre-*X Factor*, this series of *Celebrity BB* was the biggest event I'd been involved with. It was supposed to be a bit of fun at the start of the year; serious stuff wasn't supposed to happen, and if it did, it wasn't supposed to happen on my show. That was Davina's territory, right? The most we'd ever had to deal with was racing pundit John McCririck going crazy in his pants because he wasn't getting enough Diet Coke; Jackie ('Yeah, Jacky') Stallone's entering the house in order to stun her ex-daughter-in-law, Bridget Nielsen; and George Galloway calling Preston from the Ordinary Boys a 'plutocrat' for eating some cake, and drinking milk from Rula Lenska's cupped hands whilst pretending to be a cat. 'Would you like *me* to be the cat?'

Prior to the race row, the biggest controversies *that* year had been Jade accusing the film director, the late Ken Russell, of eating more than his fair share of food from the shopping list: 'Ken, we haven't got enough food, as it's all in your big belly,' and Leo Sayer escaping his perceived incarceration in the house due to the fact that he had been forced to wash his own underwear.

Suddenly, after the Jade–Shilpa argument, the place went crazy. Lawyers (those fun-loving guys) were all over the script, and we went from being a light-hearted-poke-in-the-ribs-style round-up of what had happened in the house that day, to a pretty serious news-style show that was practically devoid of anything other than, well, serious content.

Indian media went heavy on it, and effigies of Jade were being burnt in the streets. Gordon Brown, the then Chancellor, on a trip to India, condemned the show, as if somehow we were responsible for the words coming out of the housemates' mouths. And I remember a pretty pitiful edition of *Question Time*, where all the panellists were lining up to give the show a good kicking whilst all of them acknowledging they hadn't actually seen it.

For me, it was so frustrating but, in retrospect, a valuable learning experience for live TV presenting. To start with, we weren't to blame for what grown adults said – *Big Brother* is not responsible for the issues it throws up. Its responsibility is to deal with them intelligently and objectively when they *are* thrown up, but it shouldn't be condemned just because certain topics arise. Like I said, the feeling on the ground was that the issue, at least from Jade's point of view, was more to do with bullying than race (a point that both Jade and, more importantly, Shilpa, made later).

What's more, even if there was a racial element to the disagreement, then that is EXACTLY the sort of debate that *Big Brother* should have been prompting and engaging in. In my opinion, it's far better for that sort of behaviour to come out and be confronted head-on, so that we can raise issues such as what sort of language and behaviour is and isn't acceptable, and air them.

For me, both from my parents' experience and my time on TV, the British public has always shown themselves to be some of the most tolerant and accepting people in the world, and the reaction to Shilpa was an example of that. To work on a show that, albeit unintentionally, provoked debate and national reaction was something that is still a great source of pride to me.

Ultimately, Jade became a parable of a life and death played out in the public eye. She had to leave the house to a closed set, i.e. with no one there, as the police and producers were in fear of the reaction she might receive, and she was pretty fractured after that year. I bumped into her at John's office and she was broken, just so distraught with how she'd behaved and full of remorse for being a bit of a bully. As tolerant as we may be, we do love our pound of flesh, and she was properly out of sorts for a while.

John looked after her as best he could and slowly she got her life back on track, to the extent that she even took part in the Indian version of *Big Brother*. (In fact, that's when she got the first signs of cancer and received her first diagnosis.) I never saw her again, as she went downhill pretty fast and passed away in 2009, but her facing her disease with honesty, bravery and openness led to a 12 per cent rise in women between the ages of twenty-five and sixty-four going for smear tests in the United Kingdom – an increase that came after the figures had been declining year on year since 2002. Not bad for someone who thought that a ferret was a bird.

I can't think of my time on BB without thinking of Jade, which is why I feel that the theme to my best bits should be of her time on *BB*. So I've taken the Keane track that we cut the first 'Best Bits' montage to. Thanks, Goody gumdrops, xx.

SOUNDTRACK

16

'All These Things That I've Done'
by the Killers

In my heart, I suppose I've always been a TV baby (meaning, aside from my wife, family and *some* of my friends, TV is my first love). It's the way in which it feels a bit like theatre, that notion of putting on 'a show', which I guess is a little old-fashioned, but even now I can't go into a TV studio without a tinge of excitement, especially when it's live.

When the BBC sold Television Centre for flats (flats, it's always flats), I was lucky enough to work on the last-ever live transmission from the studios there, anchoring a couple of hours of *Comic Relief* with the ever-brilliant, mouth-of-a-sailor, laugh-out-loud-funny Claudia Winkleman. After our stint I went up to the gantry (the gangway a level above the studio that runs right around it) to have a moment to say goodbye. I'd done loads of shows there and when one of the old lighting boys found me and asked what I was doing, I just told him I wanted to say goodbye to the 'old girl'. He then went all misty-eyed and, knowing that he had a soulmate, told me: 'It's a disgrace what they are doing.' See, telly – it gets under your skin.

But radio? There's something magical about working in radio. Radio is fluid, it's intimate, it's immediate. It's you and the listener, and no one else (apart from the other listeners, the producers and the engineers, of course). You can get a relation-ship through radio that TV can't touch. You and (hopefully) your listeners find out who you are on the radio – there's nowhere to hide, by which I mean you can't help it – even on the BBC, where you're supposed to be fanatically impartial, which I appreciate is an oxymoron – as your opinions, your politics (with a small p), your morals and your tastes all leak out far more subtly than they do on a more physical medium like television.

I have friends who have drifted away from working on radio, and they pretty much all say the same thing: they miss it like crazy and they'd kill to be back in it. It's the medium that allows most artistic freedom. I feel like that, and I'm just trying to make a music/entertainment show. For comedians, it must be the most creative of mediums, with the fewest boundaries and red tape.

An example of this fluidity is my show on Radio 2. I can wake up on a Saturday morning, look outside and decide to change my running order, and what music I want to play, depending on the weather, my mood, the news or whatever else impinges on my consciousness (it was the way one of my cats looked at me once – I can't quite remember what I ended up playing off the back of it, but I've got a feeling it was Curiosity Killed the Cat), then go to work, change the playlist, make the show, have a drink and get home in the same time it would take in television to send a round-robin email to all involved to see if we could meet to discuss if it was a good idea to maybe send it out to a focus group before then deciding whether we should do it. Or not.

So in a book that's pretty much about the most important songs in my life, radio obviously plays a big part, from Tezza and 'The Floral Dance' to actually working on it for a living. And the one earworm that I can't shake whenever I even think about radio is the title track of this chapter.

The Killers are an anthemic, stadium-filling band from Las Vegas. They put on an incredible show that I've had the good fortune to see many times, and they've been responsible for the backdrop to some of the best nights of my life (and, as often follows, some of the worst mornings). They were the first band I played on Radio 2 and I can't think about them without recounting the terror of my first show for the biggest radio network in Europe . . . (in fact, when I put it like that, it makes me feel just as sick as I did back then).

So, after a few years away from radio once I'd left XFM (largely due to the fact I didn't entirely trust myself to be in charge of a whole studio, and therefore a whole radio station, and that I was getting a bit ticked off with having no producer, and therefore no one thinking about each week's show apart from me and a computer I hated, that randomly generated a playlist – we weren't exactly the happiest of bedfellows), I was eager to get back to working in radio.

John put the line out and I was lucky enough to land, or at least get a nibble from, the two leviathans (enough of the fishing puns) of Radios 1 and 2, both of which were great plaices to be . . . (sorry, that was definitely the last one).

This was big news for me. To start with, I thought it was a no-brainer. Like most people who were kids in the eighties, I'd been brought up on Radio 1. This was before what they called the whole 'blood on the carpet' era when a new controller, Matthew Bannister, came on board and got rid of the old guard of DJs that had become big national institutions, his reasoning being that some of them had grown a bit too old for the demographic Radio 1 was there to serve. That was as maybe, but for a child of the eighties, DJs like Simon 'Our Tune' Bates, Dave Lee Travis – the Hairy Cornflake – Mike Read, Bruno Brookes, and Steve Wright were part of the fabric of our lives. So too their characters and phrases: 'quack quack oops', 'Mr Angry', 'Smiley Miley', 'Diamond Geezer' – and the highlight of the year, the Radio 1 Roadshow. (That was something I could only dream of attending, though I think my sister went. I was deemed too young, and apparently it was a bit too lively for one of my tender years . . . thanks, MUM!)

On paper then, Radio 1 seemed the place for me to go. And it would've been an honour to work there, but after doing a couple of pilots for them, enjoyable as they were, something just didn't feel right. I was introducing music that I didn't really listen to or, in many cases, actually know. (I mean, Eric Prydz's 'Call On Me', anyone? Not really me, although in retrospect, and having just now listened to it, it was quite a tune.)

I was hit with a cold, harsh reality. It was 2004, I was thirty-one, I'd been working camera/mic-side since I was twenty-four, and for the first time in my career (and this wasn't an easy pill to swallow) I was too old to be taking a gig.

Ouch.

I mean, really, *ouch*.

It's like the first time you go back to that club you always loved as a student, only to realise within five minutes that you have no right to be there any more (other than maybe to give your daughter a lift home, and then, strictly speaking, you should be outside, the obligatory two streets away). It wasn't Radio 1 itself – they were really keen, and far more respected, older and better broadcasters were still there (John Peel R.I.P. was still broadcasting on Radio 1 until his death). It was just that the show they wanted me to do meant that I couldn't pick my own tunes, meaning I was playing someone else's choices; meaning that, in truth, I wasn't right for them.

At the same time as Radio 1 had come a-knocking (and left me feeling as if I should have been drawing my pension), Radio 2 had also shown an interest. This was obviously a huge deal. Radio 2 is now the biggest network in Europe, but even then it was a massive station. At the time, though, whilst it felt right for me, I wasn't 100 per cent sure I was right for it. I mean, Radio 2 was full of musical geniuses, so where the hell did I fit in? I LOVE my music, and I know *some* stuff (mainly the holy trinity of Springsteen/Pogues/Brendan Shine) but I've never professed or wanted to be an expert. Question me on, let's say, pre-Collins Genesis, and I'll get eaten alive. And these Radio 2 boys and girls don't mess around: I was a Christian, and I was off to the Colosseum.

It was, however, a station in transition and one person there made me feel like it was the right move for me without my even knowing it. Radio 2 had recently undergone a bit of a change (evolution, not revolution, you understand – we're far too Home Counties for any of that). The retiring controller, Jim Moir (a man I've never met but by all accounts was a saint and one of the finest dinner companions on the planet), and his heir, Lesley Douglas, were keen to inject some new faces/voices into the schedule. The first of these was Jonathan Ross.

It feels a little strange to be talking about Jonathan now, as I consider him to be a friend (I'll settle for at least a friendly acquaintance), but together with Wogan, and the drive and energy of Chris Evans, he also made me want to get into the broadcasting industry.

I first saw him on a show called *The Last Resort* back in the eighties, when I was a teenager cooking a stir fry with my sister before my mam got home from her shift on reception at the local sports centre. Within days, hours probably, I was on to my friend, Neil Butler, telling him he had to watch this show. Alongside *Vic Reeves Big Night Out*, it was the most important show of my teenage years and the one that rubber-stamped my love of TV.

It was the first talk/variety show that seemed to be genuinely irreverent and properly going for laughs. It tore down the old barriers and mystique between the audience and the programme-makers (it broke the fourth wall as they say, though I have no idea who 'they' are). Evans followed and perfected this with *The Big Breakfast* and *TFI Friday*, but for me it all started with *The Last Resort*.

Jonathan is such a great broadcaster because he is instinctive; he doesn't worry about going off script and, contrary to some, he listens (admittedly to varying degrees depending on the guest). Alongside the equally brilliant Graham Norton, he's the most accomplished talk-show host of the last twenty years.

I've got to know Jonathan pretty well over the last ten or so years. He very kindly sent me a message early on in my career telling me I was doing a good job on *BBLB* and inviting me around for dinner. (It didn't go so well as I'd just been dumped by my then girlfriend, and after a bit too much red, spent most of the evening pouring my heart out to his wife and her friend . . . it wasn't a good look.) Thankfully (hopefully), I've been able to convince him and his wife that that was an off day. And he's still to this day a big inspiration to me.

But back then, he'd just signed for Radio 2, which was seismic for the station. He was only doing one show a week, but the message of having a show based around personality was what drew many other new broadcasters to Radio 2.

So, I had a few meetings with them. As I said, to start with I was a bit nervous: the place (actually Western House, a building next to Broadcasting House in central London) and its corridors were chock full of legends, people who had had their own shows for decades. Wogan was there, king of the mid-morning Ken Bruce, the fiendishly clever Jeremy Vine, radio legend Steve Wright, the effortlessly natural Simon Mayo, encyclopaedic Paul Gambaccini and old-school daddio Bob Harris (and that's just off the top of my head).

The good thing was that it became apparent pretty quickly that Radio 2 and I were singing from the same hymn sheet (although theirs was slightly more thorough, and holy). What both the station and I wanted was to do a show where live music played a big part, and where I was in control of the music I played and who I had on.

Prior to taking the job at Radio 2, I'd done a job for BBC Three, which was in its infancy at the time. A good friend of mine, Drew Pearce (who I'd also brought in to produce/ co-present with me later in my XFM tenure), had come up with the programme, called *Re:covered*. Drew and I worked on it together and I had helped to get it commissioned. The idea was that bands came on to perform one of their current hits and then covered a song by someone who had had an influence on them. We did two series, and it's one of my favourite TV shows that I've made. I really missed working on a music show, and the idea of having bands in session, doing covers and paying homage to those who'd inspired them, especially in a place like Radio 2, was one of the things I wanted to take to my own radio show.

The minute Radio 2 agreed to this, I knew I was in the right place. In fact, they were really up for it and, crucially, as it was a weekend show, and as such subject to less restrictions playlist- wise, they were willing to let me play what I wanted – yeah, you heard me, XFM! Plus, they were happy to let me produce it myself with my own production company, which I'd recently set up (with an old producer friend from my *No Balls Allowed* days, Mark Raphael) called Murfia. So, all told, this couldn't be any better. It was a huge deal to sign for Radio 2 – it's the nation's favourite radio station, and it's not something I take for granted even now, almost ten years after starting there.

From the station's point of view, they wanted me to intro- duce new bands to their listeners. Now, it's fair to say that most of their/our listeners know their music very well, but by new bands, they meant anything a Radio 2 audience might not normally know. This included some genres of music that might be more at home on Radio 1, but through the passage of time have become part of the fabric of music. It means that even to this day I still have a little chuckle when we play the likes of Public Enemy, or the Beastie Boys, and see the emails and texts go crazy telling me that Radio 2 isn't the place for this kind of 'newfangled noise', when the record I'm playing is actually over twenty years old.

In my time at Radio 2, I've also failed spectacularly to bring the average age of the listenership down. The demographic for Radio 1 is fifteen to twenty-five years of age, so it stands to reason that Radio 2's appeal should start at around the mid-twenties, and therefore the show I do should cater for the lower range of that demographic. Well, on the last count, the average age of the Radio 2 listener is fifty-one, whereas my indie disco kids are, on average, about fifty-two. Hey ho, so long as the kids are rocking!

But this was all still to come. Back in 2004, Radio 2 had just offered me a job, to start within a month or so, which to be honest I was a teensy bit worried about as I hadn't done any radio for a while. So, in a slightly/deeply neurotic and insecure way, I piloted – test runs to get me 'match fit' at driving the desk, etc – and piloted and piloted. And then piloted some more.

As I said, by now I'd started my own production company. This was always a big thing for me – not to have an enormous company (trust me, over time I've learnt that the responsibility involved when you employ someone means it's always good to keep companies as lean as possible), but to have some input into the shows I make. So, with Radio 2 having agreed to let us produce the show out of house – that is, independent from the BBC but still under their watchful eye – we got one of our

TV development producers, a maverick genius draped in tweed called Paul Connolly, to steer the pilot and get the show on air. Once it was up and running, we'd find a specialist radio producer.

Doing a pilot for radio is tricky. With TV you can watch it back and learn from your mistakes, in every way – from how it's shot, scripted, how you react, etc. Radio is a completely different beast, it's far more instinctive and, more often than not, live, so it's hard to 'pretend' and therefore far harder to learn from. You can pilot and practise, sure, but really it's trial and error, so you never actually know how it's going to go until you actually do it.

The two things I remember from the piloting process are that on the night of two of the pilots, Kelly Holmes won gold medals at the Athens Olympics (I'll never forget the look of incredulity on her face when she won the 800 metres) and the Killers . . . always kicking things off with the Killers. I must have done ten or so run-throughs and I always chose that track as the one to open the show. So I can't think of my time on radio without it – and Kelly Holmes – popping into my psyche. The first song you play on your first-ever show on a station you've never worked on before should be one to remember, so it seems right that this is on my soundtrack.

My actual real, live non-pilot first show was like the first day at school for a not particularly smart first-year kid who happens to be at school with nothing but really brainy prefects, all of whom made me feel extremely welcome. It was pretty intimidating and, truth be told, I was pretty shit. There's no getting away from it: my first show was a bit of a disaster and it was my fault. For example, I ran a quiz in which one of the questions

was, 'What number is six the square root of?' The lady on the
end of the phone didn't know, and in a moment of panic, I
confessed I didn't know either. (Rule one of running a quiz:
make sure you know the answers to the questions.) All I remember is the reviewer from the *Telegraph* saying that at that moment
he turned off in disgust (I'm not sure if it was because of my
poor broadcasting skills or my poor maths ability). But, like
anything, the more you do it the better you get, and after a while
I settled into it, and found a format and my feet. (By the way, six
is the square root of thirty-six.)

A few months down the line, I realised just what I'd joined
when we had our first Radio 2 presenters' Christmas dinner.
This was in the grand, old 'last days of the Roman Empire' style
of Christmas dinners, the sort of thing that went on before the
BBC Trust got their hands on the reins of the licence fee and
made us cut down on such festivities (meaning we now have to
resort to a couple of mushroom vol-au-vents – rotters!).

It was at old school restaurant the Criterion, in Piccadilly
Circus, and the place was heaving with legends. It's an over-
used word but, trust me, this place was a legendorama. Knowing
I was the new boy, the controller Lesley Douglas did her best to
integrate me into the fold, sticking me between Elaine Paige
and Lulu – it was like being sandwiched between your two most
glamorous, slightly tipsy aunties at a wedding! What struck me,
though, was just the sheer diversity of the talent in the place.
There was a guy there who has a show just playing the organ –
the crown jewel that is Nigel Ogden's *The Organist Entertains* . . .
and he does. Of course, Wogan was there – it's where he gave
me that great piece of advice, 'Never be afraid of the silence.'

He's a master at that, you'll be listening to him and think he's gone outside for a smoke, he's that relaxed. The now late and much-missed David Jacobs was there. On meeting me, he asked my age and then replied with a glint in his eye, 'I was still on my first wife at thirty-one. Wonderful woman.' Wherever you looked, the place was awash with the biggest names in radio: Gambo, Tony Blackburn (a man so in love with Radio 2 he's been found in the office on days when he doesn't even have a show just to be 'around the place') and the great Bob Harris, who, like many of them, put a fatherly arm around my shoulder . . . but in his case it extended to entertaining my team and me around at his house in Didcot. (I can report that he cooks a mean shepherd's pie and is more than charitable with the red.) He even took us to see the local football team where I foolishly stood behind the opposition goal as one of his sons heckled the away team's goalie. The poor goalie looked at me as if to ask, 'Why the hell are you standing with this kid and the six other people at this end of the pitch, in the snow, giving me a hard time?' I didn't really have an answer, but I was with Bob's kid, and it was only a bit of football banter, so what was I supposed to do?

After one show in particular I was rushing down to Cornwall to spend the weekend with some friends when, in my haste to get out of London, I found myself taking a wrong turn down a one-way street. Seeing a car coming towards me flashing its lights, I pulled over. The approaching car's driver's window wound down. I thought I was about to get an earful, only to see Bob's face pop out and say in his trademark whispered tones: 'Hey man, you know this is a one-way street?'

To which I replied, 'I didn't, Bob, sorry.'

'It's cool, Derm, cool.' And with that he just drove off . . .

That night at the Christmas party was the first night that the responsibility of working for Radio 2 truly dawned on me. The people I was working with, and the station, were some of the most experienced, knowledgeable . . . and drunk people in the industry, and somehow I'd lucked out joining them.

Radio 2 has given me time to grow, and whilst I still feel pretty in awe of a lot of the people there, it now feels like home. Lesley sadly resigned after the Andrew Sachs affair (where, as regrettable as it was, the place went a little mad), to be replaced by Bob Shennan, who has picked up the baton with aplomb, and loves music as much as anyone at the station.

My company still makes the show, and the producers I have, Ben and Simon, who I've employed for almost ten years, have become dear and trusted friends who love music as much as I do. We've helped break some really good acts/bands who either send us their tracks via CDs or we see at gigs; lent our early support to the likes of Adele, who played her first radio version of 'Someone Like You' on our show; broadcast Amy Winehouse's first piece of promo for *Back To Black*; gave their first-ever radio performance to Bastille, Ben Howard and many others.

We've had a lot of fun on the radio. I think on radio, bands give you something they don't on TV, which I put down to not being as self-conscious. The show continues to be three hours a week that I cherish; it's like having your own national jukebox. We've compiled four albums of our 'Saturday Sessions' and won three Radio Academy Awards for Best Music Programme. Of all these things that I've done, it's the one of which I'm most proud, and protective. And I know that sounds a bit 'beauty queen' winner's speech, but alongside Radio 2 I also love puppies, walking in the rain, and desperately want the world to be a more caring, sharing place. Amen.

SOUNDTRACK

17

'Rehab'

by Amy Winehouse

It was 2007 and I'd been doing *BBLB* for about six years. Although in many ways it was my dream job, I knew that I couldn't do it for ever. (Well, perhaps I could have done, but I, and more likely the viewer, might have got a teensy bit bored by series forty.)

De Niro says the talent is in the choices. It's one of those back-of-a-fag-packet, pub-bore bits of philosophy I've pilfered and used as my own guide, and that mantra was about to be put to the test.

Pretty much out of nowhere John called me and told me they were considering offering me the job as host of *The X Factor*. In his Billy-Goat-Gruff, northern tone, I was told that I'd be mad if I 'didn't think about it'.

What? *Think* about it? Of course I'm going to think about it! I'm now going to think about precious little else. Obsessively, compulsively (but hopefully not disordered-ly).

Cue interrupted sleep for the next few weeks.

It *was* a tricky one. To start with, I knew Kate Thornton, who had been let go by *The X Factor*. She was a friend, and someone I knew to be a funny, smart and quick live presenter. But I know it wasn't always plain sailing for her, which did slightly disarm me. If I was going to do the job, I had to be my own man. Secondly, it was a massive step up and, to be frank, it scared me. It wasn't the job itself – I'd grown up watching Saturday-night television, so of course I wanted to host a show to the biggest audience possible – rather, it was the responsibility that came with it and the obvious challenge of working on the biggest stage there was that frightened me.

At the time, I was still doing a show that by its definition was subversive and non-formatted and, to be honest, was essentially my own little empire. I loved it. It was popular, without rating through the roof or being too mainstream, which meant you could get away with murder. In comparison, even though *The X Factor* wasn't the beast it is now, it was still the biggest show on TV.

I had by now started to do some bigger gigs but nothing that could compare to the X, and with it the pressure, scrutiny, and responsibility that hosting a flagship show for a channel entailed. These included a show on BBC One called *1 vs 100*, which was a quiz show – another one of those jobs I couldn't turn down as, even though it didn't really float my boat too much, it proved I could do a prime-time gig (in fact, if I hadn't done it, I don't think I'd have been offered *The X Factor* in the first place). I'd also done two years of a cracking awards show on Channel 4 called *The UK Music Hall Of Fame*, one of those shows that advertisers and sponsors threw money at before the arse fell out of that game in the last recession. It was sponsored by some telecommunications company that I'm not sure exists any more, and was a sort of night of musical 'Lifetime Achievement' awards for Channel 4.

The UK Music Hall Of Fame was a brilliant gig – as a music fan, I was in heaven. (Well, kind of, as most of the legends there were either in rehab, so pretty much in and out the door before temptation was thrust under their nose, mouth or any other orifice; or should have been in rehab, in which case they weren't entirely sure where they were.) One stand-out moment was when Joss Stone performed and went on a wander mid-song into the audience, and was on camera walking past Brian Wilson from the Beach Boys, who was asleep. A magical moment in itself, but it was made even more brilliant by the woman who I assume was Brian's wife, on realising what was happening, giving him a dig with her elbow to wake him up, which she did, on camera, just as the scantily clad Stone skipped by in bare feet. Poor Brian Wilson had no idea where he'd woken up (I presume he thought heaven) or, I imagine, what day it was.

Whilst these were big shows, *The X Factor* was a whole other level. So I did what any other brave young man would have done in my situation and . . . I ran away.

Well, that isn't exactly true (but it is, kind of). The brilliant and even more brilliantly titled South By Southwest festival, held in Austin, Texas (which for those not in the know is, as you might expect, in the south by south-west bit of America), was being covered by Radio 2, and they asked us to go and do our show from there. Kind of running away to America seemed like a good plan whilst I sorted my head out. Not that it needed sorting – I pretty much knew from the outset I wanted to take/bite their arm off for the gig, but I had to get my head around it, and what better way to do that than to go to a music festival and work hard/party as hard for a week or two?

South By Southwest, or 'South By', as people too lazy to add the 'Southwest' part of the title call it, is extraordinary. Think Glastonbury without the mud, better places to eat, and hotel rooms. I've not been back, sadly, and by all accounts it's changed a bit, but it's honestly one of the best festivals I've ever been to. The randomness of it all is the best thing about it, as a lot of well-established UK acts go there to start to try to break America. So you'll be walking down a side street at 2 a.m., heading back to your hotel, and you'll wander past a bar playing a song by a band/act you like (for example, on that trip, Bat for Lashes) and therefore think that said bar seems OK for a nightcap. You then walk in to find it is actually Bat for Lashes, headdress and all, actually playing beautiful, sweeping epic music to twenty or so drunk and slightly bemused Texans.

The week turned out to be a proper burning-the-candle-at-both-ends type of affair. My producers, Ben and Simon, and I would be up early to grab as many interviews as we could, then head off to the studio for the sessions/show, then eat great food and, well, drink and party a lot. It was also the festival where I first saw Amy Winehouse perform.

I'd met Amy once or twice before, in particular when, fairly early on in her career, she'd done a knockout of a session on my Radio 2 show. I'd never found her anything other than a warm, super-smart, funny and obviously gifted young lady. This was back in the days before she became addicted (or at least a time when it seemed as if she had her problems under control).

At South By Southwest, we had an appointment to get a quick interview with her before she was to do a showcase gig to a bunch of middle-management record execs at a Texas BBQ (always at a BBQ) at two o'clock that afternoon. She was head-lining a Radio 2 show later that night and this would be the only chance we'd get to speak to her, so we were keen to get her impressions of the festival, how *Back To Black* was taking off, and how she was doing.

The interview was a disaster, heartbreaking. I hadn't seen her for ages and she was in a bad way: slurring her words, not finishing sentences, drifting off mid-answer and barely focus-ing. To start with, I'm ashamed to say, I thought it was amusing, but I quickly realised she was worse for wear and wrapped the interview up in about a minute and a half. As sad as that was, at the time I honestly thought she was just drunk, with maybe a bit of afters thrown in. But much as I feared for her, watching her perform on stage to a group of people more interested in the BBQ, and even though she may have stum-bled and mumbled her way through the set, such was her talent that she still looked and sounded like a star. Eight or so hours later, however, when she headlined the main Radio 2 event of the festival, she turned up like a completely differ-ent person. She had no recollection of the interview with us earlier, and was asking how we were enjoying the festival, and what myself and the team were doing later, as maybe we'd like to hook up and have a drink? Selfishly, and thought-lessly, part of me wanted to do this, to have a legendary night out with Amy Winehouse that I could dine out on, but look-ing back now, I'm glad it didn't happen.

Fast-forward to 2011 and I'm on air on Radio 2, midway through my Saturday show. As reports started to come in that Amy had passed away, I soon began to get messages on social media sweeping in like wildfire, such as, 'Why aren't you play-ing Amy Winehouse?' or 'Why aren't you paying tribute to Amy Winehouse? You should be ashamed of yourself,' etc, etc. It was the first time social media had properly had an immediate impact on my work, and it was a deluge that was quite some-thing to witness.

The reality, though, was that we were pretty helpless: we couldn't do anything, the problem being that the BBC, quite rightly, can't broadcast news unless it's been confirmed to be 100 per cent bona fide. This can lead to people accusing the corporation of not being the quickest, however, and that day was no exception. The frustration for us, and me in particu-lar, being on air, was huge in that because her death hadn't been verified yet, we couldn't even make reference to it, let alone pay homage to her. Plus, the boys and I were pretty shocked, and added to this is the fact that my show goes out on a Saturday, so the news team isn't exactly firing on all cylinders as it would be on a prime-time weekday show. So I did the only thing I thought I could do, which was to be honest with the listener and say that yes, there were reports of something coming in, but they were yet to be authenti-cated, so as I couldn't say any more or mention the person involved, we'd just continue to play music and explain all when we could.

Twenty minutes later, the call came through confirming Amy's death, so we could at last talk about it on the radio. For the rest of the show, we played both her own songs and songs that inspired her, with just the briefest of explanations. Myself and the boys were pretty devastated – we didn't know Amy all that well, but there's a sense of big brotherly stewardship when you've had an act on your radio station in their early days and then seen them flourish . . . So, whilst we weren't grieving as such, we certainly felt numb.

Amy was just this properly unique, troubled, pure of heart, typically British talent. You only have to look at her eyes the moment she won her Grammy to fall back in love with her . . . (http://www.youtube.com/watch?v=1CSX8DxYUJk&feature =kp).

Incarceration and a reference to her favourite pub in a winner's speech. One in a million.

While I was at South By, even though I was having a great time, I was still very much aware that around the corner I had a big decision to make. Luckily, I had a bad case of jet lag, and, as I've already said, nothing gets my house in order more than waking up at four in the morning wide awake, with bugger all else to do than think. So, in this instance, with the biggest decision of my career looming over me in a you've-got-a-maths-test-tomorrow sort of a way, I decided to use the time to make a list; well, to make two lists, of reasons why I should and shouldn't take the job. Which, by the end of the week, happily told me what I knew in the first place: I'd be an idiot not to take it.

With the pros list covering two pages, including the obvious points I've already talked about, and the cons running to about two lines, including such moral dilemmas as, 'Will indie bands still like me and come on my radio show?', it was, as they say, a no-brainer.

For the most part I've always tried to make decisions based on instinct – you *know* when a show is right for you, but this was too important. So, when I got home, I discussed it with my closest friends, family, and my then girlfriend (now wife) Dee, and almost everyone was of the same opinion, which was, essentially: 'Do it! Why are you asking us?'

A couple of friends were surprised I took the job, thinking I'd be better placed going into something less mainstream, but when it comes to my career choices, the idea of what is and isn't mainstream has never really entered into my thinking.

I've simply never really seen it like that. I'd been brought up watching Saturday-night TV (in a cod-roe-smelling house), having an indoor picnic as a treat, as it was the only day of the week we were allowed to watch TV and have our dinner at the same time. Hosting a show on that day, at that time, was always the height for any broadcaster, and alongside Terry Wogan, we ate dinner accompanied by the likes of Bruce Forsyth, Les Dawson and (one of my favourites) Larry Grayson. In our household, watching Saturday-night TV wasn't some guilty pleasure – it was seen as no different to watching the news, or *Sportsnight* with my dad. Entertainment was entertainment, you didn't have to dress it up to justify it, or believe that if it was on ITV, or 'Channel 3' as it was called by most parents in those days, it was the work of the light-entertainment devil. To have that opportunity to be working and in the schedule alongside unarguable greats like Ant and Dec, and Jonathan Ross, was and still is a big deal to me.

So, I wanted the job, and the channel wanted me and the production company, but there was still one man with a reputation for being pretty fearsome who I *hoped* also wanted me, but who I still had yet to meet: Louis Walsh . . . (OK, not really).

I'd met Simon Cowell a couple of times before. I'd been on a talk show with him years previously in Northern Ireland and, after *1 vs 100* had rated half-decently, he'd congratulated me once at the National Television Awards. But, to rubber-stamp the deal for *The X Factor*, I had to fly out and meet him in LA. It was to be a 'let's see how we get on' kind of a meeting.

As I flew over the Atlantic, I tried to put it all to the back of my mind and not overthink it, for the simple reason that, if you're not yourself in meetings, if you try and be who you think people want you to be, you're going to get found out (and why would you want to be that person anyway?). But I wouldn't be human if I didn't admit to a certain amount of nerves!

Straight from the airport, I headed to the CBS studios and a recording of *American Idol*, the show on which Simon was chief judge, and the one he'd made his name with in the States.

Stepping off a nine-hour flight that gets you into LA in the afternoon (meaning you've still got the rest of the day to be on your 'A game') isn't *exactly* the best preparation for the biggest job interview of your life, so I was a trifle woozy when myself and Jane (the agent who was looking after me at John Noel at the time) rocked up to the show. But it was still insightful and valuable to see how both the process and the man worked.

I'll touch on what it's like to work with Simon in the next chapter, but it's hard not to remember your first impressions when you meet one of the most powerful and famous men in the entertainment world (or just the world, if you prefer). In short, he has 'it': 'it' being presence. Of course you could say that about anyone powerful, but he's different. He is at once charming – disarmingly so – interested (so long as he respects you) and generous with time. He's also fun. Don't misunderstand me, I'm not looking at this through rose-tinted spectacles, or trying to curry favour with my boss (our working relationship hasn't been without its frustrations), but those were genuinely my impressions during the time we spent together. I've lost count of the number of people I've met in music and television who are convinced they won't like him because of their preconceptions, only to end up loving him once they meet him. Like I said, he's got 'it'.

Over the next day or so, we met several times and talked about our shared love of TV, music (which, contrary to some opinions, he does love – he's a massive fan of all things Rat Pack – and about how we saw my role on the show. What became quickly apparent, to my relief, is that he hates a 'yes man'. That doesn't mean he wants people to be unnecessarily confrontational, but more that he encourages people to honestly speak their mind – at work, he likes to be challenged, pushed and to have fun.

The evening after our first meeting we were to have dinner together and, to be honest, I wasn't entirely sure what to expect. Yes, it was just dinner, but how would it play out? Would I have to drink the blood of a fatted calf whilst indulging in some ritu-alistic voodoo-style ceremony where I pledged undying loyalty to all things light entertainment?

Well, much as that might have made some headlines, as it turned out it was just a really charming evening with him and Jerry Springer, who was about to host *America's Got Talent*. (Jerry was great company, apart from the fact that in any given room he finds himself in, he has to run the gauntlet of banks of people chanting, 'Je-*ree*, Je-*ree*,' which must be disconcerting even if it is your own name.)

My time with Simon had gone well, we'd pretty much bonded; I felt like he could trust me with his flagship show and, in particular, he'd given me the most important assurance I needed: that I could be a ringmaster, not a traffic cop. The one rule Simon had, and has always repeated to me, was, 'Embrace the madness.' At the time I eagerly agreed, but really I had no idea what it meant . . . (eight years down the line, I've now got a pretty good idea).

Before heading home, I had another meeting, this one with another *X Factor* judge, and Simon's constant bête noire (mainly because she doesn't really give a shit who she offends), Sharon Osbourne.

It's pretty fair to say I adored Sharon from day one. She's like your mum, all loving and maternal and full of wisdom and sage advice . . . if your mam was also the queen of rock and roll, and rather than tell you to turn the other cheek in a disagreement, she tells you to send them one of your own shits in the post (or, better still, she'll do it for you herself). She is, simply and bril-liantly, in equal measure, hard as nails and soft as a kitten.

As soon as I returned home I had two calls to make. The first was to Kate Thornton to ask for her blessing. I knew I was taking the job; it just seemed like the right thing to do. She was, as ever, the lady. The second was to my then boss at the BBC, Peter Fincham, to tell him I was leaving *1 vs 100*. Peter, ever the gent, told me he understood and that, magnanimously, he hoped we'd work together again (which we do, as he's now head of ITV).

So, I was back in Britain as the new host of *The X Factor*, complete with those assurances from Simon that I could be the same style of host I was on *BBLB*, which I was still signed to do for another year. This essentially meant me starting an *X Factor* audition in a city somewhere in Britain, working until the early afternoon, then getting on, in no particular order, a plane, train, bike or car and getting to Elstree Studios, where we filmed *BBLB*, in time to go through the script, rehearse, do the show live, debrief and go through the next day's show, before heading back on said plane, train, bike or car to do the same, in the next city. It was exhausting, and not exactly great for the old social life, but I loved it.

That first *X Factor* series seems like a lifetime ago now, mainly because the show has moved on so much.

Apart from 'making it my own' (as Louis would say), the only concern for me on *The X Factor* were the so-called 'sob stories'. Now, it's important to clarify here that I'm talking specifically about 'sob stories' and not just 'stories'. The reason *The X Factor* is the show it is, and strikes a chord with its viewers, is because it's not just about the contestants' singing voices. People, for the most part, like people, or at least are interested in them, and they are far more likely to engage with someone on TV if they know something about that person – anything, in fact, rather than the fact that they can just come on stage and bash out a half-decent Celine Dion cover. Now, this can obviously be open to a bit of abuse from some people auditioning, who think a bit of plinky-plonky 'woe is me' is what the programme makers want, but whilst it's obvious that someone with a story is more interesting than someone without one, if you can't sing, or at least entertain, then, certainly in the last few years, even if your story is akin to *War And Peace*, you're not getting through to the live shows. (Well, maybe you are, but you're going out early.)

On one occasion, for example, during the audition tour, I ran into a chap in the crowd who had come along to audition (hence 'audition tour' – see, there's a logic to it all). I wished him good luck, and from nowhere he almost burst into tears, held up his baby daughter and said, 'I'm doing it for her.'

'Oh dear,' I said, obviously thinking that such an emotional outburst must mean the little girl wasn't very well. 'Is she OK?'

'Yeah,' he replied, getting into the melodrama. 'She's fine, I'm just doing it for her.'

All of which left me thinking, 'Er, OK, that in itself is commendable, but what message exactly do you think thrusting a perfectly healthy baby at me, whilst you wail like a banshee, tells us? And more importantly what effect do you think it will have on her? And whilst we're at it, aren't we all "doing it for her"? It's called going to work and looking after your family. Isn't it? Needless to say, I didn't say any of that and just wished him luck . . . (Bottler!)

The people with *actual* stories (rather than just the ability to have children), however, I have the utmost empathy for. It's just that, at first, I was a little worried about how to show that.

I'd gone from a show where I could take the mick out of people (for a living) who were having a hissy fit because they'd run out of cigarettes or Diet Coke, to somewhere where people were auditioning for the deepest of motives: a promise to a relative, a point to prove to themselves, a precocious talent as yet undiscovered, or a grafter who'd been at it for a while without the stars aligning. I wasn't sure if I could do those people justice, as I'd just try to make them laugh, or at least smile to feel better.

In my pre-show meetings, I raised these concerns and was told I needn't worry, and that I'd be given more of the lighter stories to have fun with.

Cut to my first day and I meet Niki Evans, whose father, before he passed away, had, unbeknownst to her, filled in an audition application for his daughter. What? *What?!* No one had told me this was going to happen. By the end of that day, I'd cried more than I had since my rabbit had died, when I was eleven. Weirder still, rather than feel awkward about it, I wasn't embarrassed at all, I loved it. There have been so many incredible experiences doing *The X Factor*, and it's changed my life in so many ways (OK, I'm beginning to sound like a contestant now), but one of my favourite things about working on the show has been meeting the many, many people from different walks of life that I'd never have met in any other job. Yesterday, in fact (for me now, that is – it's unlikely to be yesterday for you), I interviewed the following: a group of Chinese students who'd come over just to audition, a fishmonger, and a hypnotherapist (who can't have been *that* good at his job as he didn't get through). It's a people-based job, and for me the attraction has always been the same. There's nowt so queer as folk.

My first day was also one of my most surreal. We were filming at the Arsenal stadium, which for me (being a lifelong fan) was a big deal. As such, I and all the judges had boxes as our dressing rooms, mine being next to Simon's.

After what I thought was a pretty happy first half-day's filming, I returned to my box/dressing room to pick up any phone messages and shovel in a quick lunch, only to find that the door connecting my room to Simon's was open. Deciding to pop in to say hello, and see how his day had been going, I stopped dead in my tracks as I heard him on the phone saying something along the lines of, 'I know he's just started, but he's not working out. It's just not right and I think we'll have to replace him.'

Cut to inside my head – PANIC! Many things started to bounce around in there, but the gist of it was as follows: 'I've only just started, I've just done seven interviews, how can he sack me already? How has he seen them? Where has he seen them? Why were they so bad? I knew he was ruthless, but Jesus!' etc, etc. After I – sort of – got myself together, and had crept out without making a sound, I returned to the job feeling just a bit despondent that this would be my last day, and that I was to be dumped ignominiously on the light-entertainment scrap heap, ready for panel shows and pub quizzes to feast on my bones.

Except, clearly, it never happened. It wasn't me he was talking about. (I have no idea who it was, but that day I didn't care.) I'd survived my first day, and I'd take that as a win. It was quite a start.

It's going to be hard to whittle down what my track for that time will be, but for now, this part of the soundtrack needs to go back to Austin, to a hotel room, to a list, and to a fragile girl in her twenties who was one of the finest songwriters we've ever produced.

SOUNDTRACK

18

'Mysterious Girl'

by Ant and Seb (Peter Andre)

'Listen'

by Beyoncé

'Little Things'

by One Direction

OK, this was always going to be hard: to try to pick a song or songs that sum up my last eight (eight! Where has that gone?) years on *The X Factor*. In the end, I've had to go for three.

The first is from a pair of my favourite, what I like to call 'colourful characters' on the show – and, trust me, there have been many; so many, that it's almost as hard to pick the second track, which is a proper studio drop-dead 'wow' moment where you just knew you were witnessing something special. The third is a nod to having a front row seat as the biggest box-office group in the world were formed.

In truth, I could write a whole book on *The X Factor* (and *Big Brother*, come to think of it) – not in a 'read all about it in the daily rag, warts and all'-style exposé (I mean, obviously some decisions are made behind closed doors and, as in any work environment, it has its fair share of gossip), but rather as this is my experience of working on the show and how we make it . . . which, for the most part, can be visually summed up by this: http://www.youtube.com/watch?v=ETiwMTENG8g (For those of you without instant access to the internet, it's a clip of master plate spinner, Andrew Van Buren, on *The Generation Game*.)

You see? That's how it's done. That, my friends, is TV in a nutshell. Plate spinning. It's not that decisions aren't made, of course they are! It's just that what's required to make a television show of *The X Factor*'s behemothian proportions is less a Machiavellian master plan, more some poor runner, researcher, assistant producer, series producer, director, executive producer, even at times presenter (or all of the above), legging it around between plates in case the whole thing comes crashing down around them and before you know it, Jedward have become worldwide superstars.

It's been an incredible time to get into the industry and work on two shows that have changed the way we watch, appreciate, consume and make television. All power to them, or in actual fact, to you.

So, before I reveal, in no particular order (I never get bored of saying that, although, believe me, that *really* long pause I have to leave so that the director can get all his shots come elimination time is as long for me as it is for you . . . apologies), the reasons behind the songs I have chosen, I'll first tell you about my time on the strangest, most brilliantly mental, professional yet chaotic, inspirational yet weird and wonderful, show I'll ever have the privilege of working on.

Although I've already touched on my first year of *The X Factor*, I want to try and give you a sense of what it's like working on the show. At that time it really was a massive step up. Up until this point I'd done some good shows, some fairly big shows; but, in terms of scale, scope, resources and expectation, this was huge, another league.

Up until then, I was used to hosting and producing a show whose express purpose was to love its older brother, but also kick it in the nuts from time to time. Where I was going now was something way bigger.

To set the scene and introduce some of the gang (they won't appreciate being called a gang, though – they're a well-bred bunch), the same year I started, another rookie was dipping his toe into *The X Factor* for the first time: producer Mark Sidaway. Like me, he'd come to *The X Factor* from a sister show, *The Xtra Factor* (*The X Factor*'s *BBLB*) and together we were given the task of trying to make the live shows a little more . . . 'fun', I guess – to make it a bit more like the sister show, without ever . . . being too much like the sister show. Eight years down the line, Sid, as everyone calls him, has become a very good friend. He's literally the voice in my ear, and to me, and to many others, *The X Factor* UK is as much his baby as it is Simon's.

Together with Sid there was, and still is, Richard Holloway, Sid's immediate boss and mentor. Richard has worked in entertainment TV and film on both sides of the Atlantic, and having worked with everyone from Gene Kelly and the Muppets to Jimmy Perry (responsible for one of my favourite shows, *Dad's*

Army), he is one of the finest dinner companions I know. I love his company, and his counsel. And lastly there was Siobhan Greene, or Shu as everyone calls her. She was Simon's right-hand woman, and although she's moved on to pastures new, she was one of the keys to me enjoying the job early doors, a small bundle of energy from Huddersfield, who like me was second-gen Irish, and had the knack of always thinking like a viewer as well as a producer.

I mention these here because it seems odd to talk about my time on the X without them, so, you know, don't want to be rude and all that, thought I'd best introduce you all . . .

Early on in my first year, it became pretty apparent that we had a big shadow hanging over us in the shape of the previous year's winner, Leona Lewis. She's gone on to have a hugely successful career, and even though back then her success was in its infancy, as a team we knew that we were tasked with finding a winner worthy of following in her footsteps (which, well, we kind of didn't). The eventual winner that year (2007) was Leon Jackson, a likeable, undernourished underdog from Glasgow who suffered from pretty terrible stage fright and who was, whilst certainly not without talent, never properly cut out for life as a conventional pop star (something I don't think he'd disagree with). But that for me (and this is coming from the TV maker rather than the record-company perspective – I'm *pretty* certain they wouldn't agree with me) is the beauty of the show: the public always pick the winner. And it's rare for that winner to be who you think it's going to be early on; it's always the act that kind of comes from nowhere about four, five or six weeks in that goes on to triumph. I'm told that even Leona wasn't much fancied until she kicked off her shoes in the studio and banged out a killer version of 'Summertime'.

The point is, you never know who's going to win. The only people who know how the voting is going throughout the series are a couple of anonymous faces who work independently from the show, and live in the voting room (a kind of panic room come Churchill bunker) – that no one is allowed access to – and never even look you in the eye in the corridor (just in case their blinking at you might give something away).

And why would you want to know the outcome too soon, anyway? I mean, honestly, who would? It'd be like unwrapping your Christmas presents early. That's the whole excitement of the show, so why would anyone want to ruin it? Furthermore, it's crucial to me that people trust the show. I totally understand that people get annoyed when one of their favourites gets knocked out, or, as is quite often the case, Louis keeps one of the more 'unique' acts in, in place of someone who has a conventionally better voice, but the show's first priority has always been to be 100 per cent above board, otherwise we simply couldn't and shouldn't do it, and I for one would want no part in it.

But I digress, in a Speaker's Corner kind of way (apologies). Let's return to my first series. For those not entirely au fait with how logistics work on *The X Factor*, here's a quick run down: it's pretty much all go from the off. Firstly, we have the initial auditions, the 'open days' where all and sundry turn up. This happens (usually in the coldest places known to man) in about April time, when I'm freezing my tush off welcoming the viewer to whichever city we're in, dressed only in shirtsleeves in the knowledge that the show will air in sunny August.

After that round of auditions we hit the rooms, going to cities where the judges . . . judge *forty or so acts a day* whilst I stand outside interviewing family members, congratulating, commiserating, hugging and, in some cases, just staring awkwardly at the floor with them. Then, for the last few years, we've had the arena auditions which are hugely popular with contestants, as everyone gets to perform to 5,000-plus people, so even if they don't get through, they get to have their day in the sun.

We then move on to boot camp, which is actually like a boot camp, if the sergeant majors are pampered creative types and exhausted researchers, and the camp is exclusively for vocal chords. The contestants are all put up in the same hotel (the insurance premiums take up about half of the entire budget) and it's at this point that the judges realise, in their excitement, they've put loads too many people through, and the rest of us realise the impracticality of picking that forty-piece dancing *Glee* group, or the 80-year-old with the dicky hip who needs round-the-clock care.

From there we have 'Judges' Houses' (houses, not homes, very important legal differentiation that). Although ask me if Nicole Scherzinger owns the Dubai Jumeirah Hotel outright, or if Louis Walsh owns eight (and counting) luxury homes around the world including five Irish castles and an award-winning Spanish stables outside Barcelona, and I'll have to take the fifth. (Come to think of it, Louis does seem to know his way around those stables, so you never know.)

And lastly we have the Holy Grail (not the actual Holy Grail – Simon owns that), the place that our acts know they really need to get to, to have a shot at making singing their career: the live shows.

Fountain Studios in Wembley isn't much to look at from the outside. It's sandwiched between the suburban houses of Wembley on one side and the stadium, the arena and an industrial estate on the other. Paramount Studios it isn't. But it's always had a special place in my heart as it's not only where I do *The X Factor*, but also where I made that first television pilot, *Seaside Special* (nowhere near the sea, then – the magic of television), and the people who work there have always remembered and been good to me, so it feels like home . . . (though without the cats, dishwasher or wife).

This might sound a bit weird or perhaps sad to you, but one of the highlights of my week when the live shows start is being alone on stage, first thing in the morning (before we start proper rehearsals), going through the script links and positions for that night's show. This is as the stage is being set, so the scene dock doors open and close as the stagehands are getting it ready for the evening. There's just something about it, when the winter morning sun shines (dapples, if you will) through the studio and the cold comes in as I hug a cup of coffee and enjoy a bit of quiet work time (apart from the frequent calls of 'Out the way, Derm!' from the boys) before the day proper kicks off. That way, by the time I've rehearsed and the live show comes around, theoretically I *should* be in a position where having done my extra, private little bit of prep, I'm playing in a sand pit. (Note, *should* be.)

That's all to come, however, as I'm still telling you about my first series. So at this moment, I'm not worried about any bloody dappled anything – it's the first live show and I'm SHITTING MYSELF!

The first parts of the series had gone well. Well, for the most part. As I said, I was doing BBLB that year, and I was rushing between the two gigs, so much so that at times I couldn't remember the names of every single contestant/housemate. Sharon's 'Judge's House' was in LA that year, and it was time for the reveal of yeses and nos, as to who would get through to the studio. It's always the worst part of the whole show, a combination of crushed dreams, happy faces and always mascara on the shoulder. Cramming all the names in my head, I saw a girl called Steph on the way to get the good or bad news. 'There's Steph,' I thought, 'good, I know her, Steph, Steph, that's her name, Steph.' As she came out of the room Sharon was in, post news, before I could think I just said, 'Steph,' as a prelude to whatever I was going to say next. All I heard back was a rather exasperated, 'Kim'. It wasn't Steph, it was a girl called Kim, she'd got a no, and immediately after that I'd got her name wrong. Nice, classy.

So, we'd just finished the judges' homes . . . sorry, houses, always houses (mea culpa) . . . where after my personal lowlight, my personal highlight had been a chap called Rhydian (half-Liberace, half-Phantom of the Opera, who eventually ended up as runner-up that year) turning up to Ibiza in a massive white fur coat. The researchers informed him that he'd either have to take it off there and then or, for the sake of continuity (the TV equivalent of paranoia), leave it on for the rest of the day. He refused to take it off, which meant we had to watch him bake all day and turn progressively redder in said fur coat as the temperature soared.

If Rhydian was sweating, which he was, I was sweating even more as my first live show approached. To be honest, it was like nothing I'd done before. By then I might have been well versed in live presenting, but the lead up to that week was intense to say the least.

My weeks when the live shows start now follow the same pattern. On Wednesdays I go into the production office with my writer, Ivor, to script the links, then we rehearse all day Friday, before the off on Saturday and Sunday. But that first Wednesday, eight years ago, was when it first dawned on me: all the work the team does, all those hours, starting way back in April; the whole selection process; all those people who've put all that effort in, from my cameraman and the director to the executive producers to the runners, are, after months of graft, all relying on one person to go and hold all of that together, on screen.

Oh dear me.

The thirty seconds before the show starts are unique. Whilst I'm standing behind the screen doors on my own waiting for the off, the noise from the crowd is so loud, like a coliseum, our brilliant warm up man Roycey by this point has them in a frenzy and the atmosphere so intense that when the theme music starts, the buzz is incredible – I've never experienced anything like it.

Still now, eight series in – post my team, stylist Tom, and make-up artist Sarah (the Glam Squad), having done their best with 'The Show Pony' as we like to call me! – side of stage pre-show is the best feeling in the world, seriously; maybe even better than doing the show itself. But back then? On my first live show . . .?

Well, Holly Willoughby, who's become a great friend and is a brilliant live presenter, put it best (and it's something only a live presenter can really understand): on your first show you 'look around, albeit fleetingly, trying to catch someone else's eye, anyone, as if to say, "I don't want to do it, you do it, anyone?"' That's so true, but she and I also agree that as those doors go back and Peter Dickson, the man with the booming voice, calls out your name, you immediately feel, 'Hang on a minute, of course I want to do it! This is the greatest job in the world!'

On my first live show, there were rows and ructions before-hand between Sharon and our other female judge, Dannii Minogue. To be honest, I never saw it, partly because I was kind of preoccupied, but also because all of that stuff has never interested me. I'm not naïve enough to think we'll all get along famously all the time, but I knew Sharon and Dannii didn't get on, and I thought it was sad because they are both lovely people. I suppose it was like introducing two friends at a party saying, 'You two are going to LOVE each other!' only to find they both think the other is an arse.

Anyway, that added to the tension but, like I said, at the time . . . preoccupied. In fact, most of the show went by in a blur. I know that sounds odd, but it being my first show, I wasn't focused on having a good time and appreciating the show as I do now. That said, I was enjoying it, but it was effectively a first day in a new job (only in this case, a large proportion of the country was watching my first day in the new job), with all that that entails.

The biggest deal of that first live show was at the end of the night when it transpired that two of Sharon's category, 'The Girls' that year, were in the bottom two, which meant one of them was definitely going home (the judges have to pick one act from the bottom two to eliminate). Now, I pretty much knew she wouldn't pick between them, but I had no idea what was about to happen next.

Sharon kicked her shoes off (weird, I always remember that moment – I thought to myself, 'The shoes are coming off, on prime-time TV . . . something really isn't right') and then said, 'I'm not voting, Dermy,' before storming off. Not great that. As she said later (off camera), 'This is a reality show and this is fucking real.' Quite. Luckily, both Sid (in my ear) and I had done basic maths, so with three judges left in front of me, I figured it was the best of three to decide who went home. (Glad I retook maths.)

And that was my Osbourne-flavoured baptism of fire. My first live show. The greatest buzz of all time.

Now buzzy as that is, the only problem with a buzz is that you don't come down from the high that you're on for hours, so if you come off air at 10 p.m., after you've had dinner and a debrief, at the earliest it's 11 p.m. At this point you're still pretty high so, over time (eight years), both Sid and I have perfected the answer: go home, have two to three glasses of red (it's still a school night, as we've got a show the next day) and watch something on TV that's got nothing to do with *The X Factor* to try to calm down, with the aim of being in bed before 2.30 a.m. As a result, what's normally the case is that we now both come in on a Sunday for the results show and . . .

'Well, what did you watch?'

'Documentary about the cockleshell heroes. You?'

'*The Bourne Identity*'.

TV, it's a non-stop glamour-fest.

It also quickly became apparent that being on a show like *The X Factor* adds years to/takes years off your life. I don't mean that in a bad way, but working on a show that the whole public knows, or is at least aware of, means everyone wants to talk about it, thus doubling, possibly tripling the time it takes to do day-to-day chores. To be honest, it's actually quite nice – it's a show that people engage with, which is the goal in the first place and, as I've stressed several times already, I do love a good natter; but from October, when we hit the live shows, to December, I'm pretty much late for all my non *X Factor*-related appointments due to the fact that a trip to the shops goes from what is normally a five-minute errand to a twenty- to thirty-minute epic as I explain/agree that, 'Yes, so and so has got a lovely voice, yes, Simon/Gary really *is* like that in real life, and, yes, Louis *really* does like Wagner and Jedward.'

Like any job, once you get the first bit/goal out of the way, which in my case translates to, 'Don't get sacked in your first year,' you can start to make it your own (*X Factor* parley again – apols) and properly have fun, which is definitely what I've had.

So the first song from my time on the X comes from the early days of my second series when we were in Cardiff, and two chaps called Ant and Seb auditioned. Now, it's important to stress here that before I meet someone, I know a few basics about them (their name often helps) and I might have an inkling about their level of talent (based mostly on instinct) but, on the whole, I have no idea how good or otherwise they're going to be at performing before they walk through the door and start singing.

This means that I've been surprised countless times as some-one who might look or behave (let's be frank) a little odd, comes in and gives the audition of a lifetime. And all power to them – for me the show is all about the characters; it's what makes the show fun, and that's what it's supposed to be . . . fun.

That said, when two skinny white chaps from the valleys came in and said they wanted to be the next P Diddy and Usher . . . and Rick Astley . . . you knew they were going to have to be pretty spectacular for this audition to go well.

I'll say no more, but it's one of the standout moments from my early years on the X (apologies for the shirt, by the way – Richard Holloway wasn't impressed either, saying I looked like a young Howard Keel). Anyway, take a look: http://www.youtube.com/watch?v=KkKaTeWI3KM&feature=kp

Briefly, for those of you without internet access, they sing Peter Andre's seminal track, 'Mysterious Girl', though when I say 'they', I mean one of them sings and the other just chimes in occasionally with the odd word which I think is meant to be some form of rap. Then, when they're told, in no uncertain terms, that they're not quite up to the mark, they just won't take no for an answer and keep on and on and on . . . and on . . . even performing to me outside the audition room (as if a 'yes' from me would have done them any good). I would have given them a yes, though.

It really is the gift that keeps on giving, and, to be fair, the more I watch it, the more I think that Ant, or is it Seb . . . well, the one on the left, actually doesn't have that bad a voice. Maybe that's just me, rose-tinted glasses and the passing of time.

Now, to those of you who worry about the contestants on the show, let me assure you of two things. Firstly, the team of researchers who look after our contestants take their duty of care very seriously, so much so that I've been with them several times after hours, long after everyone else has packed up and gone, as they take calls and make sure the contestants are OK. And secondly, for the most part, when people come on the show, we do our best to make sure it's pretty much the most fun they have ever had, so much so that in some instances we can't actually get rid of them. We try and make it a wonderful celebration of British eccentricity which is how most people, including the auditionees see it.

A case in point is Colin Stacey who auditioned in 2013 by singing to a picture of his cat, Patch, a fine-looking animal. Unfortunately, Colin was *slightly* off in his timing of Adele's 'Someone Like You' and as such didn't get through. Rather than leaving with his tail between his (or Patch's) legs, though, I found him at 11 p.m. that night still in the holding room where we keep our auditionees. On asking what he was doing there, Colin answered simply that he was having a great time . . . even though by that time of night there was virtually no one else around.

So, the first few years went pretty well. I settled into the job and really enjoyed myself. I did have one slight hiccup a few years in, though, in 2010.

Cheryl Cole was a judge and she had two girls (her category that year) in the bottom two. When it came to it, she couldn't/ wouldn't choose between them, so we evoked the old Sharon Osbourne clause from my first year – majority vote, no sweat. The following Monday I was on a red carpet for the Pride of Britain Awards, a terrific show that recognises ordinary, every- day people who have done extraordinary things. It's a brilliant evening, the award winners are like superheroes and there's not a dry eye in the house. Anyway, whilst on the red carpet, I was asked about Cheryl not making the call between her two girls, to which I, innocently, and (I thought) helpfully, replied that a precedent was in place, so we had known what to do. Nothing more than that.

That Thursday, I was out for dinner with some friends when I got a call from my PR telling me that it was no biggy, but the *Sun* was running a story about what I'd said. She went on to say that it was only a small piece and that I came out of it quite well. I went back to dinner a little bemused that an innocent red-carpet interview would warrant a story in the first place, but was not especially concerned.

Cut to the next morning, where our good friends at the *Sun* had a front page, *a front page*, that read: DERMOT – IT'S A FIX

What? *What?!* I don't understand. What? I was on the phone, to John, to my PR, to Sid, to Richard, to Shu to everyone proclaiming my innocence. But by then, even though the story was utter nonsense, it was out and the damage was done. Essentially they'd taken me saying that we had a backup plan for the eventuality of one judge refusing to vote as an indication that the whole thing was fixed . . . yeah, thanks for that!

I immediately called Simon, but got his voicemail. This wasn't good. So, whilst sticking pins into my journalist voodoo doll, I texted him, trying to make light of a situation that had literally appeared out of thin air. I can't remember exactly what the text I sent said, but I went all Hugh Grant/Colin Firth and it was along the lines of: 'Hey Simon, grr, silly old *Sun*, eh? Tsk, the rotters. Oh well, as you told me, embrace the madness,' etc, etc.

I can't quite remember the one I got back, but I knew, in no uncertain terms, that the boss wasn't happy.

All I could do was put it behind me and try to put in a good shift at that weekend's show, for which I felt, as you can imagine, a fair deal of pressure. Which, when it came to it, I wasn't sure I had done, until Simon left me a message of congratulations, which was good enough for me. It was pretty much the worst week of my life since I had started on the X.

A few years down the line (2010), after a barn stormer of a year where we found One Direction and rated 19.4 million in the final, Simon took *The X Factor* to the States, taking Cheryl with him. With both Simon and Cheryl gone, and Dannii moving back to Australia, we kind of . . . well, to be frank, we didn't really have a panel at that time. It was just me and Louis, and, for all his strengths (and genuinely, I'd struggle to do my job without him), it didn't scream confidence. Thankfully, as is often the case, salvation was just around the corner.

Gary Barlow was a godsend. To be honest, I, and I'm sure most people, weren't 100 per cent certain the show could survive without Simon. Or if it could, how good it would be. But having Gary on board was a big deal. He is a hugely successful artist in his own right, and being an artist rather than a music manager gave him a different dynamic when talking to contestants. And, crucially, he didn't try to imitate Simon, which would have been a disaster. He's also a lot of fun and whilst he took his job of finding a star seriously, in person he's far more self-deprecating.

Through the last few years, we've had a run of different judges and, much like an exasperated form teacher, I've enjoyed working with all of them in different ways. Though some might give you more gold than others, as a live presenter that's the challenge – to get as much out of them as you can. That's why Louis has always been my golden egg – he always tells me exactly what he's thinking, literally, at that moment, even if some of it is, frankly, a little barmy/out there/odd, e.g. 'You remind me of a little . . .' whoever he can think of at any given moment. And there have been times when he's told his own act he thinks they are going home, much to the bemusement of the act, their family and most of the audience. That's the beauty of the man, and I can't quite believe I'm saying this, but there are times when I'd be lost without him. (OK, that felt weird.)

Others on the roller coaster include Cheryl (Fernandez-Versini), a beautiful person inside and out (to the point that when you see her she's in soft focus and your eyes get deceived into thinking they might have turned into film cameras), who is one of the best judges/mentors I've worked with: empathic, intelligent and insightful. Tulisa, a much-maligned girl who is in equal parts street-smart and tough, vulnerable and actually very sweet; Kelly Rowland, who brought with her that 'Oh my God, there's one of Destiny's Child over there' presence; and Nicole, who it's impossible not to adore. She's the most fun on a night out, having the voice of an angel and the drinking constitution of a sailor. And recently Mel B has joined the panel, the only person I've ever met whose *Bo' Selecta!* character that my old friend Leigh Francis does is actually a toned-down version of the real thing. All of them were/are great judges/mentors and are successful, empowering women who have made it in a very difficult industry. They all scrap like hell for their acts.

Despite the other, brilliant judges, Simon leaving was tough. I've been, and still am, really honoured to be the front man of his baby and it is brilliant to have him back, both on and off screen. Being in charge of a show that is proudly mainstream, he isn't afraid to be subversive; he loves to challenge convention; he is a meritocrat, judging you on talent and work ethic; and he still understands our audience, which for someone who lives in a world of private jets and chauffeurs is a rare gift.

On the flip side though, he's always late. *Always*, and he changes a lot at the last minute. Most of the calls are spot on . . . but that doesn't make it less annoying.

As a team, we really had to step up and evolve the show in his absence, something I honestly think we did. It's a show and a team of which I'm very proud to be a part.

So, how in God's name do I pick a couple of songs that sum up the last eight years. Well, much as I love doing all of the show, for me it really comes alive when we get to the studio and the live shows kick off.

The first live show of every year is always so exciting – it's the communal aspect I love the most. Just knowing that people are sitting down together and watching it at home – families, friends, people having *X Factor*-themed parties – heightens the atmosphere in the studio, and gives it something that a pre-recorded show could never touch. Back when I got offered the gig, this is what I hoped I'd feel – the same excitement that an eight-year-old kid sitting down with an indoor picnic, waiting for those Saturday-night TV moments to come into his living room, felt. (And if that reads 'cheesy' then order me up some crackers, I'm in for the long haul.)

Incidentally, I've always found the words 'light entertain-ment' odd. Why does it have to be considered 'light'? It always does it a disservice. Why can't it just be 'entertainment'? For me, there's no greater buzz than hosting a show where the aim is simply to entertain people after a hard week. For me that's not a bad aspiration to have when you first start out, and still is today.

So, to think of a song that is my soundtrack to *The X Factor* is a toughy. One of my friends said it should be the theme tune, but that would be a little odd, and would always make me think we're about to go on air. There have also been so many incred-ible 'pinch-me' moments when guest acts are playing: Coldplay, Rhianna, McCartney, Gaga – but it also seems odd to pick a moment a contestant isn't involved in. So for me, and a lot of the team, the highlight of the whole series is when the final three contestants get to duet with the stars; it's like *The X Factor* crossed with *Mr Benn* crossed with *Faking It*. It almost always creates 'a moment', whether it's Matt Cardle being almost inap-propriate with Rhianna, Robbie Williams becoming a cheerleader for Olly Murs, or Nicole showing she can mix it with the best of them in her 'Battle of the Belters' with Sam Bailey.

They're all memorable, but one duet back in the day really stole the show and, in my opinion, tops the lot. The final of 2008 was between JLS and Alexandra Burke, and although JLS went on to have the more successful recording career, the night belonged to Alexandra. Well, her and Beyoncé.

For me, this is everything I love about working on the show: it gives everyday people who have an undiscovered gift the chance to realise their potential and give them a shot at a career that, for one reason or other, has not developed yet. The duets are the chrysalis moment, putting these people on a stage with the most successful artists in the world. And the Alexandra/Beyoncé version of 'Listen' (a track that melts even the coldest of hearts) was, for me, *the* duet of the show because a) it's Beyoncé; b) Alexandra's face as she's looking at Beyoncé singing is a picture – it's as if she's thinking, 'Have I won some kind of competition to be singing here with you?' (which, in truth, she had); and c) Alexandra didn't murder the song, which, if you're going to duet with one of the biggest artists in the world, is kind of important, and you sort of want to get it right. Here it is: http://www.youtube.com/watch?v=ccthIuJOi5A&feature=kp ('Boom!' comes to mind.)

It would, however, be remiss of me to talk about the show and not include my favourite moments of more recent years, so . . . wait for it . . . in no particular order (of course), here they are, the first containing my last song choice:

1) One Direction: 'Little Things'. (Having a ringside seat as one of the biggest bands in the world gets together.)

So, it's 2010 and we're at boot camp, which traditionally I call *The X Factor* summer solstice in that it's halfway through the competition and, bar the live finals, it's also the longest day on *The X Factor* calendar as, for one day only, the judges get to see everyone perform. It stands to reason then, that this comes with a whole lot of pressure – pressure that some really good singers can't handle and they choke, so it's a messy day as people who have been tipped for great things on the show fall by the wayside.

It's also the part of the show where the judges like to take a chance or two and give auditionees who haven't done too well on their own another opportunity, by putting them together in a group.

I think it's fair to say that up until that year (2010), the strategy hadn't really worked too well. Often the members of the newly formed group don't put too much effort in between boot camp and Judges' Houses, and so are shown up by a better group who have done their homework. So, pre-1D, I was pretty doubtful that any group assembled this way could actually do well on the show. (Obviously both the boys, and the young ladies of Little Mix fame, have since proven this to be bunkam, but that is precisely because both bands are two of the hardest-working acts we've ever had on the show, and grafters win – Always.)

It's backstage at Wembley Arena and Louis Tomlinson had just come off stage after being told he was being let go. He looked, unsurprisingly, bereft so, off camera, I thought I'd go and have a word with him. We had a chat. I just tried to make him feel better: 'It's not all bad, there's always the football career with Doncaster to fall back on . . .' that sort of thing, when, as we're talking, a list of names (of which Louis' was one) were called out by Mark, our floor manager. He was asking them to get back on stage, which, when it happens, you pretty much know is a second chance about to be offered to some contestants. That was the day the boys were given theirs. Simon had seen something and decided to put Louis and the other four together, and give them another shot as a group.

By the time Simon's Judges' House had come around, you could tell the boys has done their prep and bonded enough to warrant a shot in the live shows. It's always a hard ask on a show like this, expecting a group to be able to sing and harmonise together better than just one person holding a tune on their own, and so too is it no easy ask for the public to buy into five personalities in such a short space of time. But they impressed in the studio. Not only could they sing, they were hard-working and, crucially, they were polite to, and respectful of, the team and that goes a long way.

In particular, I got to know Harry Styles well over those ten weeks. He really was an old head on young shoulders and post-show, he'd often come up to the dressing room for a cheeky under-age Corona (he was sixteen, and before I offered him the beer, naturally I checked on the Citizens' Advice Bureau website, which told me: *Any child aged five or over can drink alcohol at home or on other private premises but it is usually against the law to give alcohol to a child under five* . . . Phew), in exchange for a sausage and apple slice from his mum's bakery. But all the boys were a pleasure to have on the show. Niall was always full of positivity, although his impression of Peter Dickson doing my name was truly awful, sorry Niall; Zayn, whilst shy, was always polite and engaging; and I had history with both Louis (from backstage at Wembley Arena) and Liam, who'd auditioned way back in my first series (the Rhydian, white-fur-coat year).

That said, come final time, it was no surprise they lost out to two really good singers: Rebecca Ferguson and the eventual winner, Matt Cardle. And whilst we all thought they could go on to have a good career, no one expected them to do what they've done. It's not that their success is hard to fathom, it's the level of it that is difficult to comprehend. Being the first group that broke at the same time social media came about has a lot to do with it, but when I'm asked about it, my answer is always the same – that for what started out as a manufactured group, they are the least manufactured group you could meet. They don't dance, wisely; they wear their own clothes; and they write a fair bit of their own stuff. They are, in many ways, the anti-boy band boy band.

So it would be odd for my soundtrack not to also include a nod to the biggest act to come out of the show I've been hosting for the last eight years. And even though I'm not their demographic (at least I hope I'm not), I guess this is their most, 'Man, that shouldn't be into us,' track-like track.

Good for you fellas.

2) Ella Henderson's first audition.

There are moments in this job where you just know you've found a star: Ella's first audition was one of them. It was, without doubt, the best first audition I've ever seen on the show. At the time she was only sixteen, and yet she came on in front of an arena and delivered the performance of someone who had been in the industry for years. She sung an original composition – always a risk – about her grandfather (again, a gamble). It was, however, a mature, heartfelt and beautiful homage to a big influence in her life without being mawkish. The place erupted, and the show and public took her to their hearts. We were devastated when she got voted out early, but are so proud of the slow-burn success she's achieved. I think she is, alongside James Arthur, the most original artist we've found.

3) Wagner: 'She Bangs/Love Shack'. (Chalk it up to Louis again – even though he never once correctly pronounced his name. It's VARGner, Louis, not WAGner!)

I could have picked a classic Jedward moment, or even gone for Ryland dressed as the lady from the Fry's Turkish Delight advert as Nicole tells him he's going to the the live shows, but I've gone for a Brazilian man in his fifties.

Wagner was such a hit on the show, he even spawned a spoof Stephen Fry homage to him online. And, off the back of his performance of 'Love Shack', I petitioned (sadly unsuccessfully) for Wagner to perform every song with a segue into 'Love Shack' (it would have been great).

4) Britney.

We'd trailed the hell out of it. I don't think I did one link without saying Britney was 'coming up' (Harry Hill had a field day on *TV Burp*), but when she was there, she wasn't really . . .

there. I think I asked her who her favourite contestants were (it's a standard O'Leary classic) and instead of naming a couple of them or doing the standard fudge ('Oh, they're all so good, I couldn't possibly pick one'), she answered that she was having a great time in London, and thanked everyone for coming . . . What? Ah, the mysteries of the Spears mind . . .

5) Lady Gaga.

She's been on many times and never fails to be anything other than original and brilliant. Despite the theatrics though, she is incredibly down to earth and self-effacing, Her highlight for me was a performance of 'Bad Romance' she did in a giant bath in 2009. At the end she, alongside her dancers, pretended to be dead and stayed in character so long it was starting to become awkward. Second to that is her coming on stage to console Kitty Brucknell in 2011, after Kitty got knocked out. She then took her off for a drink, which left the rest of us who'd worked with and watched over Kitty thinking that Lady G wasn't *entirely* sure what she'd let herself in for.

6) Rylan

Just the best character we've ever had on the show. He knew full well he wasn't the most talented of contestants, but he more than made up for it in entertainment value. His on screen feud/love-in with Gary was perfect for us, bringing out the best in both of them. And crucially remembered fondly by the team, always well mannered, a perfect gent, which counts for *a lot*.

19

'You've Got The Style'
by Athlete

This is a bit awkward. Well, maybe more strange than awkward. I wanted to write this book for a couple of reasons: firstly, to see if I could (as there are only two chapters to go, I'm 98 per cent sure that that's a yes) but secondly, because I wanted to write something that was kind of like an autobiography, without being one of 'those' autobiographies – you know the ones: 'Read all about my struggle with blah, blah, blah. Only in this week's blah, blah blah'.

Music always seemed the best way into writing it, as it's been the backdrop to, and a massive part of, my professional and personal life. I also wanted to get down on paper what it's been like to work in one of the most vibrant, challenging and publically accessible and accountable industries there is. Obviously I want to be truthful and honest but for someone in the public eye, I've always been a little private. Now, let's not get carried away with ourselves, I'm not Brad Pitt (you'll have fathomed that by now. If not, you're possibly the worst Brad Pitt fan ever) and I don't have the kind of life where I'm followed by paps. (Partly because, being honest – that's never the game I've played.) Being famous is, for the most part, great, tables at restaurants etc. And, as I'm sure I've said, I have no time for people who moan about it all the time: it's the thing that you're famous *for* that's important, so people who sell every aspect of their lives and then bemoan the fact that they don't have a private life don't really evoke that much sympathy from me.

From early on, my family and friends had a pretty down-to-earth attitude to fame, though my dad did go through a run of asking for Westlife tickets for *everyone* he knew. Now, don't get me wrong, it's a really unique pleasure getting your family tickets to experiences and concerts, but you can't push it: 'Yes, Dad, I know your hairdresser likes them – a lot. But I can't get her four tickets and a backstage pass to meet Shane. Again!'

On the whole my family have always been supportive, and proud without ever getting carried away. Or letting me get carried away . . . they're always quick to remind me that that Wilf the Whale costume is never too far away.

I think at the start they'd get a bit annoyed when I'd go home to Colchester or Ireland, and they'd ask me the normal questions anyone would want to ask, such as, 'What's so and so like?' etc, etc. At the time I was pretty resistant/responded like a fourteen-year-old boy: 'God, who cares, stop probing me for gossip!' Which, to be fair, they weren't, they were just being inter-ested and curious, like families are. I'm not sure why I was so reluctant to tell them about my world – I think I just didn't want to be seen to be showing off. (Oaf.) But, over time, I've become more relaxed and they've become . . . if not less interested, then aware that famous or not, people, for the most part, are just people.

That said, we've got trouble on our hands if you put my mam anywhere within fifty feet of Michael Bublé, in which case *suddenly* the fact I'm her son becomes a very, very big deal. (I feel used. She only loves me for my Bublé.)

So, I feel a little weird then, picking a song that reminds me of my wife. Well, no, that's not quite right. I can pick the song, easily; in fact I've got a few. (It's just that we've never been the *OK! Magazine*-style couple doing a shoot barefoot on a hard-wood floor in a kitchen that's not actually ours and embracing in that weird, huggy way that no actual couple does, even when you're getting your picture taken.) I've got friends that have done magazine deals for weddings and in their cases it's worked out quite well, plus they've raised loads of money for small charities, so I'm not judging. It's just that I like to keep my private life . . . well, private.

But if this is the blasted soundtrack to my life, then Mrs O'Leary (Koppang O'Leary) has to get a shout-out. Though trust me: like any good wife would, this chapter will have been vetted to within an inch of its life . . .

So, in a series of serendipitous moments, I actually first met my wife three times before we were properly introduced. The first was in Manchester in a lift in 1999, when I was just starting out and she was doing work experience in a production company. It was a *Sliding Doors* moment, really. She had her arms full of various random props from a shoot, and I ran into the lift as the doors were shutting. After the customary awkward silence in a lift, I turned to look at her and saw that she was wearing a pair of giant prop angel wings, which I complimented her on, and we had a nice, slightly awkward lift-based chat, where it was obvious we found each other attractive. (At least, I found her attractive.) And that was that. A meet-cute in a lift.

I met her once more a few years later by chance on a London street, where she was walking with a mutual friend. She had to run, and I knew I'd seen her somewhere before, but thought I'd best keep that to myself, as it's a terrible line and I didn't want to come across too keen and all that.

Fast-forward to 2002 where I bump into the future Mrs Koppang O'Leary (kept her maiden name – quite right too – although our children will have the oddest double-barrel going) again. I was working on the BBC Three show *Re:covered* and Dee had started working in London, coincidentally for the same production company.

If you're lucky, you get a 'thunderbolt' moment once in your life. You'll know what I mean if you've been fortunate enough to have one: every time afterwards, when she/he walks into the room, your heart skips a beat, and you think of an excuse, however tenuous, to go and strike up a conversation, during which you can't keep your eyes off them. It is, I guess, the start of what love becomes, and you have to have it. Well, that is what happened with Dee.

She was all the things you look for in a partner straight off: funny, warm, smart, independent, interesting, kooky and obviously attractive. Plus the small stuff, the stuff you can't explain, the little idiosyncrasies that you have with your partner and I have with mine. The personal stuff that you wouldn't write in your book, so you'll forgive me for not doing the same.

Three people are to be credited with getting us together, and the first two are our dear friends, Amy and Drew. As I've said, I'd known Drew since *Light Lunch*, and we were working on *Re:covered* together. He knew I liked Dee and just before had got together with his now wife, Amy. She ended up moving in with Dee, so it became very much 'their project' to get us two together, by contriving to invite us both along to the same pub, party, restaurant, etc. They've become two of our closest friends, living around the corner from us in Highbury for years, and we've both played a major part in each other's lives, from Sunday roasts and weddings (we were best men/bridesmaids to each other) to births (I drove Amy to the hospital when she was in labour with their son, Noah). They live in LA now, with Drew forging a successful career as a scriptwriter and director. We miss them dreadfully, but are so proud of them.

The other hugely instrumental person was Dee and Amy's other flatmate and close friend – Lauren Laverne, a woman who has both encyclopaedic knowledge and incredible taste in music. Much like Drew and Amy, Lauren made it her mission to get us together, to the point of coming on *BBLB* just so she could bring Dee on the show to have a look around the house and meet me. (Thanks, L, btw.)

So, without wanting to get all schmaltzy with the boy-meets-girl stuff, there were a couple of months where I had to convince her that I wasn't an airhead, and that even though I was on TV I wasn't totally self-obsessed. (OK, maybe I was a bit, but I was in my twenties and who isn't self-obsessed then?)

Discovering that she was Norwegian, I did my best to impress her with my knowledge of the history of cod. (Classy guy.) For example, did you know that William Pitt the Elder (1708–78) once claimed that cod was British gold? (Yes, that sort of thing.) That kind of gem sealed the deal and, after a few months, we were going out. (This, despite that, on our first date, she was two and a half hours . . . *hours*, late. So, I really must have liked her. And developed a taste for cucumber Martinis in her absence.)

I'd never introduced a girl to my parents before. I know that sounds odd, but it's never worked out that way, so when I brought Dee back, it was obviously a big deal. It was a Sunday afternoon, the day after Neil Butler's wedding (he of Britannia music club fame), and we drove down to Colchester for the big intro.

We were all pretty much 'off the map', with no one really knowing what to do. My mam was all of a fluster, sort of every-where and nowhere (getting a bottle of wine, and not being able to find it which, trust me, is a first) which was really endearing; my dad ended up taking control, ushering Dee out to the garden to see the geraniums. Since then, they've all become close, and I too love my Kent/Norwegian side of the family. The first meet our parents all had together, Dee and I were running the London Marathon, so we left them with keys to my flat and let them get on with it. Sounds harsh, but it worked.

So, for an early birthday present one year, I decided to surprise Dee with a trip to New York. It was her first visit, and it's subsequently become a city we love, both of us having worked there. In fact, it's where I ended up proposing to her.

But at the time, back when we were green around the gills (see, more fish), and I was still wearing baggy cargo pants, she had yet to go to New York.

Now, I like to consider myself a romantic old so and so, and in a feat of military precision I somehow managed to get Dee to the airport check-in gate without revealing where we were headed – the reveal only came when I sang (quietly) a terrible version of 'New York, New York' to her. Luckily, any judgement on my singing was eclipsed by the excitement of the trip, once she'd twigged where we were headed (I think it was around verse three – I told you it was bad).

You never forget your first time in a place like New York. If you like cities, it really is the most exciting, alive, sexy place to be. London has been home now for over half my life, but New York is the only other city I could see myself living in. I read a great quote once by the author John Berger, where he said, 'Every city has a sex and an age which have nothing to do with demography . . . London is a teenager, an urchin . . . [and this is the part I love] Paris, I believe, is a man in his twenties, in love with an older woman.'

He didn't mention New York but, inspired by his words, I always think of it as a grown up alpha town (not alpha male, just alpha, you know, ballsy), e.g. 'Hey, I'm driving/walking/eating/(insert any verb) here!' It's sure of its own identity, with a swagger we kind of envy in London, but as with London, scratch the surface and the people are as friendly as anywhere else in the world.

So, we were having a blast, apart from me almost killing my future wife by poisoning her with peanut-butter ice cream. (It's a nut allergy thing – hers, not mine. Don't give me a hard time, it was early on in the relationship, and it can take a while for this kind of stuff to stick in the head.) OK, yes, maybe I should have remembered my girlfriend had a life-threatening allergy, but we'd both been drinking and having a nice meal, and you get caught up in the moment, or in my case, the dessert. It was a one-off (although there was that other time in Brazil when she almost died after eating peanuts, which was theoretically on my watch, but let's gloss over that for now too) . . . but after she survived that, then we were definitely having a nice time and all was going well.

One day we were off shopping (no doubt I needed some more cargo pants) and, just as I was thumbing through a rail of Carhartts, I heard a shout of, 'Hello, Dermot!' from behind me. Obviously I was then hoping that my new girlfriend was watching because, you know, I was getting recognised from off the telly *and* while in New York, so I simply must be incredibly cool, right? It turned out that we'd bumped into the band Athlete, who I'd met a few times before.

Dee at first didn't know who they were, obviously (at the time she barely knew who I was), but she did know their music and she loved them . . . This was good.

Athlete is a band, who, I think, at the time of writing are kind of still together, but are also all off doing their own marvellous things. They're a diverse bunch of chaps, so that can involve anything from writing for other people (very successfully) to management, to being an actuary, actually. (Very poor, sorry.) They are all from Deptford in south-east London and scored their biggest hit (number four) with 'Wires', a song that Joel, the lead singer, wrote about his daughter who was born prematurely. As you can imagine, it's a song that gets you right *there*.

I'd interviewed the boys a couple of times and had become friendly with them, along with a bunch of my mates, the *T4* boys and our mutual friends, brothers Dan and Dom Baldwin, part of my gig/Arsenal-watching set of friends, all of us becoming fans, early doors. There was also another connection in that Steve, the drummer for the band, worked on the door at the Barfly, the venue in Camden where (unsurprisingly) we filmed *The Barfly Sessions*.

Over the years, my friends and I went to see the band countless times and got to know them well, to the point where a couple of years ago, they did what Elbow hadn't quite managed to do and post-gig, actually kidnapped the Moonman to go on their tourbus overnight to Manchester. On the face of it this seemed like a brilliant, romantic, spur of the moment idea, although come six o'clock the next morning, when he found himself waking up in a car park outside Manchester with no wallet and a family function to get to in Farnham that afternoon, the glamour of it all ever so slightly wore off.

But back to 2002 and me thinking, 'Yessss, this looks quite cool in front of my new girlfriend, doesn't it?' as well as thinking how timely it was as Dee was now looking at my shopping basket of, yes, cargo pants, a tad dubiously. In fact, as a date, it couldn't have gone any better as, after saying hello, the boys then introduced themselves to Dee and invited us to their studio to hear their new album being mastered. After which we all went out for dinner and got suitably and raucously drunk together. It was like I'd planned the whole thing, and I couldn't have man-loved them any more if I'd tried.

Actually, that's not *strictly* true . . . fast-forward ten years, and I'd popped the question whilst visiting Dee out in NYC when she was working on the Victoria's Secret Fashion Show. Now, before you all roll your eyes and ask what took me so long, I'd fallen in love with Dee very quickly but we're both busy people, OK? We've both got demanding careers and we're both away a lot – in her case, typically at the time, New York. (Serves me right for taking her there in the first place, I suppose.)

I've grown up with my wife. She was twenty-three when we met and I was twenty-eight and just starting out front of camera, so she's been part of every decision I've made since and I'd pretty much be nowhere without her. But that's the way a couple should be, right? Similarly, I've watched her grow into someone who's at the top of her game – a brilliant producer and director who I couldn't be more proud of, and who is my best friend and who I love loads.

So yes, the question had been popped and, in amongst the mountainous wedding-day preparations we really, really wanted a friendly face to play at our wedding. Of course, we'd invited the Athlete boys as friends and, well, you do the maths . . . they made our day. (All right, love made our day obviously, and the food . . . come to think of it, the wine was pretty good too . . .) but you get the gist – they played at our wedding and it was beautiful, and very special.

In my humble opinion, my wife has a good sense of style. She loves her fashion, so the first song that the boys played at our wedding was the one that they played to us in that New York mixing suite back in 2002, and the one that I gave to Dee on the first mix tape I made for her: 'You've Got The Style'.

Now, get out of here, you guys – I'm welling up.

SOUNDTRACK

20

Bonus Tracks

When I started this jaunt down memory lane, it was always my intention to tell you a little bit about me growing up and what it's like to have worked in TV and radio for the last fifteen years, all against a backdrop of a soundtrack that's uniquely mine (some of which I've loved, some of which I've hated, but that's been the idea).

It stands to reason, though, when you try to tell a story chronologically, that some of the experiences and memories you hold dear will kind of fall through the cracks. Step forward then, chapter 20 . . . the saviour of the stray anecdote.

I've been a lucky boy. I've got to work in an industry I love, in some of the fields I'm most passionate about, and I've had some incredible pinch-me moments that I've been lucky enough to share with others, primarily my family and friends (and occasionally a bemused stranger sitting on a bench/the tube/in the pub who I couldn't resist telling . . .). Now I'd like to sign off by sharing them with you.

1) Macca: 'Pipes Of Peace'.

Meeting Paul McCartney would be a big deal for any music fan, but I have to be honest, I was a bit young for the Beatles. They broke up three years before I was born and whilst I've got into them retrospectively, as with the Stones, it always strikes me as weird if someone's favourite band isn't from their own era and they haven't grown up with them. (It's why Roger Moore has to be my favourite Bond – he's the one I grew up watching.)

So as much as I love the Beatles, for me, meeting Macca was all about his solo stuff from the eighties, hence my Macca choice, 'Pipes Of Peace'. I know that might seem like heresy to some (well, most of you – OK, all of you), but it's one of my favourite songs from childhood so don't give me a hard time. Blame it on the ten-year-old me . . .

My first meet with Macca was back in 2009. I was at home working when I got a call from my radio producer, Ben:

'We've thirty minutes with Paul McCartney tomorrow at his office in Soho . . . up for it?'

'Of course.' (Slightly wanting to vomit in my own mouth with sudden nerves.)

'Don't be late . . .'

(It was during *The X Factor*, so, you know . . .)

Cut to the next day and Macca is doing press for *Good Evening New York City*, a DVD that was coming out which morphed two concerts: one he'd just done to open the new Shea Stadium in NYC, and one legendary one he'd done with the Beatles back in 1965 (the first concert to be held at a major stadium). So we had plenty of things to ask him about, but reckoned we could cover it all in the thirty minutes we had with him.

As soon as I met Ben and Simon outside his office, I could tell we were all feeling the nerves in a pre-FA Cup final sort of way. You really do not want to drop the ball when you're doing an interview like this and be known around Radio 2 as the team that messed up the Macca interview – there would have been plenty at the station who'd have bitten my arm off for it.

So, as we waited for him, I went over my notes again. And again and, yes, again. Similarly, the boys must have checked the equipment over and over . . . you get the picture. All of it totally unnecessary; all of it understandable.

Ten or so minutes later, in walks Macca, fit as a fiddle. That's the first thing that struck me, what great shape he was in (he must have been late sixties at the time). He immediately sat down and started giving us anecdote after anecdote. It was going so well, in fact, that I asked him about his upcoming tour and if he'd play my favourite song, 'Pipes Of Peace'.

For what seemed like an eternity, he stared at me as if I'd lost my mind, checking to see whether I was taking the piss out of one of the greatest figures in rock-and-roll history . . . and if I'd crack.

But I didn't, as I was deadly serious. Sure, I've got favourite Beatles tracks and Wings tracks, but my favourite McCartney track *is* 'Pipes Of Peace'. I love it. Love the song, the Christmassy message and I love the video, which I have to thank for getting me interested in World War One. (He plays two soldiers in the video, British and German, and it's based on the true story of the Christmas Day truce of 1914. The characters meet in no-man's-land on Christmas Day . . . heavy stuff, especially when you're aged ten.)

So, I was staring straight back, honesty, innocence and slight bemusement etched into my face. By then, thank God, he'd obviously decided I *was* serious and told me he'd think about it.

Our thirty minutes came to an end, but when told, like any great star, Macca told his PR he'd carry on.

After another fifteen minutes or so, me, Ben and Simon were out on the street looking at each other as if to say, 'Did that really happen? Did we really just spend forty-five minutes in the company of one of the most iconic rock stars in music history and sort of become his friends?' (For 'sort of' think, 'We wish'.)

A day or so later, I was at home when a courier knocked on the door with a parcel. I opened it up to find a thank-you note, along with the original artwork from the single of 'Pipes Of Peace'. (No idea who it was from.) That . . . is class.

What was *even* better (and weirder) was that, a few weeks later, I was walking down a street near the *X Factor* office on my way to work, when, as I trotted along, I felt someone fall into step with me so that they were walking next to me. Immediately, I began thinking, 'Uh oh, weirdo alert – someone is about to have a go at me, *The X Factor*, Radio 2, or more likely, *The Marriage Ref*.' So, I turned to say hello in the hope that a charm offensive might make things not too bad . . . when I saw that *it was him*, in a street, walking next to me.

'Hello, you walking my way?' (In the direction of his office.)

'I sure am.' (I wasn't.)

We chatted and he said how much he'd enjoyed the interview. I tried to play it cool, but failed desperately. As I walked down the street, a girl caught my eye and recognised me, so I smiled. She smiled back and then noticed who was next to me, whereupon her smile changed to a face that clearly said, 'Holy shit, you're walking next to Paul McCartney!'

To which I replied (non-verbally, of course), 'I know, girl-friend. Check me out!'

I walked him back to his office in a kind of a weird, prom-date-night way, and then made the (now long) trudge back to the *X Factor* office, a nice little water-cooler moment tucked away ready to be brought out whenever a water cooler was in the vicinity . . . 'What have you been up to today?'

'Oh, nothing . . . just hung out with a Beatle. You know, the usual.'

I've met Paul McCartney and seen him in concert several times since. A couple of years after that first meeting we got to interview him again, this time about the reissue of the Wings album, *Band On The Run*, at his farm in Kent, where he has his studio.

It was for a TV show, but the radio boys and I had piggy-backed on the recording to do a radio interview whilst we were there.

As soon as Macca saw us, he invited us to have a look around his office – which was in a windmill – and was also the place where he kept his music memorabilia. We gratefully accepted. As he was showing us around, he pointed to a big, old double bass in the corner . . .

'See that?'

'Yep.'

'Elvis's bass player's double bass.' (I think Bill Black. Or it could have been Jerry Scheff – I'll just ring my new BFF Macca and find out . . .)

I asked him what it was like meeting Elvis. He said that even for the Beatles, at the level they were at, it was a big deal. He then picks up the bass, and says to us, 'Can you imagine what it was like? We heard him sing "Heartbreak Hotel". Can you imagine? I'm standing where you are and he's where I am, and we're hearing him sing . . .'

At which point he started singing, whilst playing the bass.

'Well, since my baby left me . . .'

We all just stared at each other. Yes, yes, Paul, we can imagine, *because you are currently playing 'Heartbreak Hotel' . . . to us . . . on Elvis's double bass!*

I think we can all understand what being star-struck is.

Thanks, Macca, and thanks for those veggie sausage rolls too. Very moreish.

2) Michael Jackson: 'Thriller'.

Back in 2009, I was at home with a bout of food poisoning (my fault, I'd undercooked a chicken risotto the night before . . . oaf). I'm a keen twitcher (birdwatcher) – alongside the Smiths, it's another love Joe has passed on to me – and as part of my convalescence I was enjoying having a gander at a pair of goldfinches, when the phone rang. It was my agent, John.

'How would you like to introduce Michael Jackson on stage at the 02 for his comeback concert press conference?'

'Er, yes.'

'Great, it's on Thursday.'

'Good, gives me a week. You know, to get better and all – do my research . . .'

'No, Thursday tomorrow.'

'Ah. [Why hadn't he just said tomorrow?] OK, well, I'm still in, but a bit lurgyfied, so if we could start as late as poss—'

'Great, see you tomorrow.' (Hangs up.)

So, tomorrow comes and I turn up at the 02 to have a briefing with some of the concert promoters. They are obviously very happy that MJ is going to be doing a run of shows at the venue, as am I. He might not have been in his prime, but to see him would still be a massive deal – everyone has their own MJ era, and mine was without doubt 'Thriller', so the nine-year-old kid in me was going crazy.

I was told I'd meet him before the press conference and that my job was to go out, warm up the crowd (not exactly hard at an MJ gig) and then intro the main man himself . . . generally give the event a bit of structure, in case, you know, he went off script. All no problem . . . they kind of had me when they said, 'Meet MJ.'

A couple of hours later and he still hadn't shown. The message, for about an hour, is that he's stuck in the Blackwall Tunnel which, as anyone who lives in London or has ever listened to a travel bulletin about London will confirm, is pretty plausible. However, the crowd – well, they were really, really wanting him to turn up. As was I. I couldn't delay it any longer, so I go out to do the dreaded 'fill'. To start with, the crowd was great – they were just happy someone had come out to say hello.

We played a highlights package of Jacko's greatest hits, then we talked about the tour, and then . . . well, then there wasn't really *that* much left to say.

It was nowhere near the longest 'fill' of my life, at least. *That* came when I was doing *T4* with my co-host Vernon Kay, a loveable, super-quick, six foot five inches of fun. We'd just finished doing a marathon stint on a live show from Hyde Park where we were backstage at Capital FM's 'Party in the Park'. Elton John was the headline act and he was about to go on, so we wrapped up the show, said our goodbyes, and got ready to go and see the great man. Unfortunately for Elton, but more unfortunately for us, a freak summer thunderstorm came a-calling, and water got inside his piano so he couldn't start playing until it was fixed. And so Liz, our director, had to cut back to us, to fill, for, well, as long as we had to – the only problem being that we'd kind of said everything/anything there was to say. We ended up talking, and to this day I'm still not sure what about, for fifteen minutes. Hell.

So just, *just*, as I was starting to worry a bit and the crowd were on the turn, the next thing I knew was that, thankfully, MJ had made it through the tunnel and was backstage. Cue the highlights package (again), and get ready, London, to welcome to the stage, Michael Jackson!

I've been asked loads since if I thought it was him or an imposter, to which I always answer, 'How on earth would I know?' I think what I did know was that it was a surreal experience. As soon as he came on stage he gave me a hug . . . which kind of took me by surprise. My first thought was (and I hate to say this now) how good he looked. Not in the face obviously, I mean – in the body. He had the physique of a very fit dancer, which may not surprise you when you think of old-school, vintage MJ, but at the time this guy clearly didn't seem that well (judging by his face), and yet he looked, and felt, fit!

So, as I was kind of reeling from the hug, the crowd going nuts and how toned his body was, he started to whisper something in my ear . . . at which point I was thinking, 'OK, here we go, it's Michael Jackson, the King of Pop, what's he going to say, what's he going to ask?'

I braced myself, and then he said . . .

'Is the teleprompter on?'

His voice, even when he whispered, was exactly how you would imagine it to be.

'What? Er, yes,' I stuttered back, and then in my head, 'Is that it?'

Well, it was, and away he went – although he didn't really, as he didn't stick to any of the words on the autocue as he addressed the crowd (teleprompter is more of an American term), and just said that this was his last tour and that, 'This is it, because this is it!' over and over again.

No one minded – they were just happy to see him, and more was to come. Halfway through the speech, he was kind of overcome by the emotion of it all, and looked across the stage to where I was still standing (I wasn't going anywhere!) for some support. I immediately looked behind me, thinking some manager would be there to give him an encouraging smile, only to find that there was no one else on the stage apart from me, which meant that he *was* looking at me. (Brilliant piece of deduction.) So I did the only thing I could think of doing and gave him a muggy-looking double thumbs up . . . *idiot*. Weirder still, it appeared to do the trick and he gave me a smile, finished talking to the crowd (a couple more 'This is it!'), punched the air a few times and then he was off on his own merry way.

Just over three months later, he was dead. It was an odd footnote to be a part of, but of course it's impossible not to feel glad I was there. So I'm picking 'Thriller' – MJ at his peak – for this bonus track, the way he should be remembered.

3) Mozza: 'Irish Blood, English Heart'. (Even though I should pick a Smiths song, the fact we share the same heritage, we're practically brothers, makes this seem more apt.)

Just about the hardest/most awkward/weirdly enjoyable interview I've ever done, with someone I couldn't love, adore (and therefore be a wee bit intimidated by) more, if I tried. It's Joe Griffin's fault (you remember him, way back in chapter 6). He got me into *The Queen Is Dead* and *Meat Is Murder* (and, as it turned out, gold-finches) by dint of the fact that I sat next to him in English and he didn't stop banging on about 'Heaven Knows I'm Miserable Now'. And even though (as I've said) I had a far too happy dispo-sition to be into the Smiths, I fell in love with Mozza, with Marr, with the whole kit and caboodle. I guess that's what happens when you first fall in love, or lust; you inevitably get your heart broken again and again, and so gravitate to, and find solace in, the most depressing melancholic music you can. So, 1985/6, ta da! Hey presto! Before you know it you're a Smiths fan.

So, it was with a great deal of excitement (but, if I'm honest, more nerves and trepidation) that I welcomed Morrissey into

Radio 2 in 2011. This might sound odd, or obvious, but when you interview your heroes, idols, ex-lovers (what have you), the interview takes on a different tone as, even if you don't admit it to yourself then, or ever to anyone other than yourself, a little (tiny) part of you is still that kid in 1985 who wants his album and his poster signed, and by extension wants to do his hero justice, so that – dare I say it – they like you and respect you. (But more importantly, like. Not hang out and become best buddies, though if that's on the cards then that's cool too, but really just, you know, *like* you.)

The interview was to promote a 'best of' he'd curated and I'd done my prep, thank goodness, as I was through the first five or so questions in about two minutes, which is never a good sign. The way I try to shape an interview (when I have time to do it properly) is that I script loose talking points and just let the chat flow around it, so you're having more a conversation rather than just going through a list of scripted questions. This works fine when your guest is a good talker, but when they are a little more . . . truculent, reticent, shall we say, you can get through those questions pretty quickly, in which case you'd better have something else up your sleeve.

I've only listened back to this interview a couple of times, and I still can't quite work out whether it's any good or really bad. (I'm not the only one – the radio boys couldn't work out if we should put it up for a Sony award or never listen to it, or let anyone else listen to it, ever again.) In truth, it's probably some-where in the middle (or just really bad). But I do know one thing: if I had done that interview five years ago, I would have folded immediately; instead, what I did was keep asking questions in the hope of getting a half-decent interview out of someone who is still a hero.

It's not that Morrissey was rude – far from it. He was in many ways the perfect gentleman, especially off mic, where we were actually having quite a nice, normal chat, but as soon as the mic went up, a twinkle came back in his eye and he did what he's famous for: he interviewed the interviewer. He asked about my parents; my 'octopus restaurant' (I'm a partner in a fish restaurant in Brighton, which I knew wouldn't go down well); *The X Factor*, which I can take a wild guess at that he's not the biggest fan of; and how, in his words, I was springing up all over the place, 'on the radio, on the television, in the *Radio Times*'!

I don't think he likes doing promo very much, and in some ways, I can't say I blame him. When you're a singer, you get asked an awful lot of the same questions, but at least in Mozza's case most people that interview him are fans. Plus, it's a necessary part of selling your wares so, in my opinion, you may as well enjoy it!

Weirdly, and awkward as the interview sounds, I think we both did end up having a good time. Well, that might stretch the truth somewhat, but despite it being one of the most challenging interviews I've ever done, I'm very glad I did it.

After the interview I was having a cup of coffee and going over it all with the team, feeling somewhat like I'd just finished my very own Agincourt and trying to work out what just happened, when Kevin McCabe, Morrissey's record plugger (the person whose job it is to get the artists' music played on the radio) came up. Kevin is a legend in the business, everyone respects him. He'd been seeing Morrissey into his car and told us that in the lift, Mozza had turned to him and said, 'I thought Dermot jousted rather well.'

I'm not sure I did, Steven Patrick – but I'll take that, and have you back any time. Though could you smile a bit more next time, just a little, please?

There is a small codicil to this story, however. On our honeymoon in Rome, Dee and I bumped into Morrissey, pretty much as soon as we checked into our hotel, along with ex-Everton and Manchester United manager David Moyes, although they weren't together (or at least, I assume they weren't). When I told Morrissey it was good to see him, he replied with a wry smile, 'Really? I'm sure you'd say the same thing to Barry Manilow [never met him] or Gary Barlow [I know him, he's my friend, so yes, it would almost certainly be good to see him, too].'

I persevered, and told him (wincing internally) that I was on my honeymoon.

'Ah,' he said. 'It won't last – these things never do', which might sound rude but the twinkle in his eye told me I had to work it out for myself: did he mean the honeymoon or the marriage?

And that is that – the soundtrack to the first half (fingers crossed) of my life. (I hope you've enjoyed reading it. If you have, I'll be back in forty years with a double album). From Brendan Shine to Morrissey, via Guns N' Roses and One Direction – a leap I never thought I'd make at the start of this book. But as I said at the beginning, it's my musical DNA and I suppose the soundtrack is as I should have expected from a fifteen-year career combining light entertainment and indie music.

I'm stuck with it whether I like it or not, and I do. I've had a wonderful, lucky and blessed time so far, and most of those happy moments and memories are triggered by, or trigger, my favourite songs: from eating mackerel for the first time with my lovely family on a beach in Ireland, to dancing with my soulmate on our wedding day.

I hope you enjoyed my soundtrack, and I wish you good luck and hope you have fun making yours.

See you later, bye . . . no, you hang up . . . no, *you* . . . no . . . Oh, you have . . .

ACKNOWLEDGEMENTS

Well firstly thanks for reading this, very decent of you. I hope you liked it, I've really enjoyed writing it. When I first thought of writing a book, I had romantic notions of scuttling off to the Cairngorms, complete with Arran sweater and log fire and getting it all down on paper in a couple of weeks . . . Yeah, didn't quite work out like that, it's taken a good year. But I've enjoyed every minute of it, apart from those days when your fingers and brain aren't talking, and you end up typing sentences that look like this: divjgnfhdhcovnfb.

Thanks to the scribe, to my Pharisee, my partner in ink and inner cultural turmoil, and personal editor, (everyone should have one), Ivor Baddiel. Thanks for the feedback, (most of it), for the lunches, (Ashkenazi and Sephardic) although they were around my house so strictly speaking you should be thanking me, and the endless conversations and debates about the issues, of life, politics, and religion, and the ones that really matter (Arsenal vs. Chelsea) you really are a gent (ile).

Thanks to all at Hodder who have been a marvel to work with, the guidance of the long suffering and infinitely patient Hannah Black and Briony Gowlett and a special nod to Fenella Bates who got the whole thing rolling, thanks also for reintroducing the word 'crumbs', (when presented with a menu), back into my vocab. Thanks also to Liz Caraffi, Claudette Morris, Alasdair Oliver and Kate Brunt and to Bea Long, Emma Knight and Eleni Lawrence.

To all at John Noel management, in particular Rachel Barke, Polly Ravenscroft, George Armstrong, the unflappable gent that is Jonny Wilkinson, and the big dog himself John Noel. Sorry that I said you were a bit, you know, odd, but then again you didn't sue, so there must be something in it. X

My thanks to all at Radio 2: to Leslie Douglas for giving me the break, to Bob Shennan for the constant support in all we do, for Mark Raphael, and Paul Connolly for helping kick things off, to the SMs - the unheralded genii of any session we do, to all the bands who have deemed us worthy of coming in and playing for us, to Phil Critchlow who helped us out when things got a little sticky, and especially to my producers, dear friends, and red meat/history junkies Ben Walker and Simon Ward who still make it a pleasure to go to work for three hours every Saturday and play the songs I want. Tough gig.

Thanks to all at the mighty X, and ITV for all the support down the years: Simon, Peter, Elaine, Richard, Shu, Beth, Claudia, Lee, Phil and especially to Sid, for the best part of ten years, my fellow part Indie kid, part LE lovey. It's a strangely common mix but it works for us.

Thanks also team DOLs down the years: my camera man Clifford (west country yeoman) and to Flacky, Travers, Webbo, Beaters and my producers, Michelle, Lisa, Rosie, all of whom have gone on to do great things, I couldn't be more proud of them.

Thanks to the Glam squad: Tom (Bounder) Stubbs and Sarah (Bloody) Exley, for getting the show pony ready for the gymkhana and to Polly for making the engine turn with humour, grace and a touch of class.

Thanks to all my friends who I have spent the last twenty years gigging with, and who I have shared a musical upbringing with: Neil Butler (I swear you still owe me a couple of Genesis albums), Joe Griffin, Matt Mackman, Mike Allen, Drew Pearce, Gav, Tom Curry and the Moonman gang, Chappers, Dan, Dom, Gravesy, Stocks and Dug.

Which brings me to my actual family. To my mam, dad, sister Nicky, Seanie, and Josette. Thanks for bringing me up in a house full of love, laughter, and music. I'll never formally thank you for making me sing old Irish rebel songs to Grandparents, but I was hardly conscripted so I can't really complain. Thanks for bringing me home and giving me an appreciation of the history and music of Ireland. Thanks to Mam for always making my childhood one of singing and dancing (you can still move) and to her 'Nature Boy' for the same, plus getting me backstage to meet Brendan Shine (deft). Thanks to Nicky for sharing and caring (must be rubbish being the older one, so thanks) and to Seanie for reintroducing me to Bowie, and to my niece Josette for scolding me every time I get the words to 'Let it go' from 'Frozen' wrong (deliberately).

And lastly thank you to Dee, we don't exactly share all the same musical tastes, (she's more melody to my lyrics), but when it works, it works. Thanks for the years of love and support and fun and fire, and thanks for being my best friend. Oh, and thanks to the cats Silverthorne and Totò for the welcome cuddles when I've needed a distraction from writing, although I'll thank Totò for not walking over the keyboard so much next time.

PICTURE ACKNOWLEDGEMENTS

© Alamy: 7 (middle left)/ photo Wenn. Author Collection: 1, 2, 3, 4, 5 (above), 8 (above), 11 (above and middle right), 13 (above left and middle right), 14 (middle right), 15 (below right), 16 (above right, middle, below left and right). © Adam Bowes A4M Films: 7 (above left and middle right). © Robin Bradshaw of Bullit Photography www.bullitphotography.co.uk: 13 (above right, middle left and below). © Comic Relief: 10 (below)/ photo Ray Burmiston. © Elliott Franks Photography Services: 14 (below). © Fremantle Media: 7 (below), 8 (below left), 10 (middle), 11 (below), 12 (above right), 14 (above left and right)/photos Ken McKay, 8 (middle right) /photo Jonathan Hordle, 15 (above)/ photo Tom Dymond. © Getty Images: 6 (middle left)/ photo J Quinton, 14 (middle)/ photo Dave J Hogan. © Rich Hardcastle www.richhardcastle.com: 12 (middle left). © Eleanor Kiff: 9 (middle right). © Jim Marks www.marks.co.uk: 5 (below right). © Ken McKay: 11 (middle left), 12 (above left). © NI Syndication: 9 (above left)/ photo Nick Ray. © Dee Koppang O'Leary: 7 (above right), 10 (above right), 16 (above left). © Isabelle Percival: 9 (below left). © Photoshot: 6 (below right)/photo Barry Clack, 9 (below right)/photo Chris Lopez. © Paul Postle: 5 (middle left). © Press Association Images: 8 (below right)/ photo Ian West. © Rex Features: 6 (above), 8 (middle left) and 15 (middle right)/ photos Richard Young, 12 (below)/ photo Brian J Ritchie. © Thomas Stubbs: 15 (below left). © Ben Walker: 6 (below left), 9 (above right and middle). © Byron Ward: 15 (middle). © Simon Ward: 10 (above left).

Every reasonable effort has been made to contact the copyright holders, but if there are any errors or omissions, Hodder & Stoughton will be pleased to insert the appropriate acknowledgement any subsequent printing of this publication.